Our Fellow Shakespeare

Our Fellow Shakespeare

How Everyman May Enjoy His Works

BY

HORACE J. BRIDGES

Author of "Criticisms of Life," "The Religion
of Experience," etc.

"Why, here's our fellow Shakespeare puts
them all downe!"— *The Returne from
Pernassus* (1606)

CHICAGO
A. C. McCLURG & CO.
1916

W. F. HALL PRINTING COMPANY, CHICAGO

$\mathfrak{To}$

WILLIAM JOHN JARVIS
and
FRANK LEWIS BIRCH
for twenty-five years' friendship
and the things that words
cannot express

CONTENTS

INTRODUCTION

THE making of books about Shakespeare has long outgrown the dimensions of an infant industry. Almost everybody has written one, and so a man need scarcely apologize for following the fashion and adding another to the accumulation. Especially in this year of the tercentenary of his death, it would seem almost an affectation not to join in the general chorus of praise.

The universality of Shakespeare's genius is admitted on all hands; even the Baconians, who revile the man, do lip-homage to his works. But the inference, that that which is universal should be appreciated and enjoyed by all, does not seem to be quite generally drawn. The piling up of learned studies and commentaries seems to have had an effect similar to that of the multiplication of scientific investigations of the Bible. The means for intelligent and discriminating study of the Old and New Testaments are now at every man's command; yet it is certain that the Bible is read far less than in the days when, though inevitably misunderstood, it was genuinely loved. Anyone can now readily obtain a knowledge of Shakespeare greater, perhaps, than most of his contemporaries enjoyed, and the interpretation of the works of his genius has been carried to infinite details of exact analysis and bewildering subtlety. The effect, however, has been to render Shakespeare a subject for specialists, and rather to inhibit that naïve and spontaneous enjoyment which certainly was experienced by the men of his own time, and which it was his business, as a thoroughly intelligent commercial playwright, to produce. The academic critic has laid his icy hand on Shakespeare and thrust him into cold storage.

The governing idea of the present volume is not to increase the amount of learning possible to the expert in Shakespearean criticism. My hope is rather to enable those who have thought of Shakespeare as a frigid classic to enter like little children into his kingdom. The sun and the sea are for everybody, and so is Shakespeare. Spontaneous delight should come first, and scientific knowledge afterwards — if at all.

It happens quite often that the methods pursued in our educational institutions destroy the taste for great literature instead of fostering it. There is unconsciously growing up in this country a convention that literary culture, in the sense defined by Matthew Arnold, is something reserved for the elect few,— to be tolerated in that few only upon condition that they conceal it like a vice. For the mass, there is the Sunday newspaper, with its coloured illustrations; there is the moving-picture theatre, with its mission of destroying the use and the appreciation of language; there is the cabaret, with its instrumental din to spare us the dreaded labour of conversation. The mass is there to be amused; and woe to that man who dares presume to offer it instruction!

Fiction we still must have, on account of the length of our railway-journeys; but that which is

intended for Everyman must not venture beyond
the linguistic range of an eighth-grade schoolboy.
Matthew Arnold was led by his work as an educational official in England to declare that "the typical mental defect of our school children is their almost incredible scantiness of vocabulary." This
defect is more general to-day in America than in
England, among adults as well as children.

Now, this drift in the direction of what has been
called "the extirpation of culture" is no inevitable
adjunct of democracy. If it were, democracy
would be intolerable and would have to go. Socrates, who in antiquity ridiculed the rule of the mob,
and M. Faguet, who in our own day asserts that
democracy means dread of responsibility and the
worship of incompetence, have stigmatized an accidental accompaniment of this form of government,—one, moreover, which in practice is often
enough found associated with other forms as well.
But the criticism of what is wrong should challenge
those who believe in democracy to prove that its
actual defects are not inherent, and to show that
they can be remedied without abandoning its organic
principle. The doctrine that kings should be
philosophers is no less true where all are kings than
where only one in a nation rules. The harmonious
development of all one's native powers is the right
as well as the duty of all; and democracy ought to
mean the best and most efficient means of securing
it. To-day it often means a lazy abandonment of
everything that requires effort, or brings into view
the natural and inevitable inequalities of men as
regards intellectual power and gifts of genius or
skill.

The appreciation of Shakespeare certainly does

not require, to begin with, any rare or peculiar gift for the understanding and enjoyment of masterpieces. It is possible to every child who can be made happy by *Treasure Island* or *Alice in Wonderland* or the *Leatherstocking Tales*. We persistently forget that Shakespeare's audience consisted largely of the shopkeepers and grocers' boys of London,— the kind of people portrayed so humorously in *The Knight of the Burning Pestle* — and that Shakespeare, as a good man of business, catered zealously to the wants of such people. To be sure, in giving the public what it wanted, he also gave what he wished to give. Out of the often crude materials of romance and adventure, history and fiction, that appeal universally to the healthy instinctive cravings of average humanity, he wrought achievements before which the greatest minds stand bowed in awe. But those very plays which are full of inexhaustible significance for an Emerson, a Carlyle, or a Goethe, are, at the same time, built up around the commonest framework of melodrama. It would be interesting indeed if we could have a critique of *Hamlet* or *Macbeth* written by a grocer's boy in the pit, who saw it on the night of its first public production. Indeed, for such an interpretation it would be worth while to sacrifice a vast quantity of the dry-as-dust commentary of pedantic criticism. The boy's account would remind us of the fact that Shakespeare's primary business was to amuse and entertain people who were almost illiterate; and that, whatever else he did, he never failed to aim at, and to achieve, this object. The man who was "not for an age, but for all time," was also not for a class, but for everybody. His work is in so far like the

Christian evangel, that it involves the deepest mysteries of the soul and the universe, and yet is addressed to every child of man. Its "truth embodied in a tale may enter in at lowly doors." If the lowly doors are closed against Christ's message, or if the impression obtains that unless you become as Plato and Socrates you cannot enter into his kingdom of God, then a grievous injustice has been done both to the evangel and to those who are excluded. Exactly so is it with the man Shakespeare and his magic realm.

. It was a sound instinct, as well as a principle of economy, which led Shakespeare to choose for his themes legends and stories which had already won their way into the common heart and mind. Seeing that he did this deliberately, in order to attract the very "mob" which he is supposed to have held in contempt, one cannot go far astray in insisting that his is pre-eminently a work that ought to be known and spontaneously loved by everybody who is capable of appreciating folklore. He is as full of battle and murder and sudden death, of ghosts and poisoned swords, of the love of man and woman, of masks and disguises and midnight intrigues, as are the surreptitiously devoured dime novels of boyhood. Mr. Chesterton's defence of the "penny dreadful" has reminded us that that much-maligned literature is the authentic successor of Homer and Malory, of the *Kalevala* and the *Mabinogion,* and of all the myths and legends that classical scholars spend their lives in destroying with analysis and interring under mountains of commentary.

Hence it is natural and right that the appreciation of Shakespeare should begin from the point of view of the schoolboy, or even the street-urchin, dreaming on impossible things to come. The child ought to start by loving *Hamlet* for the sake of the Ghost, the poisoning, the usurpation, the entrapping of Rosencrantz and Guildenstern, the fencing-match, the poisoned rapiers, and the envenomed wine-cup. It is fit and proper that the inexhaustible riches of *Macbeth* should at first commend themselves to minds that can appreciate only the fantastic appearance of the Witches, the thrill of the midnight assassinations of Duncan and Banquo, and the glorious stand-up fight at the close, in which the transcendent villain first slays Young Siward, and then is slain himself, crying, in the most approved Wild-Western fashion (and even with the grammatical licence of the penny dreadful), "Lay on, MacDuff; and damned be him who first cries 'Hold, enough!'" If we begin by liking the *Merchant of Venice* on account of the mad bond accepted by Antonio, the preposterous gamble of the caskets, the Gilbertian law by which Shylock is swindled, and the wholly unmerited success attained by that rakish and rather unprincipled scamp Bassanio, we begin with the very points that were seized upon by Shakespeare because they contained the promise of a box-office success.

For myself, at all events, I can only plead that my own ever-deepening delight in the magical pages of Shakespeare began in precisely this fashion. I had the rare advantage that my education was interrupted by very little schooling. One of the supreme memories of my childhood is the discovery of a complete edition of the works of Shakespeare, unaccompanied by notes or other hindrances, printed in worn nonpareil type on the shabbiest kind of paper, illustrated with elderly woodcuts that were

funny without being vulgar, and published at nine-
pence net, by a philanthropist called John Dicks,
Strand, London. Years before I realized that books
have human authors, or had ever heard of Bacon,
or of the dreary business which some grim pedant
has called "Shakespearology," I knew, as intimately as a boy may, the majority of Shakespeare's
plays.

Now, any child who has had this good fortune
imbibes unconsciously a literary taste that opens to
him a boundless realm of appreciation and enjoyment. He gains access to the best of all solaces in
sorrow, the truest of consolations against the dis-
appointments and disillusionments of life. He becomes like the man described with unbeseeming
irony in one of Mr. Shaw's plays, as "entirely contented with the best of everything." Nobody ought
to be contented with anything else,—least of all in
art and literature.

But if, instead of going straight to the fountain-
head, a boy is coerced into studying a mass of
pedantic footnotes and comments, or the grammatical structure of Shakespeare's sentences (a thing
to which Shakespeare himself was frequently quite
indifferent), the chances are that he will never be
able to overcome the repugnance thus malevolently
instilled into him. You might as well force him to
learn the chemical constituents of every dish on the
table before permitting him to eat his dinner. Let
him enjoy the meal first; then perhaps his scientific
curiosity may lead him to study the chemical composition of his food; but, if not, it doesn't matter.
So if he learns freely to love his Shakespeare, he
may or may not subsequently study with delight
Abbott's *Shakespearean Grammar* or von Dam's

Prosody and Text; but, again, it doesn't matter if he never looks into them. He will already have attained the end for the sake of which grammars and commentaries pretend to be written. If this end is reached directly, it may be the worse for us commentators, but it is the better for Shakespeare, and for the spirit that learns to live by him.

Exigencies of space have constrained me to limit this book to a consideration of less than a third of Shakespeare's plays. The Histories are entirely omitted, and only representative Comedies and Tragedies are discussed. Nevertheless, the method of study exemplified in these chapters may, I trust, serve to stimulate the reader's independent judgment, and perhaps enable him to read Shakespeare for himself with greater insight and enjoyment than before. If this hope is not disappointed, my labour will be well repaid.

Throughout this volume, the references to scenes and lines follow the "Fireside Edition," in six volumes, edited by Richard Grant White and published by Houghton Mifflin Company. It should be explained that, as a great deal of Shakespeare is in prose, the enumeration of the lines is not exactly the same in any two editions.

H. J. B.

Chicago, October, 1916.

Our Fellow Shakespeare

Our Fellow Shakespeare

CHAPTER I

SHAKESPEARE'S BACKGROUND: THE RISE OF THE ENGLISH DRAMA

IT has been wittily said that the Elizabethan dramatists are divided into two classes: Shakespeare and the others. Those "others" are now little read, save by specialists. Shakespeare bestrides their narrow world like a Colossus, and the pettier men are overlooked, because attention is centred upon him. It is unfortunate, however, that so few of us read the dramas of his contemporaries — his friends and rivals, collaborators and enemies.

"Shakespeare and the others."

In the first place, we fail to realize that if Shakespeare had not lived at all, the dramatic development of the period of Elizabeth and of James I would still have constituted a memorable chapter in the history of our literature. An age that produced Greene, Peele and Kyd, Ford and Massinger, Beaumont and Fletcher, Ben Jonson and Marlowe, would by that achievement have earned high distinction. But it must have been very annoying to the Lilliputians when Mr. Lemuel Gulliver landed among them. It is hard to remember the relative greatness and smallness of the courtiers of the Lilliputian king when they are all alike dwarfed by one, the latchets of whose shoes they are scarcely tall enough to unloose.   Interest naturally centres in the exploits of Gulliver, and we forget that, except for the activities of the pigmies, there would have been no story to tell.   Thus it is with Shakespeare.

Attempts to explain new departures of the human spirit:

It must be left to scientific historians and to philosophers of history to account for the seeming mystery of a development, within half a century, from the crudest beginnings to the greatest heights of dramatic creation that the world has ever seen. The rest of us can but listen respectfully to thinkers who can perform the feat of explaining such a sudden burst of creative power in the common mind. Yet a word of warning is necessary against the ready and easy means of dissipating the mystery of such phenomena which prevailed during the past generation.   Explanations of genius in terms of heredity are futile; they explain nothing.   If you tell me that a gifted novelist had a grandfather who was a gifted novelist, you have not thereby assigned an intelligible cause for the grandchild's gift.   You have but made two problems to spring up where before there was only one.   Or, if you say that the second novelist is explained by the first, and we politely agree to assume that these words mean something, you are still left with the same problem regarding the ancestor as you undertook to solve in the case of the descendant.

(1) By heredity.

(2) By economic conditions.

Equally unsatisfactory is the attempt to account for such a development as that of the Elizabethan drama in terms of economic demand and supply. Certainly there was money in dramatic authorship; but not much, even in the rarest cases.   Good actors earned far more in Shakespeare's day than playwrights did, and Shakespeare himself, who was a first-rate man of business, made most of his fortune as an actor and as a shareholder in theatrical enterprises. The mere author was almost continuously hard up,—as witness Greene, whose lamentations on the subject are still extant. The trade of the playwright was looked upon with disdain by the fashionable society of the period, and the social standing of actors is reflected with unquestionable fidelity by the attitude of the Lord in the Induction to the *Taming of the Shrew* and of Polonius towards the strolling troupe in *Hamlet*. There was not as yet, to be sure, the bitter religious prejudice with which in after years both Puritanism and Catholicism insulted and ostracized even the greatest dramatists, actors and actresses.[1] But even the men of letters were scornful of the player's and the playwright's art. There was an aesthetic, though scarcely an economic, demand for poems and sonnets, and a man might enhance his social standing, and perhaps secure the generous if fickle patronage of a nobleman, by dedicating to him an acceptable poem. Hence Shakespeare's careful attention to the publication of *Venus and Adonis* and *Lucrece,* which were his baits for Southampton's favour. But playwriting was looked upon with scorn, and the dramatists very seldom published their plays.[2]

Play-writing paid poorly and did not lead to social success.

[1] Voltaire's fury at the refusal of "Christian burial" to Adrienne le Couvreur, who was interred in a cattle-field, will never be forgotten. It was only with extreme difficulty that permission was obtained to bury Molière in consecrated ground. All the sacraments, *et à la vie et à la mort,* were rigorously refused to actors. This meant that they could not be married, since there was nothing but ecclesiastical marriage. Happily, times have changed,—and the Church with them.

[2] Their chief reason for this, however, was a business one. The managers deprecated publication as tending to reduce box-office receipts. It was thought that people were less

When a piece was written, it was sold outright to one of the regular companies of players, and the author in selling it parted with all future power over it. The purchasing company could cobble it to any extent they chose, could cut out scenes and replace them with new ones, change the characters to suit their *personnel* or the public taste, or hand the whole thing over to another dramatist to be revamped.

Shakespeare's 'prentice work.

It is these facts which have given rise to the most puzzling problems in the criticism of Shakespeare. He learned his craft by working over old plays which his company chanced to have in stock. Hence, in dealing with the earlier works now extant under his name, one can never be certain how much is his, and how much is the work of a predecessor or collaborator. In the case of some of the early historical plays, it is practically certain that he and Marlowe did the cobbling together, so that we have an inextricable blending of three or more elements for the *cognoscenti* to exercise their wits upon. There are critics who undertake to tell us exactly, in regard to any of these plays, which lines are Marlowe's, what scenes come from Peele, where Kyd's hand is unmis-

likely to witness a play if they had read it. But in the absence of any copyright law, the authors and managers had no protection against publishers. Anybody who could get hold of any sort of manuscript, accurate or inaccurate, whole or mutilated, could print it and sell copies for his own profit. Hence the existence of the many Shakespearean quartos, all probably unauthorized and furiously resented by Shakespeare, and for the most part grossly defective. They were issued by "pirates," against whom he had no protection or redress. Their original cost was fivepence or sixpence apiece (ten or twelve cents: worth about a dollar at the present purchasing power of money). Perfect copies of them now range in price from $1,500 to $12,000, according to their scarcity. (See Lee, *Life,* 1916 edition, pp. 544 ff.)

takably present, and, most confidently of all, what is and is not Shakespeare's. One's attitude towards such critics cannot be contemptuous, because their results in many cases have a high degree of probability. They do, however, impair their credit with us by knowing far too much. As regards Shakespeare, their rule (inherited from Coleridge) would seem to be a very simple one: Shakespeare never wrote anything that he ought not to have written.

Taking the economic explanation as usually presented, it is difficult to understand how it can account for the rapid and uninterrupted development of a man's powers. How, for example, can it explain the difference between the poorest and the best work of Greene, or give us the secret of the growth from, say, *Love's Labour's Lost* to *Lear* and *Othello,* the *Winter's Tale* and *The Tempest?*

Fallacy of the economic explanation.

We understand what is meant by the working of the law of supply and demand in regard to the multiplication and differentiation of mechanical devices, though it cannot account for the origination even of these. But we need not carry our scepticism to its full legitimate length here. Let us admit (for the sake of avoiding argument) that necessity may mother the invention of the umbrella. When the principle of umbrella-making has been hit upon, growing demand will account for the increase of the supply. Or, again, as soon as the principle of self-propulsion has been mastered, we can readily see how numerous varieties of motor-cars will come to be manufactured. But the application of this kind of reasoning to the creations of the human spirit is simply a fallacy — one of the fallacies of materialism. The demand for mental or aesthetic satisfactions is never a demand for any one definite and specific thing. It is a demand that may be equally well satisfied in many different ways. So far as the public desire for entertainment, in response to which Shakespeare functioned, is concerned, it would have been met with equal success if he had written plays like those of Molière or Sheridan or Mr. George M. Cohan. We know precisely what his public wanted; we know, too, how far he was prepared to go in giving his public what it wanted. But the whole problem is to explain how Shakespeare came to create what nobody could possibly foresee, and therefore *could not want until it was created*. To talk of economic conditions accounting for the work of such geniuses as Shakespeare and Marlowe is like saying that the shape of the river-bed is the cause of the river. The economic explanation may be valid as regards conditions; it does not account for the force which utilizes conditions. The environment does not originate that which struggles with it. You may, by pointing to the circumstances, explain how Shakespeare came to write plays and sonnets instead of novels or newspaper editorials or religious tracts. But you cannot thus explain how he was able to write *his* plays; which is the whole question in dispute. We have to assign, if we can, the cause of the development of a qualitative excellence which had no precedent and no relation to demand. Shakespeare is the creator of the standard of taste to which his mature works appeal. We have to account for his giving the public what it did *not* want.

Mistaken economic assumptions.

The assumptions underlying the economic explanation of the products of genius are two, and are very simple: it is implied, firstly, that the greater the reward offered to a man, the better work will he do; secondly, that there is always available an indefinite reserve of potential genius of every quality, the amount of such genius actualized being determined by what the public is ready to pay. Without these two assumptions, what would be the meaning of the explanation that Shakespeare went on writing better and better plays because with each success the demand, and consequently his reward, increased? Or how, without postulating them, can one treat any great collective movement, like the Italian Renaissance, or the Elizabethan drama in general, as the result of a public demand expressed in economic terms?

To reduce such reasoning to its elementary principles is to reduce it to absurdity. We are in the presence of the mystery of the spirit of man. That spirit is the source of the "explanations" which give us our control of the outer world. But we cannot turn these formulae upon their source, and account for it by means of them. The most we can do is to describe the psychological phenomena of the progress of genius. The force it manifests is at present incalculable and unpredictable. Possibly it will always remain so. The methods of physical science,— the fundamental scientific concepts of quantity, number and magnitude — which apply to space and its contents, do not apply to the spirit.

Readers of Shakespeare will derive great help from a clear vision of the world in which he lived and moved. The life around him, and the history which his nation had made and was making, introduce us to the mental and spiritual influences that played upon him, and thus enable us to follow his unique reaction to them. One cannot say, indeed, "What should they know of Shakespeare who

[margin note: Spiritual factors at present inexplicable.]

[margin note: Psychological conditions in Shakespeare's time.]

only Shakespeare know?" for the world he created
is one of the chief sources of our knowledge of the
social life, the mind, manners and morals of the
epoch in which he lived. But one may say that they
who know intimately the literature of that period,
and are familiar with its rich interplay of social,
religious and political forces, will thereby know
much more of Shakespeare, and be enabled to learn
much more from him.

The achievement of one man is in a sense the deed
of all; and a multitude of forces had conspired to
create the situation of which Shakespeare's powers
were able to take advantage.

The Renais-
sance revolu-
tion in
thought and
knowledge.

In the sixteenth century, geographical discovery
had enlarged the world. The important accident
that happened in 1492, when a Genoese gentleman
on his way to the Indies blundered on the islands
in the Gulf of Mexico and thought he had got
there, was but one of a series of fortunate disclosures. The art of printing had disseminated
throughout Europe what remained of the ancient
wisdom of mankind. The stir of thought thus
brought about had produced a religious upheaval.
Even in England this revolution took an unfortunate course, though there its effects were never so
disastrous as in other countries. In Shakespeare's
day the mischievous consequences of the upheaval
were only beginning to manifest themselves. Great
evils had been got rid of, and good results — so
necessary that scarcely any price was too great to
pay for them — had been achieved. These were
seen chiefly in a growing freedom of thought and
in a new attempt to interpret Christianity in accord
with changing views of the universe and of man's
nature and history.

Schools were multiplied, many new books were written, and whole classes of men became for the first time readers and thinkers. Vernacular translations of the Bible opened a new world to men's wonder and speculation. Popular taste for the drama had given rise to permanent theatres in London, to several troupes of players, and to a whole school of dramatic authors, before Shakespeare left his native town. One may say with full conviction that it was the existence of this demand which caused Shakespeare's unique talents to select the special channel of dramatic authorship.

One of the outstanding distinctions of this period is an unprecedented outburst of energy and joy in life. This is characteristic especially of England, but in some degree of all the chief nations of Europe. Its beginnings, as regards England, are obscure; though they certainly antedate the life of Shakespeare, and even the reign of Elizabeth. But the development up to the beginning of Elizabeth's reign had not gone far enough to enable even the keenest of prophets to foresee what was to come. Indeed, one may say that almost any thinker of the school of Buckle or Marx — almost anyone who interpreted social developments in materialistic or economic terms alone — would, in the year 1557, have been led by the history of the previous century to forecast something radically different from what actually ensued. *Gigantic energy and joy.*

That was the year before the death of Queen Mary, of irredeemable memory. It may be said to have marked the end of a century and a half of national misery and disruption. At the middle of the fifteenth century, England had been wasted by a series of foolish foreign wars, and was entering *England in the XV and XVI centuries.*

upon a new and disastrous period of internecine war. That century, thanks to these causes, was almost barren of great intellectual and spiritual achievements. In the history of English literature it is nearly a blank. When, in 1485, King Richard III was defeated at Bosworth Field and the crown placed upon the head of Henry Tudor, the new monarch and his counsellors had to set about the task of re-creating their nation out of ruins and fragments.

No sooner had the sixteenth century dawned, than a new factor of seemingly disastrous portent emerged, in the shape of the religious conflict. The Reformation, which had really originated with Wiclif in the fourteenth century, was due to resentment against social injustices and political evils, and would undoubtedly have taken place in some form in England, though Luther had never lived. The changes in theology were one of the effects, and were not the cause, of the changes in social and intellectual conditions, and of the exigencies with which these confronted the nation and its rulers. It is to be remembered that, with the standards of that age, innovations in Church government and theological opinion were certain to involve persecution, and seemed inevitably destined also to produce foreign war. The persecution duly came, but the foreign war was happily averted for many a long day, by a combination of able diplomacy and rare good fortune. Henry VIII lived and died a Catholic; but a Catholic who, for political and national reasons, very rightly objected to the temporal government, the financial extortions, and the political machinations of the Papacy. He was thus quite consistent in directing his persecution impartially against both Papists

The Reformation and its causes.

and Protestants. During the minority of his ill-starred son Edward VI (that is, when England, for the second time, was rent asunder by the very disaster against which Henry's many marriages had been intended to provide),[3] the Regency was monopolized by Protestant extremists, and persecution was directed only against Papists. Under Mary, the tables were turned. A vigorous attempt was made, by means of her Spanish marriage and the merrily blazing fires of Smithfield, to re-impose the Papal yoke, and to suppress all independent thinking as heresy.

Bearing in mind that everything is contingent before it happens, we may venture the speculation that had Queen Mary lived another ten years, or had she not been disappointed in her expectation of issue, England would have become a mere appanage of the Spanish crown. The policy of Charles V and Philip II was naturally directed to making it such. Hence Philip's long-indulged hope of contracting a marriage with his deceased wife's sister. "Reasons of State" would have atoned easily enough for the ecclesiastical irregularity of such a course, had it proved possible.

Upon the accession of our sovereign lady Elizabeth, of much-disputed character, the outlook for

The prospect in 1558.

---

[3] *I. e.*, the disaster of a disputed succession to the Crown. This had caused, in the preceding century, the Wars of the Roses. The office of the monarch was the very soul of the government in those days, and the purpose of Henry's matrimonial adventures was not to gratify any special licentiousness on his part, but simply to provide a legitimate son whose title to the Crown should be unassailable. Licentious kings did not need to plunge Europe into turmoil and imperil the peace of nations in order to secure divorces. And there is no evidence that Henry was at all an exceptional offender in the matter of sex immorality.

England among the hostile powers of the European world was black indeed. From the standpoint of *Realpolitik,* it would have seemed a fairly safe prophecy that the nation was chained and checked, and that she would need fifty or a hundred years of domestic peace and repose from foreign war to recover from past disasters and loss of blood, and to muster again her dissipated energies. It is one of the standing enigmas of history that, instead of this, England produced and utilized in various directions during the ensuing fifty years such a gigantic volume of spiritual power as she had never possessed before and has scarcely equalled since. The truth of this as regards literature is obvious: Spenser and Hooker, Shakespeare and Bacon, and the noble army at whose head they stand, are there to make it so. But scarcely less wonderful was the inexhaustible energy and resourcefulness by means of which the tiny island nation (with a population less than that of greater New York to-day) met and conquered the mightiest forces of Spain's far-flung empire. The

The defeat of Spain.

overthrow of the Spanish Armada was ascribed with piety, and possibly with truth, to the interposition of Providence; *Afflavit Deus et dissipantur:* "He blew with His winds and they were scattered." The piety is commendable, no doubt; but one may safely say that, had it not been for the English fleet, the winds of heaven would not alone have saved England from Spanish conquest. It was during this same period

Beginnings of empire.

that England's adventurous sons laid in "Virginia" the foundations of the American Commonwealth. In statesmanship, and in the enterprises of exploration and commerce, the Elizabethan epoch produced parallels to its achievement in literature. In every one of these directions the results attained seem incommensurable with the tiny means that were employed.

Turning to our immediate subject, we speedily discover that Shakespeare, although unique in degree, was not unique in kind. He is the supreme instance of a general tendency. Marlowe, born a few months before him, was killed in a tavern brawl in 1593,— that is, at the age at which Shakespeare wrote *Venus and Adonis.* Comparing his work with what Shakespeare is known to have done up to the time of Marlowe's death, it seems difficult to doubt that had his development continued at the same rate, he might in his mature years have proved, at least in tragedy, a second Shakespeare. The chronology of Shakespeare's earliest plays is not without elements of uncertainty. But of the work that he had done before 1593, *Romeo and Juliet* is the only piece that is indisputably superior to anything of Marlowe's; and in its earliest form the superiority was, in all probability, much less apparent.

Christopher Marlowe: 1564-1593.

Marlowe is the only one of the predecessors or contemporaries who manifests in drama the special Shakespearean characteristic of a seemingly boundless energy and wealth of resource. It is one thing to attain a great height by straining one's powers to their utmost limit; it is quite another thing to ascend higher than anybody else has done, and, in doing it, to give the impression that the ascent is effortless, and is a restrained manifestation of a power that could easily have gone higher. Sublimity is, indeed, to be defined as the suggestion of a reserve of unseen force, indefinitely transcending what is displayed. That is why we call the stormy sea sublime; its gigantic frolicking is but a hint of what it might do.

The Elizabethan sublimity.

This is the characteristic shared in common by Shakespeare and Marlowe, though displayed on a vastly wider scale, and with immeasurably more subtlety and complexity, in the former than in the latter. We may say, indeed, that this is the chief distinctive attribute of the Elizabethan age. It is well typified in that picturesque legend, *ben trovato* if not true, of Sir Francis Drake's insistence on finishing the game of bowls on Plymouth Hoe before putting out to sea to meet the Armada: "We have plenty of time to finish the game and beat the Dons too." Shakespeare, piling *Othello* upon *Hamlet, Macbeth* upon *Othello,* and *Lear* upon *Macbeth,* and in his last completed play creating a new genus, gives the impression that after producing a world in six days, he has no real need to rest on the seventh, but could easily turn out another next week.

In Marlowe this energy is seen in its reckless youth. "Marlowe's mighty line," the now hackneyed phrase by which Ben Jonson described his work, is no exaggeration. The force poured forth in *Tamburlaine* and in *The Jew of Malta* is for the most part crude and unchastened. Marlowe is the swashbuckler of poetry. He is a volcano, hurling out precious metal for lava,— with everything in the crude molten state. He is redundant, bombastic and swaggering. But, with it all, the chief impression left upon one's mind is that of effortless and unexhausted power. He is flinging off an output that might have been indefinitely multiplied. The rest are constructors and fabricators; Marlowe and Shakespeare are creators. Witness the riotous braggadocio of Tamburlaine:—

Tamburlaine the Great

First Part, I ii.

I hold the Fates bound fast in iron chains,
And with my hand turn Fortune's wheel about;

And sooner shall the sun fall from his sphere
Than Tamburlaine be slain or overcome.
Draw forth thy sword, thou mighty man-at-arms,
Intending but to raze my charmèd skin,
And Jove himself will stretch his hand from heaven
To ward the blow, and shield me safe from harm.
See, how he rains down heaps of gold in showers,
As if he meant to give my soldiers pay!
And, as a sure and grounded argument
That I shall be the monarch of the East,
He sends this Soldan's daughter, rich and brave,
To be my queen and portly emperess.
If thou wilt stay with me, renownèd man,
And lead thy thousand horse with my condùct,
Besides thy share of this Egyptian prize,
Those thousand horse shall sweat with martial spoil
Of conquer'd kingdoms and of cities sack'd:
Both we will walk upon the lofty cliffs;
And Christian merchants, that with Russian stems
Plough up huge furrows in the Caspian Sea,
Shall vail to us as lords of all the lake;
Both we will reign as consuls of the earth,
And mighty kings shall be our senators.
Jove sometimes maskèd in a shepherd's weed;
And by those steps that he hath scal'd the heavens
May we become immortal like the gods.
Join with me now in this my mean estate
(I call it mean, because, being yet obscure,
The nations far-removed admire me not),
And when my name and honour shall be spread
As far as Boreas claps his brazen wings,
Or fair Boötes sends his cheerful light,
Then shalt thou be competitor with me,
And sit with Tamburlaine in all his majesty.

And again:—

. . . Fates and oracles of heaven have sworn   *Ibid.* II iii.
To royalize the deeds of Tamburlaine,
And make them blest that share in his attempts.
And doubt you not but, if you favour me,
And let my fortunes and my valour sway

To some direction in your martial deeds,
The world will strive with hosts of men-at-arms
To swarm unto the ensign I support.
The host of Xerxes, which by fame is said
To drink the mighty Parthian Araris,
Was but a handful to that we will have:
Our quivering lances, shaking in the air,
And bullets, like Jove's dreadful thunderbolts,
Enroll'd in flames and fiery smouldering mists,
Shall threat the gods more than Cyclopian wars;
And with our sun-bright armour, as we march,
We'll chase the stars from heaven, and dim their eyes,
That stand and muse at our admirèd arms.

If this is the way Tamburlaine talks before his triumph, what language will he have left to boast himself withal after he has really shaken the earth with his achievements? Only Marlowe could answer the question; and this is the fashion in which he does it :—

Ibid. **V i.**

Jove, viewing me in arms, looks pale and wan,
Fearing my power should pull him from his throne:
Where'er I come, the Fatal Sisters sweat,
And grisly Death, by running to and fro
To do their ceaseless homage to my sword:
And here in Africk, where it seldom rains,
Since I arriv'd with my triumphant host,
Have swelling clouds, drawn from wide-gaping wounds,
Been oft resolv'd in bloody purple showers,
A meteor that might terrify the earth,
And make it quake at every drop it drinks:
Millions of souls sit on the banks of Styx,
Waiting the back-return of Charon's boat;
Hell and Elysium swarm with ghosts of men
That I have sent from sundry foughten fields
To spread my fame through hell and up to heaven.

This is the spring fever of youth, suddenly conscious of new and unheard-of powers. It is the riotous excess produced by the first sense of a new emancipation "from jigging veins of rhyming mother-wits and such conceits as clownage keeps in pay." Marlowe is like a schoolboy on holiday. In the "blossomy twists" of his "linked fantasies," he "swings the earth a trinket at his wrists." He outroars the reverberations of Jove's thunderbolts, and looks down upon the loneliest stars.

In subtlety of character-sense and power of psychological analysis he is out-distanced, even by the youthful Shakespeare. Yet the meditations of Barabas, the Jew of Malta, betray a nascent power that *The Jew of* might in its maturity have created other Shylocks. *Malta.* Barabas is a mere brute criminal; but there is something titanic in the malevolence of his will. His wealth, his "infinite riches in a little room," is valued for the power it gives him, and he has the deep racial detestation of the Christians, which in Shylock is transmuted into dignity and grandeur: —

> Thus trolls our fortune in by land and sea, *Act I.*
> And thus are we on every side enrich'd:
> These are the blessings promis'd to the Jews,
> And herein was old Abraham's happiness:
> What more may heaven do for earthly man
> Than thus to pour out plenty in their laps,
> Ripping the bowels of the earth for them,
> Making the seas their servants, and the winds
> To drive their substance with successful blasts?
> Who hateth me but for my happiness?
> Or who is honour'd now but for his wealth?
> Rather had I, a Jew, be hated thus,
> Than pitied in a Christian poverty;
> For I can see no fruits in all their faith,
> But malice, falsehood, and excessive pride,
> Which methinks fits not in their profession.
> Haply some hapless man hath conscience,
> And for his conscience lives in beggary.
> They say we are a scatter'd nation;

I cannot tell; but we have scrambled up
More wealth by far than those that brag of faith:
There's Kirriah Jairim, the great Jew of Greece,
Obed in Bairseth, Nones in Portugal,
Myself in Malta, some in Italy,
Many in France; and wealthier every one,—
Ay, wealthier far than any Christian.
I must confess we come not to be kings:
That's not our fault: alas, our number's few!
And crowns come either by succession,
Or urg'd by force; and nothing violent,
Oft have I heard tell, can be permanent.

Lyly's
Euphues.

Shakespeare was indebted for much to Marlowe, and for something also to Lyly the Euphuist, both of whom he subsequently satirized. The braggadocio of Glendower and Hotspur reads like a parody of Tamburlaine's. In the early comedies, especially *Love's Labour's Lost,* Shakespeare pokes fun at Lyly, and he is still doing so when in *Hamlet* he puts a string of platitudinous euphuisms upon the lips of Polonius. Yet he remained something of a Euphuist himself. His memory of Marlowe was affectionate and respectful,[4] and he was quick to apply the lessons he learned in Marlowe's school.

[4] See, for example, the reference in *As You Like It* (Act III, scene v, line 80) : —

Dead Shepherd! now I find thy saw of might:
"Who ever loved that loved not at first sight?"
The "saw" in question is from a beautiful passage in Marlowe's *Hero and Leander:* —
It lies not in our power to love or hate,
For will in us is over-rul'd by fate.
When two are stript long ere the course begin,
We wish that one should lose, the other win;
And one especially do we affect
Of two gold ingots, like in each respect.
The reason no man knows; let it suffice,
What we behold is censur'd by our eyes.
Where both deliberate, the love is slight:
Who ever lov'd, that lov'd not at first sight?

The development of the Elizabethan drama is Sources of the Elizabethan drama. from the semi-ecclesiastical morality play, with its puppet personifications of abstract virtues and vices, to the living human music of comedy and tragedy in Shakespeare's maturest period. The secular spirit of the classic drama was a powerful element in the transformation. The widespread study of Seneca and Plautus, who were popularized in translations and adaptations, goes far to determine the course of the rapid evolution. *Gorboduc,* or *Ferrex and Porrex,* is an interesting example of the mechanical Gorboduc. imitation of classic models. It was first acted by the gentlemen of the Inner Temple in 1560–61. It is as mechanical and lifeless as Plautus at his woodenest; hence it is easy to understand why it never succeeded on the stage. The demand was for action, not for narration and moralizing. Survivals of the old morality-play abstractions are still to be found in Marlowe — they doubtless suggested the good and evil angels that hover through the popular tragedy of *Doctor Faustus.* The very theme of that Doctor Faustus. play is an ecclesiastical legend of the struggle of the superhuman powers of light and darkness for possession of the soul of man. Similar echoes from the past are to be detected in the masques of Beaumont and Fletcher, and even of Ben Jonson. *Gorboduc* attempted to naturalize the Graeco-Roman chorus in Elizabethan England, but the attempt was a clear enough failure to warn later practitioners against repetitions of it.

The worst fault of Shakespeare's dramatic con- Vicious tendencies in the drama. temporaries is their unrestrained pandering to the licentiousness of popular taste. Even Beaumont and Fletcher went to most regrettable lengths in their concessions to this vicious propensity. It is easy to understand by reading them why the later Puritans raged so furiously against the theatre. They are the forerunners of those comic dramatists of the Restoration period, who called forth the grave and memorable rebuke of Jeremy Collier.[5] I mention this defect here only in order to emphasize Shakespeare's astonishing freedom from it. Undoubtedly there are many passages in his plays which, on account of the change of taste if not of moral standards, cannot now be given verbatim upon the stage, and constitute an embarrassment to the reading aloud of his works in mixed companies. We also find occasionally, at the close of a scene, an irrelevant obscenity that is probably due to a practice he complained of — viz., " those who played the clowns " speaking " more than was set down for them." There are at least two such interpolations in *King Lear*. The wonder is, however, that there should be so little of this. The study of his women characters, especially when it is possible to compare them with the originals which suggested them to him, gives a conclusive proof that he fought against the taste of his age in this matter. From Juliet to Miranda, he gives us a gallery of girls and women not approached in the works of any other writer, and all distinguished for a virtue by no means " fugitive and cloistered." He does not paint the mincing, bread-and-butter miss of early Victorianism. His women are in general alert, resourceful, thoroughly aware of the meaning of life and the dangers of the world. They are not prudish,

But not in Shakespeare.

[5] Collier's *Short View of the Immorality and Prophaneness of the English Stage* (1697), though it makes no reference to the Elizabethans, achieved a victory, the completeness of which was attested by the public contrition of Dryden. It well deserves disinterring.

and their speech does not pretend to ignorance. But they are without exception chaste, delicate, refined and charming.

It would, however, be grossly unjust to leave the impression that the dramatic predecessors and contemporaries of Shakespeare are on the whole vicious. Their works show a vivid sense of the deathward tendency of evil, and of the natural nemesis which it brings upon the heels of those who, by inflicting it upon others, inflict it also upon themselves. Marlowe's *Doctor Faustus* is there to testify to this. His *Edward the Second* is a forerunner of Shakespeare's matchless pictures of the evil monarch who by wrongdoing destroys himself. Beaumont and Fletcher in their most salacious plays insist upon the suicidal tendency of sin. *The Custom of the Country* and *The Maid's Tragedy* bear, for those that have eyes to see, a lesson as impressive as that of *Measure for Measure* or *Hamlet*.

"The others" morally sound in general.

But, after all, the chief importance of the predecessors is that they staked out the field for Shakespeare, and provided some of the raw material which his genius was to transmute. Tamburlaine's chief honour is that he is the forerunner of Richard III and Macbeth. Barabas is memorable as the prototype of Shylock. The chronicle plays gave Shakespeare the hint for his histories and defiances of history, as well as for such things as *Julius Caesar* and *Lear*. We value the forerunners for what they did, but more for what they promised. They are the "august anticipations, symbols, types of a dim splendour ever on before."

CHAPTER II

THE BACON MYTH: SHAKESPEARE'S LIFE AND EDUCATION

Misunder-
standings
due to the
Baconian
theory.

THE great mare's-nest of the Bacon-Shakespeare school has been re-discovered, as one might naturally have expected, in connection with the ter-centenary of the poet's death. The long discussion to which it gave rise, moreover, has left certain mis-understandings in the minds of many people who have never travelled so far from the path of sanity as to believe that Bacon wrote Shakespeare's plays. One of these is the idea that little or nothing is known of the actual life of the man from Stratford. Another is the impression that Shakespeare was a person of particularly scanty education, and that this fact constitutes a difficulty in the way of a convinced belief in his authorship of the plays.

*Our know-
ledge of
Shakespeare.*

It is of course true that we know less of the life of Shakespeare than we know of that of Queen Elizabeth, or of Burghley or Walsingham or Sir Walter Raleigh, or any of the great figures who stand in the full blaze of the light of history. But it is not true at all that we know nothing of Shake-speare, nor yet that we know less about him than about any of his contemporaries with whom his case may fairly be compared. We know more of him, to begin with, than we do of any other dramatist of his time. We may leave out of the question all that is speculative or disputable, and look only to the mass of incontrovertible facts set forth in the new edition of Sir Sidney Lee's *Life of Shakespeare*. When we compare this with what we know (apart from the evidence of their own works) about Greene, Beaumont, Marlowe, Ben Jonson, Fletcher, Kyd, or Peele, the foregoing assertion becomes definitely established. Or we may extend the comparison beyond the mere playwrights, and say that we know more about Shakespeare than about any other man of letters of his time who was not also thrust into the glare of publicity as a statesman or courtier. Less is known of Hooker, of Drayton or of Chapman than of Shakespeare.

To be sure, we cannot follow the dramatist from day to day and from year to year as we can follow Doctor Johnson through the ever-charming pages of Boswell. We have no collection of letters such as those of Matthew Arnold, from which, in the absence of a biography, Shakespeare's story could be reconstructed by the methods of scientific textual analysis. Shakespeare kept no diary like that of Pepys or Evelyn; or, if he did, it has not been preserved. On the other hand, we have plenty of unquestionably genuine contemporary references, all of which go to prove that he was recognized, by friends and foes alike, both as an actor and as a dramatist.

A priori arguments about his lack of education are in any case fantastic. A man's education is to be inferred from his actual works, not his possible works from his education. Once establish the fact that any given person has done a known task, and then from the evidence of that task you can reason to the person's education. If, for instance, Huxley can be shown to have written his essay on *The*

His education.

Value of Witness to the Miraculous, then all arguments to prove that he could not have done it, because he never went through a university, are out of court. Proof that he wrote that essay is at the same time proof that he knew enough to write it. He must have been sufficiently familiar with Latin to read understandingly the extant works of Eginhard. If he wrote the volume on Hume and Berkeley, and the essay on *Science and Morals,* which bear his name, he was familiar with the main currents of philosophical thought from Descartes down to his time.

The question, then, regarding Shakespeare cannot be settled *a priori,* on the strength of allegations about his ignorance. It is simply whether the mass of contemporary and nearly contemporary testimony, which represents him as the author of *Romeo and Juliet, The Merchant of Venice,* and the rest of the plays listed by Meres,[1] to say nothing of the other contents of the Folio of 1623, can be trusted. If it can, then to discover what education Shakespeare possessed we have only to read his works. A man may acquire education in many different ways. The issue resolves itself into determining the authorship of the plays. Whoever composed them possessed at least so much education as went to their making.

There is, however, a great misapprehension as to the amount of knowledge and book-learning revealed in the dramas. They by no means testify to the possession of encyclopaedic information. The writer was clearly not a person of exact or academic scholarship. The common idea that the plays betray an expert and professional intimacy with the

His
ignorance.

The playwright not a man of rare learning.

[1] See below, p. 48.

law, and its language and modes of procedure, is a complete illusion. Shakespeare was the litigious son of a litigious father, and this fact alone would be sufficient to explain his smattering of legal terminology. When we remember, further, that the use of law-terms in poetry and drama was a prevalent literary fashion of the time — when we find that Ben Jonson, Spenser, Massinger, Greene and Webster use them more freely than Shakespeare does, and with greater accuracy,— then the theory that the dramatist must have been a professional lawyer goes hopelessly by the board. The lore of agriculture, horticulture, falconry, the chase, and country life generally, which the plays reveal, is little more than what might naturally be expected of a man brought up in the country, and familiar from childhood with the life of farms and gardens and with village sports. Shakespeare's knowledge of flowers and of the animal world is by no means that of a man of science; it is rather that of a creative poet. It is the kind of knowledge that tradition and common-sense observation may give to anybody, and creative fancy to poetic minds; not that which is given in text-books or scientific lectures.

As regards history, the plays disclose only such knowledge as any fairly diligent reader could have picked up by reading Holinshed and the other chroniclers whose works were current in Shakespeare's England, and the widely circulated translations of Plutarch. Not only is the knowledge glaringly defective, but it may be positively affirmed that the writer of the plays was either seriously deficient in historic sense, or absolutely contemptuous of the kind of accuracy which it comes naturally to an academically trained mind to strain after.

Legal language.

Knowledge of country life.

History.

The knowledge of authors.

What is more, the general impression as to Shakespeare's omniscience, and the wonder expressed at it, betray a curiously naïve conception of the way in which authors go about the making of their books. People who do not write books are apt to have a notion that the men who do must possess simultaneously all the knowledge displayed in all their works. I once knew a publishers' hack who spent all his days at the British Museum Reading-room, picking other men's brains. He had put his name to a score or two of books thus manufactured. A mutual acquaintance who was not in the secret once asked me admiringly, "What is there that that man doesn't know?" Such is the assumption which lies at the root of the astonishment commonly expressed at Shakespeare's learning. Every man who has had occasion in his time to write a few volumes will feel compelled to smile, if only in his sleeve, at this sweetly childlike faith.

How books are made.

A writer of books has to "cram" for each volume he turns out. To suppose that a man knows to-day what he put into a book ten years ago is like supposing that he could to-day pass the examination on the strength of which he graduated from his university. I may be told that in thus betraying a jealously guarded secret of the bookmaker's art, I am "giving the show away" with both hands; to which I would briefly reply that that is precisely what I desire to do.

When a man is writing a book, he knows the contents of the chapter on which at a given moment he is engaged. If he is a conscientious craftsman, he knows, at the time his work goes through the press, all that it contains. He is at pains to check every statement of fact, and to see that the various parts of the work are mutually consistent. But the chances are that by the time he is reading the reviews, he has already forgotten a great deal that his book sets forth. If it treats of an academic or abstruse subject, and if after writing it the author turns his attention to other lines of study, then in a few years he has to go back and grind at the contents of his own book, almost as though it had been the product of another mind.

Now, in the case of Shakespeare, it is foolish to assume that the entire range of knowledge in all his dramatic and poetic works was present in his consciousness at any single moment. His method of work lies on the face of his plays. He crammed for each of them as the college man crams for his exam,—though with far less regard to accuracy. For his English or Scottish history he went to Holinshed. Whether what Holinshed gave was true he did not know, and he cared as little as some newspaper reporters care whether what they write is true. What he wanted was material for a dramatic story. He picked it up wherever he could find it, and, having found it, he made such use of it as he chose. For his knowledge of foreign countries he probably depended much more upon conversation than upon books. This hypothesis accounts not only for his knowledge, but also for the amazing ignorance that he frequently displays. The one kind of knowledge in which he excelled all other men — the knowledge of human character, of the loves and hates, the desires and aversions of the human heart, the knowledge of "the breaking strain of a man under temptation" — such knowledge is not to be found in books. It is here that his creative force, his unrivalled powers of observa-

How much did Shakespeare know at any one time?

tion and sympathy, came into play. Many a schoolboy might correct the historical statements and implications of *Macbeth*. Any university professor could point out anachronisms and impossibilities by the score in *King Lear, The Winter's Tale* and *Cymbeline*. But where was the school, and where were the books, from which the poet learned to describe the workings of Macbeth's soul under the strain of the impulse to murder, and under the ever-deepening horror of the sense of guilt? It is probable that Shakespeare mistook the narrative of *King Lear,* which Holinshed handed on to him from Geoffrey of Monmouth, for sober history.[2] There is nothing to show that he considered it any more fabulous than the narratives on which *Macbeth* and *Julius Caesar* were founded. Even if Geoffrey's fiction had been historical, Shakespeare nevertheless makes of it, as he does of the historical material of many of his plays, one huge and mountainous anachronism.

Difference between booklearning and insight. Book-learning will account for knowledge, but not for wisdom and insight. The latter are given, if at all, only by that wind of the spirit which bloweth where it listeth. Wisdom and insight are as exceptional and surprising in a man who has had

[2] Down to the beginning of the eighteenth century the majority of scholars believed Geoffrey of Monmouth's *Historia Britonum* to be a veritable history. Though this view of it is utterly baseless, the quaint old book is well worth reading as a specimen of early mediaeval romancing; and, as furnishing the material of *Lear* and *Cymbeline,* it is entitled to respect. The first English translation of it appeared in 1718. This was the work of one Aaron Thompson, of Queen's College, Oxford, who quite believed in his author's veracity. It is now easily accessible in the fourth volume of Bohn's Antiquarian Library, containing "Six Old English Chronicles," edited by J. A. Giles (London, 1848), and in Dent's "Everyman" series.

the highest educational opportunities which his age and country can offer, as they are in a man who by his own powers has risen from obscurity through the conquest of disadvantages. The unacknowledged assumption, the implicit premise, of those who affirm the Baconian authorship of Shakespeare's plays, is that the insight into life which those plays manifest would *not* be surprising or exceptional in the case of a man of Bacon's antecedents and academic training. The orthodox Shakespearean may perfectly well answer that these qualities would be just as amazing in Bacon as in any glover's son from any country town in England. Prove, if you can, that the plays are Bacon's, and you add many cubits to *his* stature. But you do not dissipate any shred of the mystery.

The amount of knowledge revealed by the plays, however, is not mysterious; or, at all events, it will not seem so to anybody who contemplates the facts in a realistic and unromantic spirit, and remembers what information the unschooled Browning showed in *Paracelsus* at twenty-three and in *Sordello* at twenty-eight. Shakespeare, or whoever else, was writing for more than twenty years. The mere quantity of his output is not abnormally great. It is probable that he never produced more than two plays in any one year, and it is certain that he did not average even two a year. If, then, we think of any given play as representing six months' study and thought, the learning it displays will cease to seem surprising. Indeed, the moment we drop the fantastic habit of totalizing the knowledge displayed by these works as a whole, we get a view of the mental acquirements of their author which makes him cease to seem, in this respect, exceptional.

The plays cover a period of twenty years.

The unique gift of the poet and seer not being here in question, any man's experience may fairly be brought into illustrative parallelism. Let me accordingly cite the case of an old and intimate friend of my own — one Ignoratio E. Postpropter, a laborious pedant of various acquirements. During the past ten years it has been his fate to give several hundreds of lectures, covering an enormous range of subject-matter. For every one of these, I can warrant that he took all possible pains to master and to marshal his facts. If he were now to gather up his piles of lecture-notes and make them into books, those books would display a vast deal more knowledge than he consciously possesses at the present time. If his readers treated him to any degree of the naïve reverence of the Shakespearean idolater, they would falsely conclude that he is a desperately learned person. To push the parallel one step farther: it may be imagined that some people, astonished at so much information, might think it worth while to hunt up poor old Ignoratio's antecedents. They would then discover that he had very little schooling, and that his avocations from early youth to mature years were such as (ostensibly) to leave no margin of opportunity for supplementing the rudimentary scraps of knowledge which he picked up at school. Would not the conclusion be irresistible, that Mr. Postpropter could not possibly be the author of his own books? Would not the weird habits of mind peculiar to the Baconian tribe set some of them upon the quest of another person, who might possibly have done a work of which he was demonstrably incapable?

This leads us to a further important consideration. We have perhaps disposed of the illusion that the amount of mere learning manifested in Shakespeare is abnormally great. Turn we now to the other assumption which lies implicit in all arguments against the Shakespearean authorship of the plays. This is the idea that because Shakespeare had but little schooling, he cannot possibly have had much knowledge.[3] Is it not strange that such an idea should be entertained, in face of the obtrusive fact that much of the time of college students is spent in studying the work of people who never went to colleges? Are we really so accustomed to exhibitions of gigantic knowledge on the part of people who have had academic training, and of such alone, that we have a genuine right to be sceptical of the possibility of extensive information in a man who has picked his own way through life? All the arguments based on Shakespeare's scanty schooling which are employed to prove that he cannot have written his own plays would be equally valid if used to show that Browning could not have written his poems or Dickens his novels. Who was Dickens? This child of an insolvent and impris-

Paucity of schooling need not mean paucity of knowledge:

Nor vice versâ.

[3] The work of writing this chapter is relieved by reading in a Chicago newspaper a "legal decision," to the effect that "William Shakespeare was an impostor. Francis Bacon was the author of all the literary works hitherto ascribed to Shakespeare." In the course of this decisive judgment, his Honour propounded the news that "Shakespeare was not an educated man, while Bacon was a scholar with an education equal *or superior* to any in his age. Because *literary people were frowned upon in England in his time* [that is, in the days when Queen Elizabeth spoke a leash of languages, and the youthful Lady Jane Grey read Plato in the original!], Bacon went to Paris and found favour there. Shortly after Shakespeare's death the works now attributed to him were published, and history credited him with the authorship."— *Chicago Evening Post,* April 21, 1916. Comment is not superfluous, but it would need a Samuel Butler to do justice to the theme.

oned debtor, who was working in a Southwark blacking factory when he should have been at school,— whence can he have got the knowledge and the insight possessed by the writer of *Martin Chuzzlewit* and the *Tale of Two Cities?*

The difficulty of accounting for Shakespeare's knowledge vanishes the moment we take account of a few facts, which become self-evident when we look into our own experience instead of suffering our judgment to be perverted by baseless preconceptions.

But if, after all, we feel that there is a residual difficulty in attributing to Shakespeare so much information as the author of these plays at various times possessed, what is this as compared with the immeasurable difficulty which those who believe in the Baconian authorship must find in the *ignorance* they display? I am here dealing only with quite superficial considerations. There is a fundamental reason for holding that, whoever else may have written the plays, Bacon cannot have done so. This, however, lies deeper, and will be dealt with later. At present we are concerned only with the contention that this supreme glory of English literature must have been the work of a man of profound and accurate scholarship. Now the fact is that the plays reveal, on the one hand, a knowledge of what is commonly called "low life" impossible to a man of aristocratic family and surroundings and full (as Bacon was) of caste-pride. On the other hand, they display an all-pervading ignorance or carelessness, of a kind which does not in the slightest degree detract from their value, but which in a man like Bacon would have been inconceivable.

I do not rest this argument solely upon the

Could Bacon have shown the curious ignorance betrayed by the plays?

familiar list of petty anachronisms which any The well-known anachronisms.
reader can cull from the pages of the plays as he
goes through them.   To be sure, one cannot imagine
Francis Bacon introducing a striking clock in the *J. C.* II i 192-3.
days of Julius Caesar or Macbeth, or making King
John refer to artillery.   The academic mind would *K. John* I i 26.
recoil from putting jokes about Calvinistic theology
into the play of *Cymbeline,* the period of which is *Cym.* I ii 23.
either the first century B.C. or the first century
A.D.   The reference to Aristotle which Shake-
speare puts upon the lips of Hector in *Troilus and* *T. & C.* II ii 166-7.
Cressida, eight hundred years before Aristotle was
born, would have made Bacon, or any scholarly-
minded man, faint.   The sea-coast of Bohemia in *W. T.* III iii.
The Winter's Tale, the journey from Verona to
Milan by sea in *The Two Gentlemen of Verona,* the *T. G. V.* I i 71 and II iv 50.
embarking of Prospero on a ship at the gates of
Milan in *The Tempest,* the black skin of Othello, *Tempest* I ii 144.
the unmistakable allusions to events of 1606 in
Macbeth and *King Lear,* the description of Imo- *Macb.* II iii 1-10.
gen's bed-chamber as that of a sixteenth-century *K. L.* I ii 95 ff, and elsewhere.
palace,— these, and scores more, are so many
camels for the capacious throats of the Baconians *Cym.* II iv 66 ff.
to swallow.   But let us assume them to be all dis-
posed of.   As they recede from view, there emerges
a more gigantic difficulty.   These blunders and
absurdities *are not exceptional,* as they are commonly assumed to be.   When you hunt for anachronisms in Shakespeare, you are not looking for
needles in a haystack; you are looking for hay in
a haystack.

The tragedy of *King Lear,* for instance, is not a
synchronistic production, marred by incidental
anachronisms.   The account of the cockney strik-
ing the eels, and of the man who, " in pure kindness II iv 118-21.

to his horse, buttered his hay," Kent's description of the cringing Oswald in terms that could not possibly have been used by anybody except an Elizabethan Englishman — these things are strictly of a piece with their context. The anachronism is the whole play, not the occasional stray reference. Shakespeare's method in "Jumping o'er times, turning the accomplishment of many years into an hour-glass," is always to telescope the period with which he professes to deal into his own age. No matter what the stage directions may say, the period of his play is the month in which he writes it, and the scene is always laid either in London or in the rural districts of England. The mob in *Julius Caesar* is a crowd of cockney artizans; the minds of the conspirators against Caesar are as Elizabethan as the hats which they draw down over their brows and the cloaks in which half their faces are buried. The wood in the *Midsummer Night's Dream* may be "near" Athens, for distance is a relative conception; but one may swear that it is much nearer Stratford-on-Avon. The Forest of Arden (though it contains both deer and lionesses!) is the forest of Henley-in-Arden. The sheep-shearing, where Autolycus swindles the Clown, and gulls Mopsa and Dorcas with lies more breath-bereaving than Falstaff's, was certainly held in Warwickshire, in the days of King James I.

If we are wise, we shall love our Shakespeare all the more for this kind of procedure. But can anybody imagine Francis Bacon, with his scientific, legal, and scholarly mind, going to work with such a blissful unconsciousness or such a superb indifference to consistency? In Bacon's utopia, *The New Atlantis* (where life is as merry as a physics

II ii 13-20.

I i 1-31.

II i 73-4.

As You Like It II ii and IV iii.

W. T. IV iii and iv.

How Bacon labours after consistency.

laboratory, and nobody ever laughs), he feels constrained to resort to a miraculous intervention of Providence to explain how his Atlanteans had come by their Christian faith. He recounts how, about "twenty years after the ascension of our Saviour," a great pillar of light appeared at sea off the eastern coast of Atlantis. Putting out in boats to find what this might mean, the people discovered that it was a supernatural manifestation. Approaching closer, they found a cedar chest containing a book and a letter. The book comprised the entire contents of the Old and New Testaments (including, as Bacon specifically states, *those parts of the New Testament which were not then written*)! The letter was from the Apostle Bartholomew, explaining, to anybody to whom God should send it, that salvation should come unto them with the chest and its contents. So oppressed is Bacon by the necessity of removing every inconsistency, even at the cost of a miracle, that he tells us that this book and letter were read and understood by means of a supernatural gift of tongues.

Now, the difficulty thus laboriously circumvented would never have presented itself to Shakespeare as a difficulty at all. Is it conceivable that a writer so sensitive as Bacon to the danger of anachronism, so concerned to articulate in a consistent context every detail of the land he is describing, could have allowed himself the divine carelessnesses of Shakespeare? We must remember that the statement that Bacon wrote Shakespeare's plays is exactly equivalent to the statement that Shakespeare wrote Bacon's works,— including *The New Atlantis*. Who does not feel intuitively that the dramatist would have depicted the Atlanteans as Christians without

Shakespeare never troubles about such points.

C. E. V i. the slightest hesitation or misgiving? *The Comedy of Errors,* being a re-hash of the plot of the *Menaechmi* of Plautus, is presumably pre-Christian in its period; yet Shakespeare introduces a Roman Catholic priory and a Lady Abbess into it without turning a hair. The period of *The Winter's Tale* is some indefinite date B.C. Classical paganism is still extant, and the Delphic Oracle is going strong.
IV iv 213-22. Yet in this play Autolycus sells gewgaws unknown to mortal woman before Elizabeth's day, and describes himself as having gone about the country
IV iii 87. with a puppet-show depicting the story of the Prodigal Son! In no case could Bacon have done this kind of thing; but we do not need to rest on *a priori* arguments. We have in *The New Atlantis* his clumsy attempt at an imaginative work. We see by what far-fetched devices he goes about to avoid a difficulty that the author of the plays would have swallowed unconsciously.

Fundamental difference between Shakespeare and Bacon: But, as I have already remarked, these peculiarities of Shakespeare, impossible as they make the Baconian hypothesis, are less weighty than a fundamental consideration which it yet remains to urge. This is the fact that Bacon and the author of the plays represent two radically different types of volitional organization and canalization. Or, to express it less clumsily, the mind and will of Shakespeare are oriented on a totally different principle from the mind and will of Bacon. Shakespeare is
Shakespeare is a spectator of existence; the fascinated and fascinating onlooker at the game of life. He is what Addison pretended to be — a spectator. He observes all time and all existence; he has an eye for every various manifestation of human character and idiosyncrasy. What he thus observes he reports with a penetration and a power

of sympathy never equalled by any other student of
the pageant of human life. His is an insight which
never seeks to translate itself into social action. He
never preaches. He does not say that because ambition like Macbeth's is the way to hell, therefore we
must suppress the ambitious man. He does not
urge reform in Church or State; he does not plead
for the extension of human knowledge, for the
abolition of poverty or the moral cleansing of cities.
His will and reason, and the impulses which animate
them, are fulfilled and satisfied when he has painted
his wonderful pictures of things as they are,— of the
roots and the fruits of human conduct.

Bacon, on the contrary, though within his limits
no mean observer, is first and foremost a player
in that game of which Shakespeare is a spectator.
From first youth to the end of his days, Bacon took
all knowledge to be his province,— not for the sake
of knowledge, but in order that he might inaugurate
a new epoch of mastery over nature in the interests
of man. He is the statesman of science. Whereas
Shakespeare seeks to entertain and to delight his
audience, Bacon is always prodding at the will of
his reader. He would have you arise and increase
your knowledge, that you may co-operate with him
in the instauration of the *imperium hominis,* the
kingdom of man. Whoever has studied the immortal works of Bacon without feeling this constant
pressure upon his will, has conned him with little
sympathy.

Now, a man may have a good deal of versatility,
but he cannot be two totally different people at the
same time. He cannot be both a negro and a white
man. If he is intermediate between these, he is
neither, but a third thing. Yet the difference be-

Bacon is bent on re-mould-ing the human order.

tween such a type of mind as that of the writer of
the plays on the one hand, and that of the author of
the *Novum Organum* and the *De Augmentis* on the
other, is deeper than that between a white man and
a negro.   And as their attitude towards life is thus
radically distinct, so their observation and interpretation of life are quite differently motived.   The
lightest work of Bacon is the writing of "Counsells
Civill and Morall."   When he is not labouring at
his chosen task — a task which he knows he can
never complete, but which whole generations and
nations of men must work at after him — he recre-
ates himself by pouring forth advice for the regu-
lation of individual lives.   No man ever formulated
so exhaustively or with such insight as Bacon the
ideal conditions of the scientific habit of mind.   His
catalogue of the idols of the tribe, the idols of
the cave, the idols of the theatre and the idols of the
market-place, together with his description of the
various types of error and delusion into which these
false images lead man, is the evidence of a kind of
insight which can be generated only by a will that is
strenuously bent upon knowledge as a means to
action.   Already in 1592 (at the age of thirty-one)
he complains to Burghley that he "waxes somewhat
ancient."   He needs place and money, that he may
devote himself to the reconstruction of the entire
world of science and the inauguration of a new
epoch : —

Bacon's
Essays.

*Novum
Organum,*
Book I,
Aphorisms
xxxviii-
lxviii.

His letter to
Burghley
[1592].

> If I could purge it [*i. e.,* knowledge] of two sorts
> of rovers, whereof the one with frivolous disputa-
> tions, confutations and verbosities, the other with blind
> experiments and auricular traditions and impostures,
> hath committed so many spoils, I hope I should bring
> in industrious observations, grounded conclusions, and
> profitable inventions and discoveries — the best state

of that province. This, whether it be curiosity, or vainglory, or nature, or (if one take it favourably) *philanthropia,* is so fixed in my mind as it cannot be removed.

Nor was it removed. Bacon was loyal with an unswerving loyalty to the early chosen mission and purpose of his life. His great political miscarriage was due in part to the laudable wish for means to prosecute his researches on a larger scale. He rested not day or night in obeying what was for him the heavenly vision; and he met his death through rashly making a scientific experiment in winter-time. His whole mind and will being caught up in this one purpose, he seldom relaxes even into a contemplative, never into a playful mood. His literary style, rich, copious and scrupulously polished as it is, is a means to an end, never an end in itself. It is never at leisure to rejoice in its own felicities. It is always an exhortation to us to arise and exert ourselves in the acquisition of that knowledge which is to provide "a rich storehouse for the glory of the Creator and the relief of man's estate."[4]

His lifelong adherence to his mission.

Adv. of Learning, Book I.

[4] The ablest student of Bacon in the nineteenth century, and the best friend his reputation has ever had,— James Spedding, his vindicator against Macaulay's eloquently unjust detraction — was not only convinced that Bacon had nothing to do with the authorship of Shakespeare's plays, but thought it probable that he had never seen them. There is a passage in the *De Augmentis,* Book II, cap. xiii, in which Bacon speaks disparagingly and superficially of dramatic poesy, which he thinks far inferior to "Parabolical Poesy." Bacon's paragraph, as might be expected, betrays not the slightest knowledge of, or interest in, contemporary drama, which he thinks corrupt and trifling. Upon this Spedding comments as follows : —

"It is a curious fact that these remarks on the character of the modern drama were probably written, and were certainly first published, in the same year which saw the first collection

Now, a serious belief in Bacon as the author of Shakespeare's plays is possible only to one who either does not know the works of the two writers, or who is singularly lacking in power of insight and discrimination.   Let me offer the closest parallel that suggests itself to my mind.   Suppose someone

Italics mine.

of Shakespeare's plays; of which, though they had been filling the theatre for the last thirty years, *I very much doubt whether Bacon had ever heard.*   How little notice they attracted in those days as works of literary pretension, may be inferred from the extreme difficulty which modern editors have found in ascertaining the dates, or even the order, of their production.   Though numbers of contemporary newsletters, filled with literary and fashionable intelligence, have been preserved, it is only in the Stationers' register and the accounts kept by the Master of the Revels that we find any notices of the publication or acting of Shakespeare's plays. In the long series of letters from John Chamberlain to Dudley Carleton, scattered over the whole period from 1598 to 1623,— letters full of the news of the month; news of the court, the city, the pulpit, and the bookseller's shop; in which court-masques are described in minute detail, author, actors, plot, performance, reception and all;—we look in vain for the name of Shakespeare or of any one of his plays.   And yet during that period *Hamlet, Twelfth Night, Othello, Measure for Measure, The Merchant of Venice, Macbeth, Lear, The Tempest, The Winter's Tale, Coriolanus,* and several more, must have appeared as novelties.   And indeed that very letter without which we should hardly know that Shakespeare was personally known to any one in the great world as a distinguished dramatic writer,— I mean Lord Southampton's letter in furtherance of a petition from him and Burbage to the Lord Chancellor Ellesmere — proves at the same time how little was known about him by people of that quality. 'This other' (he writes, after describing him as his especial friend and the writer of some of our best English plays,) 'hath to name William Shakespeare. . . . Both are right famous in their qualities, though it longeth not of your lordship's gravity and wisdom to resort unto the places where they were wont to delight the public ear.'   This was in 1608; and yet only six years before, when Ellesmere received Elizabeth at Harewood, *Othello* had been acted there for her entertainment. Even now a writer otherwise unknown hardly becomes known as the author of a successful play."

(a Chicago magistrate, for example) were to take seriously the hint flippantly dropped above, and declare that Dickens could not be the real author of the works that bear his name. Suppose then that the cryptogram-and-cipher mania should take possession of this critic's mind, and he should notice the startling circumstance that the initials of Charles Dickens are also those of another man — the greatest scientific mind of England in the nineteenth century: Charles Darwin. He would at once be put upon the trail of a mare's-nest as magnificent as that discovered by the believers in Baconspeare. How obvious, he would say, is the pseudonym of Darwin! Casting about for a name under which to publish those novels which he was naturally too much ashamed of to father in his own person, he asks himself, " Now, what the dickens shall I call myself?" A flash of inspiration crosses his mind, and he replies, "Well, why not Dickens? Charles Dickens! the very thing!"

As impossible to believe Bacon wrote Shakespeare as to believe that Darwin wrote Dickens.

I admit that the hypothesis here suggested is monstrous, absurd, and incredible; also, that it is absolutely superfluous. But may I not point out (with the utmost delicacy in the world) that these are the exact characteristics of the Bacon-Shakespeare theory? How fantastic, it may be said, to dream that Charles Darwin,— whose whole soul was so organized about his scientific work that he would watch a pot of earthworms for a day and a night on end; who was so modest and circumspect that he kept his discovery of natural selection to himself for twenty years; and who never was known to show any glimmerings of a sense of humour,— should have been the creator of Mr. Micawber, Dick Swiveller, Sairey Gamp, and Sam

Weller! Fantastic it is. But I maintain that a reading of Francis Bacon's works and a study of his life creates an irresistible conviction that there was precisely this same kind of impossibility to prevent him from creating the characters of Falstaff, Doll Tearsheet, Touchstone and Autolycus.

Bacon should be compared with Shakespeare in detail.

Or take another simple test: Let any man of the most ordinary literary discrimination read first the *Novum Organum* and then the *Midsummer Night's Dream* and *The Tempest,* and he will feel that these can no more have come from the same mind than the works of Mark Twain could have come from the mind of Herbert Spencer. Or, again, let anybody read Bacon's essay on Love, with its dry, cold, cynical, contemptuous analysis, and then read *Romeo and Juliet;* or, for that matter, any of the plays of Shakespeare which contain a pair of lovers, — from Valentine and Sylvia in *The Two Gentlemen of Verona* to Florizel and Perdita in *The Winter's Tale,* or Ferdinand and Miranda in *The Tempest.* Bacon writes thus: —

Bacon on Love

You may observe that amongst all the great and worthy persons (whereof the memory remaineth, either ancient or recent,) there is not one that hath been transported to the mad degree of love; which shows that great spirits and great business do keep out this weak passion. . . . It is a strange thing to note the excess of this passion, and how it braves the nature and value of things, by this; that the speaking in a perpetual hyperbole is comely in nothing but in love. Neither is it merely in the phrase, for whereas it hath been well said that the arch-flatterer, with whom all the petty flatterers have intelligence, is a man's self; certainly the lover is more. For there was never proud man thought so absurdly well of himself as the lover doth of the person loved; and therefore it was well said that

It is impossible to love and be wise. . . . This
passion hath its floods in the very times of weakness;
which are, great prosperity and great adversity;
though this latter hath been less observed: both which
times kindle love, and make it more fervent, and
therefore show it to be *the child of folly.*[5] They do
best, who if they cannot but admit love, yet make it
keep quarter; and sever it wholly from their serious
affairs and actions of life; for if it check once with
business, it troubleth men's fortunes, and maketh
men that they can no ways be true to their own ends.
I know not how, but martial men are given to love;
I think it is but as they are given to wine; [5] for perils
commonly ask to be paid in pleasures.

Was there ever such a worldly-wise man of affairs,
impatient of the headstrong follies that distract men
from business? Who can imagine the creator of
Orlando and Rosalind making love and lust synony-
mous, or perpetrating that comparison between love
and the addiction of soldiers to strong drink? Who
can think of the creator of Juliet and Portia
speaking solely from the point of view of men,
as though women existed only as a nuisance to
men, and had no feelings worthy of psychological
analysis? Observe, too, that Bacon is cynically consistent. For the same reason that he objects to
love, he objects also to marriage and parenthood. and Mar-
In his essay "Of Marriage and Single Life" he riage.
lays it down that "He that hath wife and children hath given hostages to fortune, for they are
impediments to great enterprises, either of virtue or
mischief."

Sir Sidney Lee has said of the attempt to make
Shakespeare's plays, by the aid of a cipher, mean
something other than they say, that it is "unworthy
of sane consideration." One is almost tempted to

[5] Italics mine.

pronounce in similar terms about the entire Baconian case. Nobody would be willing to argue with a critic who maintained that the pictures of Van Dyck were painted by Velasquez. Why then should we argue seriously with those who cannot see the difference,—"gross as a mountain, open, palpable,"—between the work of Bacon and that of Shakespeare?

Alleged correspondences between Bacon and Shakespeare.

But, it is argued, there are identities of phrase, similarities of style. So there must necessarily be between men living in the same age and country, and writing in the same language. There are far less of such resemblances between Bacon and Shakespeare than there are between Shakespeare and most of the poets of his day. Any argument that Shakespeare's plays were written by another *poet,*—though it were Robert Greene or Drayton or Chapman,—would be sane and scientific as compared with the attempt to ascribe them to Bacon. Whoever may have written the contents of the First Folio, the proposition that Francis Bacon did *not* write them is as certain as anything in the whole of literary history.

Known facts of Shakespeare's life.

The known facts of Shakespeare's life are so numerous that it would be impossible, were it not unnecessary, to set them forth here. The exhaustive treatise by Sir Sidney Lee (of which the edition of 1916 is in large part a new work) renders it superfluous for any subsequent writer to tell the story again. We can trace Shakespeare from his baptism, through his schooldays, his youth, his marriage, his disappearance from his native town, and then, after a lapse of some years, through step after step of his upward progress to the position of the greatest popular success and the admittedly best dramatist of his time. The records of his life show him to be constantly associated with the very kind of men with whom we should naturally expect a dramatic author to be connected: the Burbages and their troupe, Fletcher, Jonson. He is a member of the leading company of actors of his time. He becomes a shareholder in their enterprise, he makes a fortune out of his work with them, and, after his retirement, when making his will, he thinks affectionately of some of his old "fellows," and leaves souvenir legacies[6] to them. Seven years after his death, the reciprocated affection of these "fellows" leads two of them to perform an act of piety to Shakespeare's memory, and a service to mankind greater than they dreamed of, by publishing as many of his dramas as they were able to lay their hands upon.

Shakespeare is a Stratford figure, and the traditions of him are confined to Stratford and London and the roads between. The provincial dialect of Warwickshire is found again and again in his plays, and the tradition that represents him as at loggerheads with the local magnate, Sir Thomas Lucy, is borne out by his revenge upon that worthy in the *Merry Wives of Windsor* and in the Second Part of *King Henry IV*. The character of Justice Shallow in those plays is unmistakably meant for Lucy. The Induction to *The Taming of the Shrew* introduces us to actual personages known to have lived in the neighbourhood of Stratford. These references and allusions do not appear in the old play which Shakespeare worked over. Wincot is the

Local indications in the plays.

---

[6] To John Heminges, Henry Condell, and Richard Burbage, 26s. 8d. apiece to buy memorial rings.

name of a place within four miles of Stratford. Burton Heath, to which Kit Sly describes himself as belonging, was the home of an aunt of Shakespeare and her family. The name of Hacket, the fat alewife, is that of a family traceable in the parochial records of Wincot. The reference to William Visor of Woncot and to Clement Perkes of the Hill allude to a Gloucestershire locality and to actual persons living there, and the description is such as only one intimately familiar with the local nomenclature would have written. There is no kind of evidence which could trace these significant details to any other source than the man Shakespeare.

John Shakespeare. Shakespeare's father was something of a Micawber, who, after prospering in business and rising to such rank as his little town could bestow upon him, fell for many years into comparative poverty. To this fortunate circumstance we owe, among other things, the plays of William Shakespeare. Despite John's troubles, he was able to send **The Stratford Grammar School.** his son to an excellent school,— excellent, that is, for its day,— where, without expense to his father, the boy got a sufficient grounding in the fields of knowledge then most generally cultivated. The writer of the plays does not, as we have said, give any evidence of profound or finished scholarship. He was a man who could read Latin and Italian when he had to, and French when he liked. The power to do this is precisely what any lad of more than mediocre intelligence and literary bent could well be expected to acquire at the Stratford Grammar School. It was probably a fortunate circumstance that the boy had to be withdrawn from the school before his masters had had a chance to make

a pedant of him, or to sterilize his imagination and
destroy his taste for literature.

Shakespeare's early marriage, probably under
shady circumstances, and the known poverty of his
family, make the poaching stories perfectly credible. *The poaching
stories.*
They at least explain the cause of his permanent
enmity to the chief landowner of his locality. They
also provide a plausible explanation of his sudden
disappearance from Stratford, and his absence from
his native town and his family for about ten years
on end. There are several little hints in the plays
which lead one to suspect that the writer was not *Tempest
IV i 14-23;*
very happily married. The allusions to the misery
resulting from pre-marital intimacy, and from a *Twelfth
Night
II iv 29 ff.*
man's being married to a woman older than himself,
chime perfectly with the little that is known as to
Shakespeare's relations with Anne Hathaway.

Of the poet's first ten years in London, as *Early days
in London.*
would naturally be expected, scarcely anything is
known. Shortly after his arrival there he was in
close relations with one Richard Field, a Stratford
man of exactly his own age, who had settled in
London a little before Shakespeare's coming, and
set up in business as a printer. This man it was
who printed *Venus and Adonis,* the "first heir" of
the poet's invention to be published. The tradition
of Shakespeare's beginning by holding horses at the
theatre door, which goes back to D'Avenant, is
unconfirmed, but there is nothing in the least incredible about it. There has been dispute about the
statement of William Castle, parish clerk of Stratford in the seventeenth century, that Shakespeare
entered the theatre first as a servitor, and about
Malone's assertion that he began as call-boy. But
how would one expect a raw country youth to begin

—as heavy lead or stage manager? If the traditions alleged anything different from what they do affirm, there would be reason to doubt them; as it is, though necessarily unprovable, they are entirely probable. What we do know is that by the end of those ten years Shakespeare was universally recognized as an actor and playwright, as the author of two long poems (published by himself and dedicated to the Earl of Southampton) and of a number of sonnets, which were circulating in MS., after the fashion of the day, among his friends and acquaintances. Already in the year 1598, at the age of thirty-four, he was acclaimed by Francis Meres as the best dramatic writer then in England.[7]

Position ten years later.

At this period we find Shakespeare in a position to rehabilitate the fallen fortunes of his family, and to aspire for himself after a position in the social world, by seeking from the Heralds' College a grant of arms, for which, as was customary, he applied in the name of his father. His income, from this time onwards, was comparatively large. By 1597 it was probably not less than £500 a year, the purchasing power of which was equal to that of

Shakespeare's income.

[7] References to Meres appear in many works dealing with Shakespeare. As his volume is somewhat rare, it may be advantageous to cite his actual words. His book is entitled "*Palladis Tamia: Wits Treasury: Being the Second Part of Wits Commonwealth.* By Francis Meres, Maister of Artes of both Vniuersities." (London, 1598.) One section of this work is called "A Comparative Discourse of our English Poets, with the Greeke, Latine, and Italian Poets." The chief passages in this section referring to Shakespeare are the following (though there are several others):—

"As the Greeke tongue is made famous and eloquent by Homer, Hesiod, . . . so the English tongue is mightily enriched, and gorgeouslie inuested in rare ornaments and resplendent abiliments by sir *Philip Sidney, Spencer, Daniel, Drayton, Warner, Shakespeare, Marlow,* and *Chapman.* . . .

$20,000 in America at the present day. There is conclusive evidence that after 1599, in which year he became a shareholder in the Globe Theatre Company, it increased considerably. Moreover, his various expenditures at Stratford were all investments, and as such were more or less productive. He let his house and farmed his land by proxy, spending most of the year in London down till 1611.

During the last five years of his life, he is traceable as living in retirement in his native town, whilst keeping up business connections with his old professional associates in London. His will shows him **His will.** to have been, like several others who stood at the head of their profession, a person of comparative affluence. He has considerable landed and house property to devise, and quite a large sum of money, besides a lengthy list of " goodes " and " chattells." His theatrical shareholdings are not mentioned in his will; but neither does Burbage in his will refer to his holdings. Both Burbage and Condell also left considerable sums. Alleyn, who died in 1626, had during his lifetime acquired for £10,000 (equiva-

---

" As the soule of *Euphorbus* was thought to liue in *Pythagoras:* so the sweete wittie soule of *Ouid* lives in mellifluous & hony-tongued *Shakespeare,* witnes his *Venus* and *Adonis,* his *Lucrece,* his sugred Sonnets among his priuate friends, &c.

" As *Plautus* and *Seneca* are accounted the best for Comedy and Tragedy among the Latines : so *Shakespeare,* among ye English is the most excellent in both kinds for the stage; for Comedy, witnes his *Gentlemen of Verona,* his *Errors,* his *Loue labors lost,* his *Loue labors wonne,* his *Midsummers night dreame,* & his *Merchant of Venice:* for Tragedy, his *Richard the 2. Richard the 3. Henry the 4. King Iohn, Titus Andronicus* and his *Romeo and Iuliet.*

" As *Epius Stolo* said, that the Muses would speak with *Plautus* tongue, if they would speak Latin : so I say that the Muses would speak with *Shakespeares* fine filed phrase, if they would speake English."

lent in purchasing power to $400,000) the estate at Dulwich on which he built the college which has ever since borne his name. By his will he disposes also of nearly £2,000 in money, and provides for the building and endowment of thirty almshouses. Compared with Alleyn, Shakespeare was a poor man; but the testaments of Condell, Pope, Burbage, Alleyn and others corroborate the independently established fact that it was possible for a successful actor, whether playwright or not, to acquire a fair competency by his profession.

Shakespeare died on April 23, 1616, this being, according to tradition, his fifty-second birthday. It is not absolutely certain, however, that he was born on April 23, 1564, though it is certain that his birth took place within a day or two of that date.

CHAPTER III

SHAKESPEARE'S APPRENTICESHIP: TYPICAL EARLY PLAYS

How plays were made, re-made,

THE conditions of dramatic authorship in the Shakespearean period make it extremely difficult in many cases, and sometimes impossible, to assign a play, in whole or in part, to any particular author. The MS. became the absolute property of the theatrical company that purchased it. If, upon production, any part of the play did not take, it would be handed over to another dramatist, or to the literary man of the company, to be cobbled. Upon a revival, new scenes might be inserted, or a whole new part vamped up to suit some particular actor. The liberties thus taken with the text of plays must often have been as extensive as those perpetrated at a later date by Mr. Vincent Crummles.

It was, however, to these conditions that Shakespeare owed his apprenticeship. As Emerson puts it, he "esteemed the mass of old plays waste stock, in which any experiment could be freely tried." To them also we owe those delightful difficulties about the composition of the various parts of the early works of Shakespeare which have provided copy for generations of commentators, and which, being insurmountable, will, by the grace of Providence, furnish a harmless and delightful occupation to the Shakespeare Societies of generations yet unborn.

and
published.

I have already mentioned the fact that the theatrical companies objected to the publication of their plays. In the absence, however, of any law securing the author's copyright, they had no legal redress against piratical printers or publishers who chose to put forward any sort of version or perversion of a drama, and ascribe it to any author whose name was likely to take with the public. Thus it came about that several plays were at various times ascribed to Shakespeare, in which he had no hand at all; and several collections of poems were fathered upon him, without authority and without truth. Many of the quarto editions of authentic plays present a text extensively corrupted.[1] The first quarto of *Hamlet* is a glaring instance of this. Sometimes the printer would purchase a stage copy from some venal actor or hanger-on of the theatre. At other times he would employ a shorthand-writer to take down a piece from the lips of the performers. It is well-nigh impossible even for the most expert modern shorthand-writer to get a correct rendering of a play in this manner. The delivery of the actors is invariably too rapid, and the poetic vocabulary constitutes in itself an enormous strain upon the skill of any stenographer. The piratical printers, however, cared nothing for accuracy; they were merely tradesmen anxious to get the market.

Plays taken
by " brachy-
graphy."

Sixteen of Shakespeare's plays were published in these cheap quartos during his lifetime. There is no evidence that his sanction was obtained to the

---

[1] " Many times . . . the Lord Chamberlain in behalf of the acting companies warned the Stationers' Company against 'procuring, publishing and printing plays,' 'by means whereof not only they [the actors] themselves had much prejudice, but the books much corruption, to the injury and disgrace of the authors.' "— Lee, *Life,* ed. 1916, p. 546.

publication in any single instance. The destruction by fire of the Globe Theatre on June 9, 1613, is probably responsible for the disappearance of Shakespeare's own MSS. The copies on which the Folio is based were obviously defective at many points. It sometimes happens that for isolated passages the quartos give us a better text than does the Folio. In *King Lear,* for example, the whole of scene iii in Act IV is omitted from the Folio, although it contains some of the most impressive lines in the entire tragedy. From the second quarto of *Hamlet* the Folio text has been extensively supplemented. The extreme shortness of *Macbeth,* which is little more than half the length of *Hamlet* or *Lear,* is probably to be ascribed to the fact that the Folio text, our only authority, follows an abbreviated playhouse copy.

What became of Shakespeare's MSS.?

Despite these difficulties, the extensive labour which piety has bestowed upon the analysis of the Shakespearean text justifies us in affirming that we have in the early Comedies undoubted works of Shakespeare, though with occasional touches from other hands, and survivals from older plays which were worked over by him. In the case of some of the Histories, particularly the three parts of *King Henry VI,* we have instances of collaboration between Shakespeare and Marlowe, and perhaps others.

One of the perennial problems of Shakespearean criticism is the case of *Titus Andronicus.* This tragedy is included in the Folio of 1623, and it is one of those mentioned by Meres in 1598. Yet there are only two passages in it (with the exception of an individual line here and there) which the

The mystery of *Titus Andronicus.*

reader can possibly feel to come from the author of
Romeo and Juliet or *Love's Labour's Lost*,— to say
nothing of their greater successors. The two passages in question are the following : —

II ii 1 ff.

The hunt is up, the morn is bright and gray,
The fields are fragrant, and the woods are green :
Uncouple here, and let us make a bay,
And wake the emperor and his lovely bride,
And rouse the prince, and bring a hunter's peal,
That all the court may echo with the noise.
Sons, let it be your charge, as it is ours,
To attend the emperor's person carefully.
I have been troubled in my sleep this night,
But dawning day new comfort hath inspired.

. . . .

II iii 10 ff.

My lovely Aaron, wherefore look'st thou sad,
When everything doth make a gleeful boast?
The birds chant melody on every bush ;
The snake lies rollèd in the cheerful sun ;
The green leaves quiver with the cooling wind,
And make a chequered shadow on the ground :
Under their sweet shade, Aaron, let us sit,
And, whilst the babbling echo mocks the hounds,
Replying shrilly to the well-tun'd horns,
As if a double hunt were heard at once,
Let us sit down and mark their yelping noise ;
And, after conflict such as was supposed
The wandering prince and Dido once enjoy'd,
When with a happy storm they were surpris'd
And curtain'd with a counsel-keeping cave,
We may, each wreathèd in the other's arms,
Our pastimes done, possess a golden slumber ;
Whiles hounds and horns and sweet melodious birds
Be unto us as is a nurse's song
Of lullaby to bring her babe asleep.

Mr. Oliphant Smeaton ventures the assertion that
such passages " are *assuredly* the contributions of
Shakespeare to the play, in his capacity either of
collaborator or reviser." But such transmutation

of possibility into certainty is the bane of Shakespearean study, as of literary criticism and science in general.

Of external evidence against Shakespeare's authorship of *Titus,* we have none save the long-belated assertion of Edward Ravenscroft, who, when issuing a new edition of the play in 1678, said, "I have been told by some anciently conversant with the stage, that it was not originally his [*i. e.,* Shakespeare's], but brought by a private author to be acted, and he only gave some master-touches to one or two of the principal parts or characters." Even without this rather vague statement, however, one would feel certain, from internal evidence, that the ascription of this ghastly abomination to Shakespeare was a mistake. The characters in it are not like human beings at all. The whole thing is a welter of treachery, slaughter, lust and mutilation. The central character, though deeply wronged, cannot for an instant command our sympathy, being himself guilty of every description of senseless savagery. One's impulse would be to ascribe *Titus Andronicus* to Kyd, the author of *The Spanish Tragedy.* It displays a good deal of literary ability, and, with the exception of a very few passages, such as those quoted above, it gives a strong impression of unity of authorship. Meres's testimony is a real difficulty. One might hazard the conjecture that there was a genuine play of Shakespeare's under this title, which has been lost, and that the editors of the Folio printed the extant text by mistake. I offer this merely as a speculation, for which, in the nature of the case, it is impossible to find evidence. One learned Shakespearean, the Rt. Hon. J. M. Robertson, has

External evidence: Ravenscroft (1678).

Internal evidence.

Is Shakespeare's *Titus* lost?

gone to the trouble of writing a whole volume[2] to prove that Shakespeare was not the author of the Folio text of *Titus*. It is not easy to understand why anybody should have given himself the labour thus assumed by Mr. Robertson. The negative cannot be proved by external evidence, and the internal evidence is such that no discriminating reader of the other plays could suppose this one to come from the same hand. It may be Kyd's or Peele's, or the "private author" mentioned by Ravenscroft may be an otherwise unheard-of person, who committed this one offence and then curled up into obscurity for the rest of his days. The point cannot be decided, and it is of little importance. It is, however, as certain as it is astounding that *Titus* was once popular on the stage; as witness the remark of Ben Jonson in the Induction to his *Bartholomew Fair* (1614): "The man who will swear *Jeronimo* or *Andronicus* are the best plays yet, shows that his judgment hath stood still these five and twenty or thirty years." Incidentally, this is eloquent testimony to the task Shakespeare and others had to face in educating the taste of their public.

Dates of composition.

As to the dates of composition of Shakespeare's early plays, a small element of certainty has to be eked out with a liberal allowance of conjecture. If we were to take quite literally the statement in the Dedication of *Venus and Adonis,* published in 1593, that that poem was the "first heire of my inuention," we should have to conclude that no play of Shakespeare's had seen the light before that year.

[2] *Did Shakespeare Write "Titus Andronicus"?* (London: Watts & Co., 1906.)

But this would be to strain the phrase to the break-ing-point, as well as to ignore the difference between his attitude towards his plays and towards his poems. *Venus and Adonis* was certainly the first thing he printed, though the date of printing is no necessary clue to the date of writing; but we must not forget the enigmatic peculiarity of the author with whom we are dealing. He was a man who would take scrupulous care about the publication of such a poem, intended to secure the countenance of a noble patron, and would write *Hamlet, Macbeth, Lear* and *Othello* in the ordinary way of business, and, so far as we can discover, take no steps whatever to ensure their preservation.

One of the fixed points of the criticism of Shakespeare is the fact that he did not think of his plays as literature. He thought of them exclusively from the point of view of the stage and the box-office. Their lines are written for the ear, not for the eye. They presuppose spectators and auditors, not readers. Such plays as were published during his lifetime were printed in defiance of his wishes. The probable destruction of his best MSS. by the Globe fire elicited from him no word of regret that has come down to us, and he seems not in any way to have made provision for the work completed by Heminge and Condell in 1623. This lifelong carelessness of every extra-theatrical aspect of his plays justifies the inference that Shakespeare is not thinking of them when, in 1593, he writes of *Venus* as the first heir of his invention. It may be added that if we do interpret these words as including the plays, we shall have to credit Shakespeare with producing, within five years, eleven of the twelve plays mentioned by Meres in 1598 (omitting *Titus Andro-*

Shakespeare's attitude towards the plays.

nicus), together with the *Lucrece* and nearly all of the Sonnets.

Love's Labour's Lost, 1591.

By the consensus of opinion among the best critics, the comedy of *Love's Labour's Lost* is the earliest of Shakespeare's own productions. It was almost certainly written in 1591 and produced in the spring of 1592. The plot is of the class defined by Professor Moulton as that of "Complication and Resolution," but, as in *The Comedy of Errors,* the breath of new life is imparted to a scheme handled mechanically by the classical practitioners. If the story was borrowed, it was from a source

Characters. now unknown. The names of the chief characters are those of actual leaders in the French Civil War of 1589–94. Biron and Longaville were the two chief supporters of the real King of Navarre. The name of Moth commemorates a French ambassador named La Mothe, who during his stay in London, which closed in 1583, won a popularity which long survived in the memory of playwrights and play-goers. Don Adriano de Armado, the "fantastical Spaniard," recalls a half-crazed personage of that nationality, who for some years haunted the Court of Queen Elizabeth. The scene in which the leading characters appear "in Russian habits, and masked," follows the description of a reception tendered by the ladies of Elizabeth's Court in 1584 to a Russian embassage which had come to seek among them a wife for the Tsar.

The play is full of the spirit of youth and of boisterous and irresponsible fun. It shows many traces of the influence of Lyly; and the preposterous phraseology used by Armado, "a man of fire-new words, fashion's own knight," satirizes the

Euphuistic craze to which Lyly's most famous book had given rise. The rural Constable, the Schoolmaster, and the Curate are the first representatives of a long line of lovable comic characters. In this play, Shakespeare already manifests his habit of pressing into service every scrap of his experience. Even fragments of his school Latin grammar are turned to account. By the age of twenty-seven, he has already made close and discriminating observation of persons in many walks of society. Indeed, the experience and wisdom the comedy displays, together with certain peculiarities of phraseology and versification, have led some critics to the opinion that the extant text represents a fairly extensive revision made by Shakespeare in his "second period." We know that it was touched up in 1597 for a Christmas performance at Court, since in 1598 an edition of the play, "newly corrected and augmented," was published, "as it was presented before her Highness this last Christmas." It is on the title-page of this volume that Shakespeare's name first appears as that of the author of a play. The strict formalism of the blank verse, the abundance of rhyme, the endless punning and the following out of jests to the point of exhaustion, are unmistakable stigmata of Shakespeare's early manner. Biron's brilliant diatribe against study is a typical example of some of these peculiarities:—

Later revision.

Metrical peculiarities.

Why, all delights are vain; but that most vain
Which with pain purchas'd doth inherit pain:
As, painfully to pore upon a book
  To seek the light of truth; while truth the while
Doth falsely blind the eyesight of his look:
  Light seeking light doth light of light beguile;
So, ere you find where light in darkness lies,
Your light grows dark by losing of your eyes.

I i 72 ff.

Study me how to please the eye indeed
　By fixing it upon a fairer eye,
Who dazzling so, that eye shall be his heed
　And give him light that it was blinded by.
Study is like the heaven's glorious sun,
　That will not be deep-search'd with saucy looks.
Small have continual plodders ever won
　Save base authority from others' books.
These earthly godfathers of heaven's lights
　That give a name to every fixèd star,
Have no more profit of their shining nights
　Than those that walk and wot not what they are.
Too much to know is to know nought but fame;
And every godfather can give a name.

In Shakespeare's first play, too, he uses a device
to which he recurs in many subsequent works —
that of a masque or play within a play. The
ludicrous performance by Costard, Sir Nathanael
and the rest of the duffers in the fifth act fore-
shadows the "lamentable tragedy" of Pyramus
and Thisbe in the *Midsummer Night's Dream.*

Plot.

The structure of *Love's Labour's Lost* is of the
simplest. The King of Navarre and his three
friends, Biron, Longaville and Dumain, have sworn
to study for three years, and during that time to
see no women. The Princess of France and her
three ladies, visiting the Court of Navarre on an
impossible embassage, allure them into breaking
their oath. Each of them secretly concocts a poetical epistle to his adored one, and there is riotous
fun as they find one another out. Two of these
compositions are notable examples of the sonnet
style of Shakespeare, and the one addressed by
Longaville to Maria affords positive proof that
Shakespeare, at the beginning of the last decade of
the sixteenth century, was already capable of anything in the extant Sonnets. I mention this because,

for the purpose of supporting a rickety hypothesis about the poet's connection with Pembroke and Mary Fitton, certain writers have dated the Sonnets as late as 1608 or 1609: —

> Did not the heavenly rhetoric of thine eye, IV iii 55 ff.
>   'Gainst whom the world cannot hold argument,
> Persuade my heart to this false perjury?
>   Vows for thee broke deserve not punishment.
> A woman I forswore; but I will prove,
>   Thou being a goddess, I forswore not thee:
> My vow was earthly, thou a heavenly love;
>   Thy grace being gained, cures all disgrace in me.
> Vows are but breath, and breath a vapour is:
>   Then thou, fair sun, which on my earth dost shine,
> Exhal'st this vapour-vow; in thee it is:
>   If broken then, it is no fault of mine:
> If by me broke, what fool is not so wise
> To lose an oath to win a paradise?

The humour of the play, even allowing for the fact that many of the jests are done to death, is a rich achievement, as well as a prophecy of better things to come. IV i 60 ff. There is nothing in Shakespeare more superbly idiotic than the epistle of Don Adriano to Jaquenetta, and the Song of the Seasons at the end of the play has the characteristic Shakespearean lyric lilt. The Page-boy Moth, with his supreme impudence, his impossible cleverness, and his daring wit, is a predecessor rather of Puck and Ariel than of any human character. The long dialogues in rhyme are consistently clever, often surprisingly poetical, but always artificial. The love-making is unconvincing, and suggestive for the most part of a young man who is observing it from without. It is evident that Biron, Longaville and Dumain are only falling in love for a lark.

*The Two
Gentlemen,
1591.*

The Two Gentlemen of Verona, which in all probability goes back to the same year as *Love's Labour's Lost,* is characterized by all the mannerisms and peculiarities which we have noticed in the former play. The plot can be traced to earlier sources, and particular incidents were suggested by a number of works current at the time. In the play as it stands, there is nothing to account for the curious conduct of some of the characters, particularly that of Valentine and Thurio. The plot is mechanical, and in many ways unnatural. The infidelity of Proteus to Julia is as absurd as his repentance; indeed, his double treachery stamps him as a soulless rogue, unworthy of the good fortune bestowed upon him at the close of the play. Decidedly the most notable of the characters are those of Launce and Speed, the precursors, as Sir Sidney Lee remarks, of a long line of whimsical serving-men. One cannot refrain from adding a tribute of praise to Launce's immortal dog,— though unfortunately his owner's speech about him is not suitable for reading aloud. The song "Who is Sylvia?" containing the great lines —

Launce and
Speed.

IV iv 1 ff.

> Love doth to her eyes repair
>   To help him of his blindness,
> And being helped inhabits there —

is another evidence of the early ripening of Shakespeare's lyric genius. We have already remarked on a number of the impossibilities of the play, such as the embarking of Valentine on a ship at Verona to travel to Milan.

It is in this play that the "fine filed" phrases which have passed into current speech begin to appear. At the very outset we have the line, "Home-keeping youth have ever homely wits," and, in Act V, scene iv, "How use doth breed a habit in a man!" The overdone device of the girl disguised in masculine attire—a trick of the southern romancers which was peculiarly useful to dramatists providing for companies that contained no actresses — is used by Shakespeare for the first time in this play. There is abundance of rhyme, and the blank verse is marked by regularity of form and the completion of the thought with the end of the line. The comedy also testifies to a steady development of poetic power, as witness the following lines, which some critics (heaven knows why) have declared to be a description of the Avon at Stratford:—

The first disguised girl, II vii, IV ii, &c.

> The current that with gentle murmur glides,
> Thou know'st, being stopped, impatiently doth rage;
> But when his fair course is not hindered,
> He makes sweet music with the enamell'd stones,
> Giving a gentle kiss to every sedge
> He overtaketh in his pilgrimage;
> And so by many winding nooks he strays
> With willing sport to the wild ocean.

II vii 24 ff.

The Comedy of Errors dates itself by internal evidence among the earliest of Shakespeare's dramatic productions. It was never published in quarto form, the Folio text being the only authority. It is probable that the play performed before the benchers and students of Gray's Inn on December 28, 1594, was Shakespeare's comedy, though it may have been an earlier composition (now lost), entitled *The Historie of Error,* which had appeared in 1576. In the form in which it has come down to us, *The Comedy of Errors* is the shortest of Shakespeare's plays. The abundance of rhyme, the regularity of the blank verse, and the monotony with

Comedy of Errors (1592?).

which the thought, sentence or speech ends with the end of the line, together with the perpetual punning and the piling of pun upon pun, are unmistakable indications of early date. The description of III ii 115-16. France by Dromio of Syracuse as "armed and reverted, making war against her heir," must be understood as referring to the French Civil War of 1589–94. On the whole, the conclusion, both from internal and from external evidence, is that the farce was composed at some time between 1591 and 1593.

Its peculiar characteristics. On many grounds, this play deserves minuter study than has commonly been bestowed upon it, or than we can give to it here. A work of Shakespeare's unripe youth, in form a mere imitation of one of the "classical" comedies, tied down (a very exceptional feature in Shakespeare) to the classical "unities" of time and place, it yet displays such freedom of treatment, such bold defiance of tradition, such originality of structure and dexterous management of complicated plot, as to make of it an important innovation and a gracious prophecy of the unmatched achievements of its author's later years.

Source. In the first place, *The Comedy of Errors* is an adaptation of the plot of the *Menæchmi* of Plautus. That time-honoured composition, however, as usual with Plautus, is dull, mechanical and artificial to the last degree. Following timidly the established tradition of its time, it gives us farce so unqualified as to cut it off altogether from the realities of life. Its characters are sordid, greedy, thievish and contemptible. The conditions of the Roman stage conspired with the tradition to prevent the introduction of the slightest touch of verisimilitude.

Shakespeare, while still in the imitative stage, is free enough to create new characters (those of the two Dromios in particular), to depart from the unnatural theory that a play must be either all comic or all tragic, and to change the characters of his source from lifeless lay-figures into living men and women. It cannot, of course, be pretended that the two Antipholuses and the two Dromios, Adriana and Luciana, the Abbess and the Duke, are individualized as are the characters of Shakespeare's maturer years, or even as are Mercutio, Juliet and Romeo. The "unity" of time — the completion of the action within a single day — gives little scope for that gradual disclosure of character which is the charm of the freer drama. On one point of detail, it may be remarked, Shakespeare's farce is, if possible, more absurd than its wooden Roman original. Plautus does at least attempt to explain the fact that his one pair of twins both have the same name: the relatives give the name of the first to the second after the first has supposedly been killed. Shakespeare does not feel it necessary to inform us why the two patrician twins were both called Antipholus, or why the two plebeians were both named Dromio. In a farce in which consistency is deliberately disregarded, why break the rule by attempting verisimilitude on such a point?

To every story-teller, certain initial assumptions must perforce be granted. You may not dispute the *conditiones sine quâ non* of the story. That there should be two sets of twins with identical names, so alike not only in bodily appearance but also in dress, in manner and in speech, that the one is mistaken for the other by his double's wife and by all his friends (although they have been separated from infancy

Shakespeare's departures from Plautus.

Farce demands acceptance of impossible situation.

and reared in different countries) — this is not a matter to be dismissed because it is impossible. That trifling detail is, of course, self-evident; but in order that there may be a play, you must forget it, or believe it, as Tertullian did his theology, because it is impossible. The dramatist does not say, "I will undertake to prove that such resemblances can exist." He says, "Let it be assumed that such resemblances exist, and I will show you what must follow."

Double confusion of identity destroys the basis of sanity.

What does follow is the suspension of the normal working of people's rationality — the removal, so long as the confusion lasts, of the basis of sanity. When the wife of Antipholus I is speaking with Antipholus II the rational bond which is the presupposition of all human intercourse is snapped. When Dromio II is beaten for not having discharged an errand on which Dromio I was sent, this is because illusion has for the moment so far prevailed as to sever the spiritual nexus of society. The complication, involved as it becomes, is only the working out of this confusion of personal identity, this unconscious abandonment of the absolute of logic, the principle that $A = A$.

Departures from the classical tradition.

III ii.

I i and V.

Most interesting from the critical standpoint, however, is Shakespeare's unhesitating introduction, first of the note of tragedy, and secondly of the serious interest of the wooing of Luciana by Antipholus of Syracuse. The grey and sorrow-stricken Egeon, bereft of wife and children, and exposed by a barbarous law to violent death; the magnanimous Duke Solinus, pitying and desiring to save the victim of the law which nevertheless he is bound to execute; and the sad abbess-mother, who has abandoned the human world which had so dispiteously used her — all these are truly tragic figures, and as such, according to classical standards, are quite out of place in a farce. The love-making of Antipholus II and Luciana, being genuine, is by the same token illicit. Luciana obviously resists his overtures only because she mistakes him for her brother-in-law; she admits that he accosted her "With words that in an honest IV ii 14. suit might move"; and we are left with the certainty that there will be a wedding soon after the curtain falls.

Another partial lapse into seriousness is the discussion between the wife and the maiden sister on II i 1 ff. women's rights, the wife demanding why men should have more liberty than women, and the sister urging the submission of women on the analogy of the animal world:—

> Why, headstrong liberty is lash'd with woe. *Ibid.* 15 ff.
> There's nothing situate under heaven's eye
> But hath his bound, in earth, in sea, in sky:
> The beasts, the fishes and the wingèd fowls
> Are their males' subjects and at their controls:
> Men, more divine, the masters of all these,
> Lords of the wide world and wild watery seas,
> Indued with intellectual sense and souls,
> Of more pre-eminence than fish and fowls,
> Are masters to their females, and their lords:
> Then let your will attend on their accords.

Holding this view, she consistently concludes:—

> Ere I learn love, I'll practise to obey.

Neither the avoidance of the absurdities and artificialities of Plautus, however, nor yet the rich humour of the two Dromios, can make of *The Comedy of Errors* a success, as we understand that term in relation to Shakespeare. Pure farce is not his line: the very lapses into seriousness which we have instanced serve to prove as much. The reality of life is too strong for him. Precisely because his creatures are living and not mere puppets, they fail to respond flexibly to the mad environment of unmixed farce. He reduces, to be sure, the tiresome improbability of the situation by the very natural and life-like process of doubling it.[3] Life is but a collection of impossibilities familiarized to us by their perpetual recurrence. Hence it is easier to tolerate the situation of the two Antipholuses when they are kept in countenance by the twin absurdity of the two Dromios. Yet we feel, as we laugh at the boisterous horseplay of *The Comedy of Errors,* that this kind of thing is unworthy of Shakespeare's steel, and we are glad that his own good judgment, or the counsel of friends, or the public disapproval, so convinced him of this that he never again attempted a play of the same kind.

The period of this comedy is impossible to assign. Ostensibly belonging to the days of paganism, it yet introduces an abbess and a priory. The Ephesian currency appears to include marks, guilders, and English sixpences. The geography of Europe, as discussed between Antipholus and Dromio of Syracuse, is not that of Imperial Roman times, but that of the sixteenth century of the Christian era. Even America and "the Indies" are dragged in, to complete the admirable confusion. The intricate and masterly mechanism of the structure, here as elsewhere, stands out in contrast to the headlong heedlessness with which periods of time are jumbled

I i 21; IV i 4; and I ii 55.

III ii 106 ff.

---

[3] "The introduction of twin servants as well as twin masters is due to Shakespeare, who rightly saw, on this as well as on later occasions, that two improbabilities buttress each other, and have a greater plausibility than one."— Oliphant Smeaton, *Shakespeare: His Life and Work,* p. 89. (Everyman Series.)

together. That is Shakespeare's <u>little</u> way of reminding us that he is himself, and <u>not</u> Bacon.

With the tragedy of *Romeo and Juliet* we pass
into a new stage of Shakespeare's development. Indications abound that in its original form the play
goes back to 1591 or '92, but external and internal
evidence combine to convince us that the received
text belongs in great measure to a later year. Such
was the popularity of this play that three quarto editions appeared in Shakespeare's lifetime, a fourth
undated, and a fifth some years after the publication
of the Folio. Already in 1598 a satirist testifies that
the lovers of that time were speaking "naught but
pure Juliet and Romeo." An indirect testimony to
the finality of Shakespeare's handling of the theme
is supplied by the fact that, whereas before his time
this plot had been used by many writers in many
tongues, it has furnished since he treated it the
material of only one drama, the *Castelvines y Mon-
teses* of Lope de Vega, the great Spaniard.

The tale of the star-crossed lovers has been traced
as far back as the second century, but for the modern world its first embodiment is in the *Novellini* of
Masuccio, towards the end of the fifteenth century.
In the sixteenth century there were two Italian versions of it, one of which was translated into French
and from French into English. Prior to or con-
temporaneously with Shakespeare's use of the story,
it was dramatized by French, Italian and Spanish
writers. It is probable that Shakespeare sought his
material in the French and Italian versions as well
as the English, although he has most closely followed the verse rendering published by Arthur
Brooke in 1562. As generally happens, Shake-

Romeo and Juliet, 1592.

Its vogue.

Sources.

speare's work upon his sources is parallel to that of the mighty wind which in Isaiah's vision caused the dry bones to live and to rise up on their feet, an exceeding great army. He has departed only in details

Shakespeare's innovations.

from the sequence of events in his material. It is he who makes Mercutio a humorous gentleman, and gives to the Nurse her prominence in the plot. Needless to say, the rich poetry, the individualization of the characters, and the splendid emotional contrasts are due to him alone. The presence of many of the peculiarities of his earliest comedies, such as the frequent punning and the love of verbal quibbles and conceits, side by side with depths of sympathy and felicities of expression characteristic of his much later work, bears out the hypothesis that five or six years after its original appearance the play was extensively overhauled and in large part rewritten. The first quarto appeared in 1597, and its text is extremely corrupt. The second, published in 1599, is far more accurate; but, as usual, the definitive authority is the Folio version.

The first unique masterpiece.

This is the first play which is definitely beyond the powers of any writer then living, Shakespeare alone excepted. Marlowe could never have combined the many facets of character which Juliet and Romeo and their entourage exhibit. His dead blacks and whites never express the richness of intermediate shading, of which his eclipsing pupil was from a very early stage the easy master. The caricatures of Ben Jonson and Beaumont and Fletcher do not belong to the same world as the living men and women of Shakespeare. To him is also peculiar the power of presenting a crescendo of agony without once violating good taste by morbidity or by the introduction of gratuitous horrors. He alone has the secret of introducing comic relief without descending to bathos or marring the dignity of the tragic development. And, all the time, his poetic power is unfolding itself with ever richer form and content. The Balcony scenes, in the wealth of their imagery and in their power of suggesting by the slightest phrase the agonized ecstasy of contending emotions in the lovers, were never surpassed by Shakespeare in any of his later works: which is the shortest way of expressing the fact that they have not been surpassed at all. When Sir Sidney Lee asserts that *Romeo and Juliet* "as a tragic poem on the theme of love has no rival in any literature," he is voicing the general verdict of criticism.

The advance in Shakespeare's power, and his growing independence of his exemplars, is shown in this play not only in the central characters, but very markedly also in the minor personages. To class Mercutio in this category may seem unjust, even though we do not accept the suggestion of his worshipper Dryden, that Shakespeare "was forced to kill him in the third act to prevent being killed by him." The fact of his disappearance at that juncture, however, must serve to justify our relegation of him to a seemingly inferior position. Our classification at least has the merit of leaving him to share the ineffable society of the Nurse, that radiant ancestress of Mrs. Nickleby, the goddess of irrelevance and humorous absurdity. Mercutio is not merely the wit of the play. His account of Queen Mab and her peregrinations is one of the most delightful passages of imaginative description in the whole of Shakespeare. Already we discern the protended shadows of Puck and Ariel, with all their airy rout: —

Minor characters: Mercutio.

The Nurse.

I iv 53 ff.

Oh, then, I see Queen Mab hath been with you.
She is the fairies' midwife, and she comes
In shape no bigger than an agate-stone
On the forefinger of an alderman,
Drawn with a team of little atomies
Athwart men's noses as they lie asleep;
Her waggon-spokes made of long spinners' legs,
The cover of the wings of grasshoppers,
The traces of the smallest spider's web,
The collars of the moonshine's wat'ry beams,
Her whip of cricket's bone, the lash of film,
Her waggoner a small grey-coated gnat,
Not half so big as a round little worm
Pricked from the lazy finger of a maid;
Her chariot is an empty hazel-nut
Made by the joiner squirrel or old grub,
Time out o' mind the fairies' coach-makers.
And in this state she gallops night by night
Through lovers' brains, and then they dream of love,
O'er courtiers' knees, that dream on curtsies straight,
O'er lawyers' fingers, who straight dream on fees,
O'er ladies' lips, who straight on kisses dream,
Which oft the angry Mab with blisters plagues,
Because their breaths with sweetmeats tainted are:
Sometime she gallops o'er a courtier's nose,
And then dreams he of smelling out his suit;
And sometime comes she with a tithe-pig's tail,
Tickling a parson's nose as a' lies asleep,
Then dreams he of another benefice:
Sometime she driveth o'er a soldier's neck,
And then dreams he of cutting foreign throats,
Of breaches, ambuscadoes, Spanish blades,
Of healths five fathom deep; and then anon
Drums in his ear, at which he starts and wakes,
And being thus frighted, swears a prayer or two
And sleeps again.

The youthful gallants.   Tybalt, Mercutio, Benvolio and the County Paris are creatures of the type of the Three Musketeers of Dumas, brave, generous, " jealous in honour, sudden and quick in quarrel." Life is for them a pro-

tracted revel, interspersed with the still fiercer joy
of combat. The riotous torrent of their wit cannot be stopped even by the approach of death, as
is shown by the punning of Mercutio when he is
dying : —

> *Romeo:* Courage, man, the hurt cannot be much.   III i 89 ff.
> *Mercutio:* No, 'tis not so deep as a well, nor so wide
> as a church door; but 'tis enough, 'twill serve: ask for
> me to-morrow, and you shall find me a grave man. I
> am pepper'd, I warrant, for this world. A plague o'
> both your houses! Zounds, a dog, a rat, a mouse, a cat,
> to scratch a man to death! A braggart, a rogue, a
> villain, that fights by the book of arithmetic! Why
> the devil came you between us? I was hurt under
> your arm.
> *Romeo:* I thought all for the best.
> *Mercutio:* Help me into some house, Benvolio,
> Or I shall faint. A plague o' both your houses!
> They have made worms' meat of me: I have it,
> And soundly too: — your houses!

Already in *The Two Gentlemen of Verona* we   Household
noticed certain of the phrases which have since taken   words.
root in language. In *Romeo and Juliet* these begin
to fall thick and fast: "He jests at scars that never   II ii 1.
felt a wound"; "Virtue itself turns vice being mis-   II iii 21-2.
applied, and vice sometimes by action dignified";
"a gentleman, Nurse, that loves to hear himself   II iv 132.
talk"; "a plague o' both your houses"; "What's in   III i 85.
a name? That which we call a rose by any other   II ii 43-44.
name would smell as sweet"; "my poverty but not   V i 75.
my will consents." This power of minting instan-
taneously phrases that will remain authentic currency so long as the language lasts, is one of the
indisputable signs of genius; and that Shakespeare
possessed it more richly than any English writer
before or since is a fact that can be established by a

mere process of arithmetic. The Bible alone rivals his plays for the number of unimprovable quintessential phrases that form part of the mental stock of the English-speaking world.

CHAPTER IV

"THE MERCHANT OF VENICE": THE TRAGEDY OF
RACE-PREJUDICE

ON August 25th, 1594, there was produced a play entitled *The Venetian Comedy*. Whether this was or was not the first draft of Shakespeare's *Merchant of Venice* is uncertain, but in all probability it was. Just before the production, there had been an outburst of anti-Semitism in London, awakened by the execution of Dr. Roderigo Lopez, a Jewish physician of great distinction, who had been first in the service of the Earl of Leicester and afterwards in that of Queen Elizabeth. He was accused of having conspired to poison the Queen and a Spanish refugee named Antonio Perez. The evidence was incomplete, but he was convicted of treason. For a long time the Queen delayed signing his death-warrant, but at last, on June 7th, 1594, he was executed. Sir Sidney Lee points out the curious coincidence that a Christian named Antonio should have caused the ruin both of the greatest Jew in Elizabethan England and of the greatest Jew in the drama of that period. From this, as well as from the correspondence of the dates, he argues that Lopez was probably "the begetter of Shylock."

The influence of Marlowe upon Shakespeare is traceable in this play for the last time on any considerable scale. The characters of Shylock and

Circumstances attending first production.

Life, ed. 1916, p. 135n.

Indebtedness to Marlowe.

[75]

Jessica are obviously suggested by Barabas and his daughter Abigail in *The Jew of Malta*. Together with this proof of dependence, however, we have the demonstration of the way in which Shakespeare had outranged the powers of his exemplar. Shylock is a tragic and even a sublime figure as compared with the grasping brute depicted by Marlowe; and, as we shall see, there is clear evidence that Shakespeare had reacted both artistically and ethically against the vulgar race-prejudice which characterized his time, and which had been exhibited with particular grossness in connection with the death of Dr. Lopez.

Sources:

The sources of *The Merchant of Venice* are definitely known, and consequently they furnish no occasion for a critical quarrel. The story of the Jewish creditor, the defaulting Christian debtor, and "the lady of Belmont" who rescues the latter, comes from

Il Pecorone.

a collection of Italian stories called *Il Pecorone,* by Ser Giovanni Fiorentini; that of the Caskets is told (not for the first time) in a Latin collection of stories

Gesta Romanorum.

entitled *Gesta Romanorum.* There is some evidence that these had been combined in a previous English play. Certain hints, too, were taken from a play

R. Wilson.

(now lost) by Robert Wilson, entitled *The Three Ladies of London,* which had been printed in 1584.

Structure.

In structure, *The Merchant of Venice* is one of the most elaborate and masterly of Shakespeare's productions. A whole series of separate actions are artistically combined, in such wise that they act and react upon one another in a manner that seems perfectly normal. Tragedy and comedy mingle as naturally as light and shadow,— as they do in real life, but as the classical tradition affirmed that they ought not to do in drama. We have the love-stories of Bassanio and Portia, of Gratiano and Nerissa, and of Lorenzo and Jessica. We have the tragedy of Antonio and Shylock, the comedy of the Caskets, and, at last, the delightfully humorous episode of the two rings, which comes to relieve the strain of the Court scene, and to reveal the sweet girlish mischief of Portia, in brilliant contrast to her stern and mannish demeanour in the conflict with Shylock. Readers who wish to appreciate the wonderful craftsmanship by which these elements are blended into a perfect symphony should study the excellent analysis of the play in Professor Moulton's *Shakespeare as a Dramatic Artist,* a work which not only throws a flood of light upon the plays with which it deals, but also furnishes the basis of a liberal education in the science of inductive literary criticism.

R. G. Moulton's analysis.

Whether *The Merchant of Venice* is to be regarded as a comedy or as a tragedy depends in some measure on the point of view of the reader. With his indifference to exact classification and his scorn for the iron rules of the Graeco-Roman tradition, Shakespeare may have deliberately left us in doubt upon the subject. His own favourite type of play is that which he has described by the mouth of Polonius in *Hamlet:* "tragical-comical-historical-pastoral, scene individable, or poem unlimited." That phrase expresses his contempt for the established rules of technique,—"such conceits as clownage keeps in pay,"—a contempt which saved him, and some of the other Elizabethans, from the deadening slavery in which the French classic drama of the seventeenth century remained fettered. When one holds the mirror up to nature, one does not find the reflection behaving itself according to the rules of any established school of art. And so of *The Merchant of Venice* we may say that it resembles life

Comedy or tragedy?

Hamlet II ii 375.

truly in this, that one man's comedy is another man's tragedy.

Who is the hero?

Who is the hero of this "poem unlimited"— Antonio or Shylock? Or are Bassanio and Portia the hero and heroine? Sir Sidney Lee gives a bold and unhesitating answer: "It is Shylock (not the merchant Antonio) who is the hero of the play, and the main interest culminates in the Jew's trial and discomfiture. That solemn scene trembles on the brink of tragedy." We may be told that the original title, *The Venetian Comedy,* and the present title of *The Merchant of Venice,* settle the question in favour of Antonio as the hero, and therefore of comedy (in the strict sense) as the nature of the play. The answer to this, however, is twofold. First, Shakespeare is notoriously careless about titles; witness the *insouciance* of such phrases as *Twelfth Night, or What You Will; As You Like It;* and *Much Ado about Nothing.* Secondly, and consequently, the question can only be settled, if at all, by appeal to the internal evidence, which, as we have already noted, is decidedly ambiguous. An author who practically invites you to call his plays anything you please must not be held with excessive rigour to the exact implications of any particular title, especially when it may very well be that the title was chosen by his colleagues, with a view to advertising purposes.

Contrast between material and treatment.

As Shakespeare's art matures and his work becomes profounder and more subtle, the contrast between his raw materials and the use he makes of them grows ever more striking. Think of his choosing the *opera-bouffe* theme of the bond whereby Antonio, in default of payment, is to forfeit a pound of his own flesh, and the card-sharper's trick by which the disguised Portia swindles Shylock of what Antonio never doubted was justly due to him; and then think of the skill with which these twin absurdities are made to yield the breathless tragedy and the incomparable poetry of the Court scene! Take, IV i. again, the old folklore story of the Caskets, the monstrous incredibility of which is almost completely disguised from us by the art with which Shakespeare makes the meditations of the two unsuccessful suitors betray their characters, and by the keen II vii, ix, and III ii. emotion awakened by Portia's solicitude for Bassanio's success. His sense of poetic fitness is happily illustrated by the exquisite device of the song and the accompanying music, which covers the silence in which Bassanio makes his felicitous choice. What material,—and what a product! It is as though the poet had grasped at the heaviest possible handicap, that his transcendent power might be the more amazingly displayed. One is reminded of those pregnant words of Browning's *Abt Vogler:*—

. . . Here is the finger of God, a flash of the will that can,
  Existent behind all laws, that made them, and lo! they are;
And I know not if, save in this, such gift be allowed to man,
  That out of three sounds he make, not a fourth sound, but a star!

As regards his own moral judgment upon the Shakespeare's estimate of his characters. characters he presents and the conduct he describes, Shakespeare does not trouble to arrive at complete consistency. Had he accepted the ordinary conventions of his day, he would have represented Antonio, Bassanio and their friends as completely in the right, and Shylock as a mere fiend, devoid of any claim to human sympathy, and deserving only to be persecuted as mercilessly as possible. If, on the other hand, he had taken the attitude of uncompromising revolt against these conventions, he would have depicted Shylock as a wholly sympathetic character, and exposed Bassanio, Gratiano and the rest as snobs, self-righteous prigs and unscrupulous thieves. But he does neither of these things with "foolish consistency." His insight and his irony prevent him from being deceived as to the true character of the ruffling gallants who marry for money, and rob a lonely old man both of his riches and of his daughter. By a marvellous transcending of the prejudices of his time, he sympathizes profoundly with Shylock, and turns what another playwright would have represented as mere vicious perversity into an intelligible and dignified assertion of racial patriotism and natural, though not laudable, revenge. Yet he clearly sees how blameable Shylock's conduct makes him, and how many redeeming features there are in the characters of his enemies.

Jessica's conduct.

He shows us Jessica acting with unpardonable perfidy towards a father who had loved her as the apple of his eye. He shows her incredibly false to her faith and to her race. And yet he makes her to the end, from the young men's point of view, a consistently charming girl. We are left convinced that Lorenzo will never have occasion for apprehension lest the infidelity he has taught her to commit against her father shall be practised upon himself. Only once does the culpability of her conduct appear to flash upon her, when she exclaims:—

II iii 15 f.

> Alack, what heinous sin is it in me
> To be ashamed to be my father's child!

Her desire, however, for a freer life than she could hope to enjoy in the gloomy house of a fanatical member of a proscribed race, together with her love for the handsome swaggerer who had wooed her, makes her ready to call herself a Christian. We cannot doubt that she would have been equally ready to become a nominal Mohammedan, had such been the profession of her suitor.

The place of woman in the play reflects the semi-barbarous social and moral standards of the period. To Shakespeare's audience, no doubt, it seemed altogether natural that Portia should submit uncomplainingly to the horrible conspiracy by which her deceased father had disposed of her unconditionally to any sot or savage who might happen to select the right casket. The notion that by marriage the woman and all her worldly goods became the absolute property of the husband was taken for granted as unquestioningly by women as by men. If any of Portia's earlier suitors had been led by luck or judgment to the leaden box, Portia, despite her own feelings, would have held herself bound to accept the doom of marriage with him. The Neapolitan prince, who "doth nothing but talk of his horse"; the French lord, Monsieur le Bon, of whom she pithily remarks, "God made him, and therefore let him pass for a man"; the young German, "the Duke of Saxony's nephew," whom Portia likes "very vilely in the morning when he is sober, and most vilely in the afternoon when he is drunk";—any one of these she would have felt compelled by honour and duty to accept had he chosen the right casket, for her decision is firm that "I will die as chaste as Diana, unless I be obtained by the manner of my father's will."

Social status of woman in XVI century: Portia's submission to her father's plot.

I ii 30 ff.

The character of Bassanio.

Of Bassanio we know only that he is perfectly respected by the best among his contemporaries. Yet he is quite frankly presented as a man who has never done an honest day's work in his life. Having gambled away his fortune like a spendthrift, he thinks it entirely honourable to rehabilitate himself, if he can, by marrying, simply for the sake of her money, the richest heiress he can fascinate. Against such a method of living, at least in the aristocratic class, it had never occurred to the sixteenth century that there was any ethical or economic objection to be raised. Antonio is a frugal merchant, whose wealth represents years of careful study and prudent investment; yet he feels honoured by the friendship of the sponging parasite Bassanio, the scion of a class above him, and is very willing to pledge his credit to advance that noble youth's fortunes.

Moral blindness as to treatment of the Jews.

To the people of Shakespeare's time it also seemed consistent with morality and religion that Christians should act with diabolical cruelty and perfidy towards a Jew, but that the Jew, if he imitated them, should be condemned as a monster of iniquity. Even his strictly legal revenge might fairly be thwarted by a palpably dishonest trick. The Jew was there to be robbed and trampled upon, for the glory of God and the advantage of such estimable citizens as Bassanio, Lorenzo & Co.

The " salvation " of Jessica.

Again, the conscience of the sixteenth century had no misgivings as to the curious method by which Jessica secures her eternal salvation. The way for her to gain entrance into heaven after death was to rob her father, lie to him and desert him, and embrace the exalted faith of the instigator of these virtuous deeds. Lorenzo ranks as an honourable man. Far from losing caste by his exploit (de-

scribed by himself as "playing the *thief* for a   II vi 23.
wife"[1]), he rises in the estimation of all his friends
by his shrewdness and his good luck.

The astonishing thing is that, living in an age   Shake-
which held such standards, Shakespeare should have speare's
entertained any misgivings about the business at all. originality:
We have many proofs of his unparalleled power of Shylock.
self-identification with other human beings, but nowhere has he so transcended the limitations of his
age, and of the morality he inherited, as in his sympathy with Shylock, and his perception that the Jew's
resentment of the unspeakable treatment he had received, even from the good Antonio, was natural, if
not just:—

> *Salarino:* Why, I am sure, if he forfeit, thou wilt III i 41 ff.
> not take his flesh: what's that good for?
> *Shylock:* To bait fish withal: if it will feed no-
> thing else, it will feed my revenge. He hath disgrac'd
> me, and hindered me half a million; laughed at my
> losses, mocked at my gains, scorned my *nation,*
> thwarted my bargains, cooled my friends, heated mine
> enemies; and what's his reason? I am a Jew. Hath
> not a Jew eyes? hath not a Jew hands, organs, dimen-
> sions, senses, affections, passions? fed with the same
> food, hurt with the same weapons, subject to the same
> diseases, healed by the same means, warmed and
> cooled by the same winter and summer, as a Christian
> is? If you prick us, do we not bleed? if you tickle
> us, do we not laugh? if you poison us, do we not die?
> and if you wrong us, shall we not revenge? If we
> are like you in the rest, we will resemble you in that.
> If a Jew wrong a Christian, what is his humility?
> Revenge. *If a Christian wrong a Jew, what should
> his sufferance be by Christian example?* Why, re-
> venge. *The villainy you teach me, I will execute;* and
> it shall go hard but I will better the instruction.

[1] Antonio also, in the Court scene, speaks of him as having
lately *stolen* Shylock's daughter.

In this familiar passage, the two most important points are frequently overlooked. The one is Shylock's deep feeling that Antonio had scorned his *nation*. The other is the emphatic and undeniably just insistence that Christian example warranted him in seeking the fullest revenge he could attain. He had been *taught* the villainy he sought to execute. He had been outrageously wronged, and the most intolerable humiliations had been heaped upon him; yet any attempt on his part to do as he had been done by is rebuked in the name of mercy,—by those who, in their dealings with the Jew, had never dreamed of showing mercy.

Shylock's wife's ring.

In the interview between Shylock and his co-religionist Tubal there is one exquisite touch, which quite destroys the vulgar impression that Shylock is a mere miser, groaning over the loss of his money. No doubt the mass of the audiences in Shakespeare's time thought it merely funny when Tubal told Shylock that Jessica had purchased a monkey with his ring. The ordinary dramatist, or even Marlowe, at this point would simply have made Shylock groan the disappointed usurer's groan. Notice, however, what Shakespeare does with the incident:—

III i 96 ff.

> *Tubal:* One of them showed me a ring that he had of your daughter for a monkey.
> *Shylock:* Out upon her! Thou torturest me, Tubal: it was my turquoise; I had it of Leah when I was a bachelor: I would not have given it for a wilderness of monkeys.

The ring was a gift from his dead wife before they were married! That is why he values it! How deeply this touch of sentiment stirs our sympathy with Shylock, and how incredibly despicable does it make Jessica's act appear!

The culmination of the play, regarded as tragedy, is of course the Trial scene, from which the tragic hero goes forth disgraced and ruined, bereft of most of the means of life, forced to profess an alien faith, and to swallow the last bitterness by bequeathing what Antonio's cruel mercy has left him of his goods to the insulting son-in-law who had robbed him. Of this scene I shall venture to suggest an interpretation which, so far as I know, is new; and I offer it, as I shall offer later my reading of *Hamlet,* not dogmatically, but as a challenge to the independent thought of the reader. I suggest that the Trial scene in *The Merchant of Venice* is a masterpiece of irony. It has its ostensible meaning — the conventional comic or melodramatic vanquishing of vice in Shylock's person, and the rewarding of virtue in the persons of Antonio and Bassanio. That meaning is for the groundlings. An explicit statement of the author's real feelings and intentions would in his day have been fatal to his success as a playwright. A century and a half later, Hume had to cover with irony his real opinions on the subject of miracles, and Gibbon had similarly to veil his sceptical interpretation of the rise of Christianity.

Shakespeare was writing at a time when the twin superstitions of monarchism in the State and divine despotism in the governance of the universe were still sacrosanct and virtually unchallenged. It was a received part of the current code that the Jew, as unbeliever, was to be hated and despised. The Golden Rule and the Parable of the Good Samaritan constituted no part of orthodox Christianity as it was practised towards " Turks, heretics, and infidels." Only by means of irony could a man venture to express his sense of this situation. He must perforce take refuge in the safe principle, "He that hath ears to hear, let him hear."

A satire upon

(1) race-prejudice,
(2) self-righteous-ness,
(3) lawyers and the law.

Such, I venture to suggest, is the procedure of Shakespeare in depicting the mock trial of the issue between Shylock and Antonio. He is in fact pouring vitriolic scorn upon race-prejudice, and upon the blind self-righteousness of the Christian parties to the affair. He is further writing a satire upon lawyers and their procedure which is only paralleled in literature by the trial of the celebrated suit of Bardell against Pickwick.

The meaning of the bond.

To take the last point first: the bond by which Antonio pledged himself to refund to Shylock the amount of his loan to Bassanio had been entered into with the full expectation on Antonio's part that its penalty would be exacted in the only possible manner if the three thousand ducats were not duly repaid by the stipulated date. Antonio was fully prepared to face the music. When he entered into the contract, he deliberately challenged Shylock to act not as towards a friend but as towards an enemy:—

I iii 122 ff.

> I am as like . . .
> To spit on thee again, to spurn thee too.
> If thou wilt lend this money, lend it not
> As to thy friends; for when did friendship take
> A breed for barren metal of his friend?
> But lend it rather to thine enemy,
> *Who if he break, thou mayst with better face*
> *Exact the penalty.*

Antonio, of course, is confident that he will not forfeit his bond; but he has given the Jew no reason to spare him, should the chances of the market place him in Shylock's power.

The Court's dishonest evasion of it.

Now, what Shakespeare shows us is a supposed lawyer, with the full assent of the head of the State, placing upon this contract a construction which had never entered the minds of either of the parties who between them drew it up. The advocate also attaches to it conditions which are not merely impossible of observance, but which, if foreseen by the parties, would have restrained them both from entering into the agreement. What is it but the work of a satirist to depict a learned advocate thus deliberately resorting to barefaced chicanery in order to pervert the course of justice?

The special interest of this famous judicial interpretation consists in the fact that Shakespeare's exceptional knowledge of the law is offered us as evidence that he must have been a member of the legal profession. The Baconian mare's-nest is chiefly hunted by lawyers, and one cannot doubt that it is their professional pride which, in part at least, inspires their attempt to prove Bacon's claim to the authorship of the plays. That Shakespeare's knowledge of the law was really but slight can be demonstrated from many passages in his works; but one need not enter upon any such investigation. We shall be quite safe in staking the whole issue upon the Trial scene in the play before us. Would a professional lawyer have emptied out the whole bag-of-tricks of his sophistic and casuistical avocation as Shakespeare does? The knowledge of law here displayed (if that may be called knowledge which is really grilling caricature), and the temper in which law is regarded, are suggestive rather of a many-times-swindled litigant than of an attorney. If the irony leaves the legal withers unwrung, that is but an evidence of the deficiency in sense of humour which is often charged against gentlemen of the long robe, and which, by their advocacy of the Baconian theory, some of them exemplify.

Shakespeare and the law.

The " bull " of the Venetian charter.

The mention of the Baconian theory makes it appropriate to point out that in Shylock's first speech in the Court scene he refers to the *charter* of the city of Venice:—

IV i 38 f.

> If you deny it, let the danger lie
> Upon your charter and your city's freedom.

This is one of the innumerable proofs that the dramatist was lacking in the very kinds of detailed knowledge and accuracy which to such a man as Francis Bacon must have become a second nature. Venice was an independent oligarchy, and as such, of course, it had no charter. Shakespeare naïvely takes it for granted that Venice stood in precisely the same relations and had exactly the same constitution as Stratford-on-Avon or the city of London.

Irony of the appeals to mercy.

The irony of his exposure of the lawyers, which to me seems as obvious as that in Dickens's pictures of Messrs. Dodson and Fogg, Mr. Serjeant Buzfuz and Mr. Justice Stareleigh, is altogether surpassed, however, by the veiled scorn in his presentation of the Christlike appeals to mercy made by Portia. I would invite the reader to go over Portia's exalted

IV i 178 ff.

answer to Shylock's question—"On what compulsion must I be merciful?"—and compare it point by point with the earlier conversation between Shylock

I iii 50 ff.

and Antonio. In that conversation, we have a graphic and uncontested description of the kind of mercy which Antonio had consistently exhibited towards the Jew.

Position of mediæval Jews.

We must remember, in the first place, exactly what treatment had been meted out to Shylock's nation. Most of the avenues in life had been closed to them, so that they had been driven into the professions of finance and money-lending. Now, this business of lending out money at interest had been declared a sin by the Church, and prohibited under the severest ecclesiastical penalties. Thus there arose the following situation: The Jew was virtually forced to be a money-lender; he was declared a sinner and a criminal for doing almost the only thing which he was permitted to do; yet he could not have done this thing except with the co-operation of those who condemned him for doing it![2]

Shylock describes how Antonio had again and again interfered with the money-lender's business, publicly berated him about it, and, by lending money gratis, brought down the rate of usance. He further recalls the opprobrious epithets and the disgusting behaviour of the Christian gentleman towards him. With incontestable fairness, he asks whether, in return for these courtesies, he can be expected to advance money to relieve the necessities of his avowed enemy. There is a further point to be noted: Shylock never promises that, should the bond be forfeited, he will not exact the penalty; although, to be sure, he could not have much hope that Antonio would default, and so be brought within his grasp. The sequel shows plainly that it was by a quite unforeseeable freak of ill fortune that Antonio's ventures were reported (albeit erroneously) as having all miscarried together. He was perfectly confident, at the time of making the contract, that a month before the expiry of the stipulated period he would become possessed of " thrice three times the value of this bond."

Shylock's indictment of Antonio, I iii 32 ff.

[2] See the details of the intolerable treatment accorded to the Jews throughout medieval Europe in the sixth chapter of Lecky's *Rise and Influence of the Spirit of Rationalism in Europe.*

Lorenzo's
treatment
of Shylock.

Portia's "Quality of mercy" speech should also be compared with the kind of mercy confessedly shown to Shylock by Lorenzo, the unrepudiated friend of Antonio. The merchant and his circle knew full well how Lorenzo had induced Jessica to play the burglar in her father's house, to rob him even of the jewels which her dead mother had given him, and then to elope with one who professed himself a Christian; thereby bringing upon her father what, in orthodox Hebrew eyes, was the last disgrace. For this, Lorenzo had incurred no rebuke from Antonio; nor had that gentleman ever asked himself how he would have judged the situation had it been reversed,—had *he* been treated by Jews as Shylock by Christians. It is evident that these Venetian Christians regarded the Golden Rule very much in the light in which Mark Twain cynically describes it,— as something which, being of gold, was too precious for everyday use. All opportunities of religious freedom and social equality were closed to the Jew, and measureless indignities were heaped upon him, merely because he refused to profess a faith and an ethical code which Antonio and his circle no less decidedly refused to practise. But the moment there comes a possibility of the tables being turned, the Christian gentleman and his advocates invoke without a blush, as binding upon the Jew, that rule of action by which they had never dreamed of governing themselves in their relations to him.

The
" mercy "
Portia had
prepared for
Shylock.

To make the irony perfect, only one further revelation was needed, and that Shakespeare has not failed to give us. We are to read the Mercy speech in the light of our knowledge of *the mercy that Portia had up her sleeve for Shylock while she was in the act of uttering it.* She comes to the court after having devised a conspiracy by which the luckless Jew is to be denied his covenanted revenge, robbed of his principal, and deprived of his entire wealth, his lands, and his life. Having perfected this pretty little plot down to the last detail, Portia rises, in all the majesty of her beauteous youth, and urges upon her victim a passionate and exquisite commendation of the quality of mercy!

To go beyond this is almost like painting the lily. Yet Shakespeare does not hesitate to spice the cup with one last piquant ingredient. He shows us the perfect "quality of mercy" bestowed, when the tables have again been turned, by the triumphant Antonio upon his ruined and humiliated victim. Half Shylock's goods, it appears, are forfeited, under the conveniently pliant Venetian law, to the State; and the other half to the man against whose life he has conspired. Antonio generously suggests that the State should accept a fine in lieu of the half to which it was entitled, upon three conditions: first, that he (Antonio) is to have *his* full half for his present use, and to hand it over upon Shylock's death

> unto the gentleman
> That lately *stole* his daughter;

secondly, that, for this favour, as he humorously terms it, Shylock shall immediately ("presently" in Elizabethan usage = immediately) become a Christian; and, thirdly, that he shall, upon the spot, execute a deed binding himself to bequeath all that he might die possessed of to his virtuous son-in-law and his no less virtuous daughter. Antonio, to do him justice, was no coward. He, we may be sure, would have felt insulted by the suggestion that he would not rather have died ten deaths than embrace the Jewish religion. Yet he thinks it honourable and

Antonio's mercy to him.

pious to insist that Shylock shall abandon the passionately held faith of his forefathers, and accept that creed which had been so alluringly commended to him by the conduct of his Christian acquaintances! What a triumph for Christianity, to gain such a recruit by such a method of suasion!

Modern Jews and *The Merchant of Venice.*

I understand that certain Jewish rabbis and schoolmasters in our own time object to *The Merchant of Venice,* and do not care to have it taught to their children or performed before Jewish audiences. To me, I confess, this attitude is unintelligible. Were I a Jew, there is nothing in literature that I should feel more tempted to have my children study, as a luminous confession of the bitter prejudice and injustice with which their race has been treated throughout the Christian period.

Shylock's character.

Shylock, to be sure, is no saint. Shakespeare does not pretend but that it would have been infinitely finer in him to have shown the magnanimity which Portia and the Duke demand of him. The old money-lender is very human in his passions and prejudices, and his desire for revenge, however natural,— and however equitable as against those who indulge in the utmost measure of revenge against him—is still the proof of an unregenerate nature. But he is very far from being the mere infamous miser that he is commonly taken to be. After being perfidiously robbed by his daughter (a wrong for which, apparently, he has no legal redress), he refuses thrice the amount of the loan which Antonio owes him. The motive that prompts him to do this is racial revenge. He is mainly angered by An-

I iii 40.

tonio's hatred for "our sacred nation." Now, racial revenge is not, to be sure, an eminently ethical motive. But it is enormously finer than the squalid,

Ralph Nickleby money-grubbing that is vulgarly imputed to Shylock.

In any case, a fair analysis of the play cannot fail to show us that the conduct of Shylock is, to say the least of it, not more ignoble than that of the virtuous Christians with whom he has to deal. A horde of them have wronged him to the utmost of their power; not only so, but the whole of his life, like the entire history of his people, has been one long story of similar bitter oppression. That oppression was inflicted by men who professed a religion which condemned every part of their conduct, but who, without a blush, expected their enemies to live by the code which they themselves consistently violated. Towards the close of the fifteenth century, the Jews of Spain had been read a precious and memorable lesson in the justice and fidelity of a Christian State: they had been robbed, decimated, betrayed and banished. At the moment when Shakespeare's play was first produced, as we have seen, the populace of London was clamouring to revenge upon all the Jews among them the sins, or the alleged sins, of one individual member of the race. And in the face of all this Shylock is treated to the crowning and exquisite hypocrisy of the appeal of Portia and the "generosity" of Antonio! No wonder his last words betray a feeling of nausea:—

Christian treatment of the Jews.

> I pray you, give me leave to go from hence;
> I am not well: send the deed after me,
> And I will sign it.

IV i 389 f.

Thus ends the tragedy of Shylock, in whose woeful figure is epitomized the history of his race, from the days of the Egyptian captivity to the last Russian pogrom and the grinding of the Jews of Poland

and Galicia beneath the alternate Juggernaut cars of
Russia, Austria and Germany. Well may Mr. Zang-
will in his sonnet complain:—

> A whit long-spun, O Lord, the epic play,
> The Wandering Jew in nineteen hundred acts!

**Effect of
persecution
on persecu-
tors.**

But the evil that men do recoils on them. A persecuted people inevitably develops characteristic
vices, but also it inevitably obtains a "capable and
wide revenge," because the infliction of persecution creates corresponding faults in the ascendant
race that is guilty of it. Socrates of old was scientifically sound, and not sentimental, when he declared it worse to do evil than to suffer it. The
craft and the cunning of Shylock are, in biological
jargon, protective devices, necessitated by his struggle for existence. A blind self-righteousness overtakes those who persecute him, and judge him, by a
standard which they never apply to themselves, for
the faults themselves have engendered. This is the
nemesis of their own headlong inhumanity.

**Shake-
speare's
moral
greatness.**

That the ill-tutored countryman of Stratford, the
foundling of fortune, exiled from those privileges
and refinements of life which he would have graced
and honoured, and doomed to live "by public means
that public manners breed,"—that *he* should have
seen the pitiful irony of this situation, that his catholic sympathy should have pierced through the ada-
mantine barrier of prejudice erected between Jew
and Christian, is one of the greatest moral triumphs
in the whole of his unmatched achievement. Having
attained it,—having strained his own soul, and har-
rowed the more sensitive among his audience, by his
courageous presentation of this terrific indictment,—
he turns to laughter and revelry to refresh himself,

and to assuage the sympathetic sorrow of his humaner auditors.

Portia, after her little hour of usurped eminence, after unwittingly judging herself and the Christian world by the judgment she passes upon Shylock, resigns her borrowed robes and abdicates her unconsciously symbolic function. She becomes again the human girl, her heart full of the joy of prosperous love and of the playful mischief which delights in vexing the object of its affection. From the grateful Bassanio she beguiles the ring which she herself had given him after pledging him never to part with it. Nerissa, following the example of her mistress in this as she had done in her marriage, plays the like trick upon Gratiano. And then the magician waves his wand again and transfers the scene to the happy bower of Belmont, where, in the serene twilight, Lorenzo and his love pour out their souls in poetry to the sound of music. The end is the resolution of all perplexities, the enlightenment of Bassanio and Gratiano as to the triumphant strategy of their wives, and the completion of that edifice of happiness erected over the mangled spirit of Shylock.

Episode of the rings.

To enjoy the play as comedy, we must place ourselves unreservedly at the point of view of an average bourgeois in the Elizabethan audience. We must accept Bassanio and Lorenzo as Portia and Jessica accept them. We must suspend the moral judgment which, from our modern standpoint, we cannot help passing upon the spendthrift who unfolds to Antonio the story of his prodigal squandering of his estate, and the heiress-hunting plot by which he proposes to recoup his fortunes. We must forget the ingratitude of Jessica towards Shylock, and the still meaner baseness which could prompt Lorenzo to

Conditions for appreciating the play as comedy.

I ii 120 ff and 160 ff.

suggest the filching of Shylock's substance. The play grows, indeed, all the finer when we appreciate the subtle irony to which I have directed the reader's attention. But the recognition of the tragedy does not debar us from the joy of appreciating the lyric happiness of the lovers, and the deft magic of the dramatist's spontaneous poetry.

XVI-century and XX-century ethics.

The principles of morality are unchanging, but its concrete and positive rules vary from age to age. I have here depicted Bassanio and his compeers as any man whose conscience is enlightened by the morality of to-day must see them. But it would have been unjust to expect them to see themselves and their conduct in this light, or to expect an Elizabethan audience so to see them. In the last hundred years we have learned something of the inequity of making a wife and a wife's substance the mere chattels of a husband. The claims of the moral personality of woman as an autonomous spirit are now self-evident to us, and we know precisely what to think of the fortune-hunter who makes the legal theft of his wife's property his means of access to a life of self-indulgent idleness. It goes without saying that in twentieth-century England or America no man would dream of acting as Bassanio did, even if he had the chance; or, if he did, no million-dollar heiress would dream of accepting him. Nevertheless, we must abstain from reading back into the benighted sixteenth century the ethical verdicts prompted by that fuller radiance in which we walk to-day.

The self-sufficiency of Portia.

Of the feminine characters in *The Merchant of Venice,* the leading figure, of course, is Portia. Having already admitted the injustice involved in the social status of woman in Shakespeare's time,

I would now confidently commend Portia as an object-lesson to those mistaken feminists who treat us to fancy pictures of woman in the past as the mere slave and toy of man. Portia is one of a worthy sisterhood, which includes Rosalind, Beatrice, Helena, Cordelia, Imogen and Perdita, who show us how alert-minded human beings can make of their very disadvantages the means of outward and inward triumph. Shakespeare's women are frequently the most efficient people in his plays. Nor is this true only of the good women. It is Lady Macbeth who, at the hour of crisis, is eyes and hands and will to her irresolute and vacillating husband. Shakespeare never showed greater insight into woman's character than when he depicted the clear-eyed Portia as knowing exactly what she wants and how to get it, and having the determination to use her knowledge to the full. The fainting dolls of later fiction and romance are a libellous caricature of what the eighteenth century used to call "*the* sex."

John Stuart Mill has declared that one of the chief differences between men and women in the present stage of evolution is the greater power of women to react with sensitive alertness to the sudden demands of a concrete situation. The so-called intuitive power of woman,— that gift of rapid judgment, which reaches its conclusion so promptly that it cannot pause to analyze the steps by which it has travelled,— is the source of this alert efficiency. Bassanio, confronted with the news of Antonio's predicament, is helpless. His wife, on the contrary, is able immediately to devise the plot by which the merchant is to be saved; and, whatever we may think of its morality, we cannot deny it the praise of in-

Feminine psychology.

genuity. Portia outwits everybody; and no doubt, like her fellow-Christians, she even outwits herself. I have indicated the hypocritical irony of her speech in praise of mercy, but I would not suggest that the irony and the hypocrisy were fully present to her consciousness at the moment of delivering it. The power of self-deception is one of the most universal, as well as one of the most effectual, safeguards of human self-respect. What we really pray for is the gift of *not* seeing ourselves as others see us, and as we insist on seeing them; and our prayer is by no means in vain! We can now see readily enough the absurdity of assuming that everything is right for the Christian and wrong for the Jew. Yet this assumption underlies every action of Antonio and his associates, as well as every word and deed of Portia in her relentless pursuit of Shylock. Still, we cannot doubt that they made it unwittingly, and never advanced so far in self-criticism as to become aware of the real nature of their conduct.

" Slavery " of women countered by bamboozling men.

But it is not seriously to be supposed that, whatever the laws of property and the accepted theory of the relation of man and wife might be, women of the type of Portia and Nerissa were ever really the slaves and tools of such men as Bassanio and Gratiano. Just as the Jew, under stress of an artificial struggle for existence, had evolved qualities of character that secured his survival, so women in general, and our ladies of Belmont in particular, had developed in their legal and social servitude a subtlety which enabled them to twist their duller-witted lords and masters round their little fingers. So be of good cheer, ye feminists. Bassanio will not be permitted to squander Portia's heritage, nor shall he indulge on his own account in a second crop of those wild oats which he had sown before he found his salvation in the leaden casket. Law and ordinance may say what they will, yet, as Huxley puts it, "Witless will serve his brother." Still more certain is it that Witless will serve his wife. Sir James Barrie has given us a famous perversion of *The Taming of the Shrew,* wherein he represents Petruchio as the hoodwinked fool of a gentle Katherine, who pretends to be a shrew in order to entrap him. Shakespeare knew, we may suspect, that when Katherine absolutely obeyed the will of her lord, it was only because she had first, against his knowledge, imposed her own will upon him. Certain it is, at all events, that, in the partnership of Bassanio and his lady, the "little body" who has professed herself "a-weary of this great world" will to the end have freshness and initiative enough to steer him on the course she wants to follow; and, when she is most completely having her own way, will most easily convince him that he is having his.

CHAPTER V

TWO POINTS IN HAMLET'S SOUL

Vogue of
Hamlet and
its discus-
sion.

THERE is not in secular literature another composition so universally known and so interm-
inably discussed as the tragedy of *Hamlet*.   While
it is certainly not Shakespeare's best play, and does
not contain his greatest poetry, it is indubitably to-
day, as it has been for three centuries and in every
land, the most popular of his works.   All the
extravagances of idolatry are illustrated in the
multitudinous commentaries upon it.   Yet even
these extravagances bear indirect but potent testimony to the living force of the dramatist's work.
One of the sanest utterances which comments upon
it have evoked is that of Edgar Allan Poe.   In
his *Marginalia,* Poe warns us against the attempt
to expound the characters of Shakespeare, to account for their actions, and to reconcile their inconsistencies —

> not as if they were the coinage of a human brain, but
> as if they had been actual existences upon earth.   We
> talk of Hamlet the man, instead of Hamlet the
> *dramatis persona* — of Hamlet that God, in place of
> Hamlet that Shakespeare, created.   If Hamlet had
> really lived, and if the tragedy were an accurate
> record of his deeds, from this record (with some
> trouble) we might, it is true, reconcile his inconsist-
> encies and settle to our satisfaction his true character.
> But the task becomes the purest absurdity when we

deal only with a phantom. It is not (then) the
inconsistencies of the acting man which we have as a
subject of discussion (although we proceed as if it
were, and thus *inevitably* err), but the whims and
vacillations, the conflicting energies and indolences of
the poet.

This radical error, as Poe calls it, has given rise to
an entire literature, wherein Hamlet is treated as
though he had been an historical personage, and
theories of his character are discussed with portent-
ous and rather ridiculous solemnity. But perhaps
Poe may be answered by saying that the "phan-
toms" of Shakespeare are more real than most historic characters, few of whom we know so well as
we know the *dramatis persona* of Elsinore.

Now there is scarcely a play of Shakespeare in
which carelessnesses of construction and inconsistencies both of characterization and of episode are
so glaring as in *Hamlet*. A careful reading of the
accepted text (which is the result of a close revision
of the version in the Folio of 1623 and that of the
second quarto, published in 1604) betrays a series
of evidences of headlong haste, and of the incon-
gruous combination of elements from the sources
with Shakespeare's own inventions and reconstruc-
tions. The duration of the action is impossible to
determine precisely, as is also the age of Hamlet
(for we can scarcely trust the accuracy of the First
Grave-Digger's chronologizing); while, as to the
hero's character, there is an entertaining variety of
opinions.

In this connection I must insist upon the elementary considerations to which I have elsewhere
alluded. We must set out with such a criticism as
would have been passed upon the play by the
grocer's apprentice who is introduced to us in *The*

*The struc-
ture of the
play.*

*For whom it
was written.*

Knight of the Burning Pestle; for it was he and his kind that Shakespeare had prominently in mind in furbishing up the antiquated materials of which in *Hamlet* he availed himself. He chose the theme because it was a tale of intrigue, incest, murder and usurpation, a tale with two appearances of a ghost, a tale of "occulted guilt" at last made apparent, a tale that ends with an orgy of poisoned swords and wine-cups and a stage full of corpses. These are the things that attracted the groundlings, and it was the fact of the story's attractiveness to them that induced Shakespeare to make use of it. He wrote *Hamlet* because a previous play on the same theme had been a popular success.

The First Quarto (1603).

How much of this older play he took over is not known, because its text is lost. The first quarto, which appeared surreptitiously in 1603, to the great indignation of the author and his fellows, is a mass of absurdities, which can best be explained on the hypothesis that its text was not based upon a MS. copy (unless possibly of some of the smaller parts), but upon notes taken by an incompetent shorthand-writer, and supplemented by the disastrous efforts of his memory or invention. To none of the quartos probably do the angry words of Heminge and Condell " To the Great Variety of Readers," in their preface to the Folio, apply so unreservedly as to this mischievous perversion of *Hamlet:* "You were abus'd with diuerse stolne, and surreptitious copies, maimed, and deformed by the frauds and stealthes of iniurious impostors, that expos'd them."

Sources.

The tale of Hamlet goes back to the *Historia Danica* of Saxo Grammaticus, who "flourished" in the latter half of the twelfth century, and even by him was retold from Scandinavian sagas of indefinite antiquity. The earlier play was not Shakespeare's only source. In his time the old story had figured anew in the *Histoires Tragiques* of Belleforest, to which it is most probable that he had access, either in the original or in an English version of part of them, entitled *The Hystorie of Hamblet, Prince of Denmark.*

Following his usual practice, Shakespeare adhered as closely as he conveniently could to the intrigue and the action of his sources. But through that action, which in the sources was that of a barbarian, he has put an intensely civilized and sophisticated modern (*i. e.,* Elizabethan) gentleman, thereby creating an abundant supply of perplexities for the critic. He has also removed the old motive for certain acts, while retaining the acts themselves. Why, for instance, should Hamlet feign madness? In the *Hystorie,* there is a very evident reason — namely, to protect himself from the revenge of the usurping King. That usurper's guilt was known; and therefore Hamlet, if he remains sane, must either overcome his supporters and slay him or be slain by him. Here we have a sufficient motive for the assumption of insanity; one, however, which Shakespeare's subtler presentation of the situation destroys and does not replace. But he leaves his hero adopting a line of conduct prompted by, and only intelligible upon, the motive that he has removed.

The real reason, no doubt, is the simple fact that Hamlet's sham madness makes excellent playing, and had already been popular in the older play; while the piquancy of the whole situation is greatly enhanced by making the King's guilt unknown to his entourage. Shakespeare was not out primarily

Treatment of material.

to solve complex problems in psychology. His first
business was to make a play that would crowd the
Globe with the kind of "groundlings" (*i. e.,* standing auditors in the pit) for whom he had the same
amount of respect as Hamlet expresses: "groundlings who for the most part are capable of [*i. e.,* can
understand] nothing but inexplicable dumb shows
and noise." And so for him the first question was
not, Is it consistent that Hamlet should feign madness, when in the modified situation he could be
safer and could plan his revenge without any such
antic behaviour? It was, Shall we get a full house
by showing him as he appears to Ophelia and as he
mocks Polonius?

The fact that the play was huddled together
hastily and from hand to mouth is further shown
by such inconsistencies, "gross as a mountain," as
those of Hamlet's relations with Horatio and of his
remarks about immortality after his interview with
the Ghost. He at first greets Horatio as one with
whom he had previously had but the slightest acquaintance: "Horatio,— or I do forget myself?"
How is this possible, when Horatio has been about
the Court for not less than two months, having
come from Wittenberg to see the late King's
funeral? Consistently with this, however, Horatio
appears as *a foreigner* in Denmark, and to him as
such Hamlet explains the barbaric customs of his
native country. Why should Horatio, if he too
were native there and to the manner born (as
Hamlet's differential description of himself clearly
implies that Horatio is *not*), have to ask whether
it was the custom for the ordnance to be fired when
the King "keeps wassail, and the swaggering up-
spring reels"? And yet, in the second scene of

III ii 9, 10.

Contradic-
tions evi-
dencing
hasty work-
manship:

(1) The
status of
Horatio,
I ii 161.

I iv 7, 12 ff.

Act III, Horatio is deep in Hamlet's most intimate confidence, and is addressed in terms only applicable to a lifelong friend:— *III ii 47 ff.*

> Since my dear soul was mistress of her choice, *Ibid. 56-59.*
> And could of men distinguish, her election
> Hath seal'd thee for herself; for thou hast been
> As one, in suffering all, that suffers nothing, &c.

Hamlet has even confided to him the circumstances *Ibid. 70.* of his father's death, although after his interview with the Ghost he had put off Horatio, just as he had put off Marcellus, with chaff, and with "wild *I v 133 ff.* and whirling words," swearing them both to secrecy as to what they had seen and disclosing no syllable of what he had heard. At the very end of the play, *V ii 319 ff.* this lifelong friendship is again presupposed, and Horatio, like an antique Roman (though now, in spite of Act I, scene iv, a born Dane!), wishes to die with his adored prince and friend. It is idle to resort to subtle theories to explain away a frank and obvious inconsistency, and one that is quite naturally accounted for by the hypothesis of hasty or careless workmanship.

Now let us turn to the second gross self-contradiction above mentioned. Hamlet, at the very outset of the play, hears of a ghost, which presently he sees and talks with. Whatever may be the nature of the later appearance in his mother's chamber, *III iv.* this first apparition is certainly no mere creation of his own subjective fantasy, for it is seen by Marcellus, Bernardo and Horatio, as well as by himself. Yet, in the famous "To be" soliloquy, Hamlet speaks of what lies beyond death as "the undiscover'd country from whose bourn *no traveller re-* *III i 79-80.* *turns.*" It would need a reconciler of Kantian antinomies to explain the utterance of these words

(2) The Ghost and the "To be" soliloquy.

by a man whose whole course of life is due to a conversation with a returned traveller from the said country. And when the reconciler had done his work, he would only have made a small addition to the world's collection of jokes.

Shakespeare forgets both Hamlet and the Ghost, and expresses himself.

Here again the most obvious explanation is the best. Shakespeare becomes interested, as he well might, in the theme of the soliloquy; and in the act of writing it, carried away by the joy of self-expression, he forgets all about the ghost. He also forgets that Hamlet is a prince, and makes him talk like an unsuccessful man of the middle classes, familiar with all kinds of discouraging experiences which can never have crossed the path of an heir-apparent to the Danish throne. What do princes know of " the proud man's contumely, . . . the law's delay, the insolence of office, and the spurns that patient merit of the unworthy takes " ? Shakespeare was evidently not incapable of forgetting for the moment who the inappropriate speaker of these lines was supposed to be. And how, if not by sheer carelessness, did he manage to mix the metaphors as he does in the opening lines of the soliloquy? Do we need any other explanation than carelessness or haste, when a man of Shakespeare's known powers speaks of taking arms against a *sea* of troubles, and makes a character, who has talked with a ghost from purgatory, call the after-life inscrutable? And what of the earlier soliloquy, in which Hamlet speaks of the Everlasting having " fix'd His canon 'gainst self-slaughter," when there is no such " canon " in the Bible?

The initial mixture of metaphors.

(3) Hamlet's relations with Ophelia : I iii 5-51, and 88 ff. II i 75 ff.

Further perplexities confront us regarding the relations between Hamlet and Ophelia, and also regarding Ophelia's fate. The conversations of

Ophelia with Laertes, and immediately afterwards with Polonius, imply a fairly continuous recent intercourse between her and the Prince. Somewhat later (a few weeks or months at most) she again describes to her father an interview, that moment ended, between herself and Hamlet, whom she describes as palpably insane both in demeanour and in conduct. Yet, at her next appearance, presum- III i 90 ff. ably but a day or two afterwards, she has no notion when she meets him that there is anything the matter with his mind, until his astounding questions provoke the discovery, which overwhelms her with horror and despair. Observe, too, that this interview commences by her asking him,

> How does your honour for *this many a day?*

and by her offering to return his presents,

> That I have longèd *long* to re-deliver.

The death of Ophelia, again, is described by the IV vii 164 ff. Queen to Laertes and the King, in the plainest possible language, as an accident, for which the grief-maddened girl was in no wise responsible: the bough of the willow-tree broke and precipitated her into the brook. Yet on the very next page we find the two Grave-Diggers questioning whether it was not suicide, and concluding that it was — the Second speaking for both when he declares: "If this had not been V i 22. a gentlewoman, she should have been buried out o' Christian burial." The Church concurred with its lowly retainers, for the "maimed rites" accorded to the corpse betokened that its owner had been guilty of self-slaughter. To the protest of Laertes the Priest replies: —

> Her obsequies have been as far enlarg'd Ibid. 208 ff.
> As we have warrantise: *her death was doubtful;*

> And, but that great command o'ersways the order,
> She should in ground unsanctified have lodg'd
> Till the last trumpet. . . .

The chances are that Ophelia in the old play killed herself. Shakespeare, with exquisite taste, made the change denoted by the Queen's beautiful speech, —and then forgot to harmonize the Graveyard scene with his modification.

Such haste or carelessness in construction is of a piece with the information that Hamlet and Horatio went to the school of Wittenberg, which was founded in 1502, although the incidents of the play are supposed to have transpired somewhere about the tenth or eleventh century. At no later period would it have been conceivable for a Danish **III i 167.** monarch to send to England "for the demand of our neglected tribute," or to count upon obedience **IV iii 59-60.** from England, "since yet thy cicatrice looks raw and red after the Danish sword."

Theatrical competition in first years of XVII century. Now, at whatever cost of seeming irreverence to the infallible idol of the Coleridgeans, we must insist that these anachronisms and inconsistencies are palpably due to the fact that *Hamlet* was written in a great hurry, by a comparatively ignorant man of transcendent genius, whose chief purpose was to vamp up a successful play to meet the demands of the illiterate London public, at a time when new and dangerous competition was confronting him and his "fellows." The discussion about theatrical **II ii 310-41.** affairs between Hamlet and Rosencrantz, in which we hear of "the late innovation" and the "aery of children, little eyases," who "are now the fashion," ludicrously anachronistic as it is, opens up a precious mine of information as to the real history of Shakespeare's work. The young players were seriously interfering with the receipts of his company. When Hamlet asks, "Do the boys carry it away?" Rosencrantz replies, "Aye, that they do, my lord; Hercules and his load too." This apparently cryptic remark is explained by the fact that the sign of the Globe Theatre was a picture of Hercules bearing the world on his shoulders. It therefore means that the boys had recently been attracting the audiences which were formerly wont to resort to the Globe.

The position, then, is so far a simple one. Shakespeare, working probably against time and certainly with a keen eye to business, grasps at an old and well-tried story, full of the melodramatic, and to us often repulsive, incidents which had been proved to attract the London public. Manipulating these materials, he turns the old puppets into living creatures, transforms the barbarian prince into a reflection of his infinitely active-minded and subtle self, and puts wingèd poetry on the lips of all his characters, simply because, like Luther, he could do no other. Absorbed in this joyous task, he was sometimes oblivious to the necessity for chronological consistency, and for conformity between character and character, episode and episode, speech and speech. To think of him as having first elaborated a theory of Hamlet's character, and afterwards devised incidents and speeches to conform with his *a priori* conception, is merely to bemuse ourselves. His principle of economy was to change as little as possible of the old material on which he worked. Hence the survival from the old play of that preposterous scene in which Hamlet observes the King at his prayers, and bethinks himself of a reason for not then slaying his victim;—a reason which, in

Shakespeare's procedure.

III iii 73 ff.

its naked savagery and imbecile superstition, is indescribably out of key with the conduct and character, " most like a gentleman," that he elsewhere manifests.

The fancy picture of Hamlet as moody philosopher incapable of action or of prompt decision:

The usual theories of Hamlet's character are based upon the impossible assumption which, following the wise counsel of Edgar Allan Poe, I have emphatically rejected. There is, however, an answer to be made upon the ground of internal evidence, as well as on *a priori* grounds, to the common argument that Hamlet was conceived by Shakespeare as a distraught philosopher, a man of introspective mood and hyper-intellectuality, which unfits him for the grievous practical task that is laid upon him. This interpretation is given classical expression by Coleridge, in the following passage: —

Coleridge.

" Notes on Hamlet," in Coleridge's *Essays & Lectures on Shakespeare,* &c. (Everyman series), pp. 136-8.

If there be an over-balance in the contemplative faculty, man thereby becomes the creature of mere meditation, and loses his natural power of action. Now one of Shakespeare's modes of creating characters is, to conceive any one intellectual or moral faculty in morbid excess, and then to place himself, Shakespeare, thus mutilated or diseased, under given circumstances. In Hamlet he seems to have wished to exemplify the moral necessity of a due balance between our attention to the objects of our senses, and our meditation on the workings of our minds,— an *equilibrium* between the real and the imaginary worlds. In Hamlet this balance is disturbed: his thoughts, and the images of his fancy, are far more vivid than his actual perceptions, and his very perceptions, instantly passing through the *medium* of his contemplations, acquire, as they pass, a form and a colour not naturally their own. Hence we see a great, an almost enormous, intellectual activity, and a proportionate aversion to real action, consequent upon it, with all its symptoms and accompanying qualities. This character

Shakespeare places in circumstances, under which it is obliged to act on the spur of the moment: — Hamlet is brave and careless of death; but he vacillates from sensibility, and procrastinates from thought, and loses the power of action in the energy of resolve. Thus it is that this tragedy presents a direct contrast to that of Macbeth; the one proceeds with the utmost slowness, the other with a crowded and breathless rapidity.

The effect of this over-balance of the imaginative power is beautifully illustrated in the everlasting broodings and superfluous activities of Hamlet's mind, which, unseated from its healthy relation, is constantly occupied with the world within, and abstracted from the world without,— giving substance to shadows, and throwing a mist over all commonplace actualities. . . . Hamlet . . . looks upon external things as hieroglyphics. His soliloquy,—

Oh, that this too, too solid flesh would melt, &c.—

springs from that craving after the indefinite — for that which is not — which most easily besets men of genius; and the self-delusion common to this temper of mind is finely exemplified in the character which Hamlet gives of himself: —

It cannot be

But I am pigeon-livered, and lack gall
To make oppression bitter.

And later, in the " Rogue-and-peasant-slave " soliloquy, Coleridge thinks he finds " Shakespeare's own attestation to the truth of the idea of Hamlet which I have before put forth." *Ibid.* p. 150.

The most eminent English critics since Coleridge, down to Sir Sidney Lee, have done little but echo that master's voice. Thus Hazlitt gravely informs us that " Hamlet is as little of the hero as man can well be. . . . He seems incapable of deliberate action, and is only hurried into extremities on the spur of the occasion, when he has no time to reflect." Hazlitt.

Richard Grant White, in the footnotes to his useful R. G. White.

edition, joins this chorus, informing us that Shakespeare imagined Hamlet "a weak, imperfect, morbid creature, but a kind-hearted gentleman," and assuring us that another passage is "merely a procrastinating fetch of Hamlet's, a subtle manifestation of that intellectual dawdling and paltering to which he confesses to himself that he is wont." Upon Hamlet's adjuring the Ghost,

III iv 127 f.

> Do not look upon me;
> Lest with this piteous action you convert
> My stern effects:

Mr. White informs us that this is "another nascent excuse for flinching and procrastination."

Dissent from Coleridge:

Readers whose independent searching of the text has led them to a radically different conclusion will be relieved, after this, by the note of reality and common sense in the words of Professor Bradley, who, in the third of his valuable lectures on *Shakespearean Tragedy,* says of Hamlet, "The text does not bear out the idea that he was one-sidedly reflective and indisposed to action. Nobody who knew him seems to have noticed this weakness. Nobody regards him as a mere scholar who has 'never formed a resolution or executed a deed.' In a Court which certainly would not admire such a person, he is the observed of all observers."[1]

Bradley, *op. cit.,* 2nd edit. (1915), p. 108.

[1] Wishing to form as unbiassed a judgment as possible, I deliberately refrained from reading either Professor Bradley's book or the German critics translated in Furness's *Variorum Hamlet* until this chapter was written. The interpretation I have set forth first suggested itself to my mind some twenty years ago; later I was gratified to find that it had been independently reached by my valued teacher and revered friend, Dr. Stanton Coit, whose literary judgments and instincts, as I have learned to know, can never be disregarded, and cannot safely be set aside without the deepest study.

Professor Bradley's interpretation of Hamlet's character, I

My interpretation is opposed to that of the school of Coleridge only in so far as the latter maintains that Hamlet is deficient in his power of responding to the challenge of life's practical exigencies. That he is given to philosophic meditation need not be denied. The doctrine which I oppose has been recently stated anew, in its most challenging form, by Mr. Oliphant Smeaton, who declares that the popularity of *Hamlet* is due "not to any well-proportioned or interesting plot, . . . for *of plot there is next to none,* but simply to the marvellous analysis given of an ultra-introspective tempera-

rejoice to find, is in some essential points consistent with that set forth in the text (though, in fairness to him, it must be added that he rejects this view as formulated by Werder). Dr. Bradley's doctrine is that Hamlet has had a moral shock through the horrible conduct of his mother — a shock which accounts for his melancholy and his longing for death, but which destroys his power of action only so far as concerns his mother and uncle. In all other relations of life, Hamlet is as alert and efficient as ever. The only criticisms I can venture here are that Bradley's interpretations often seem subtler than the problems require, and that he has overlooked certain considerations which make for my position without destroying his special thesis.

In view of the silly and tiresome parrot-cry that the Germans understand Shakespeare better than the English, I take this opportunity of saluting Mr. Bradley as one of the most discriminating expositors Shakespeare has ever had. Most of the German criticism (the exceptions, however honourable and distinguished, being astonishingly few) is metaphysical pedantry, devoid both of poetic insight and of understanding of Shakespeare's spirit and historic background. Whoever doubts this can settle the matter for himself by observing how the German critics assail each other. From the days of Ben Jonson and Milton to those of Bradley, Shakespeare has been best understood, most spontaneously loved, and most adequately expounded in his own country, and in the country which inherits his spirit and his speech — the United States of America.

ment, with that *complete paralysis of the active powers* which results therefrom." [2]

A page or two later this verdict is in part cancelled by such phrases as "the marvellous drama of *Hamlet*," and "one of the greatest dramas the world has seen." It would surely be somewhat paradoxical that these boundless eulogies should be deserved by a composition which had next to no plot. A little later still, with super-Emersonian scorn for consistency, Mr. Smeaton gravely replies to the alienists who urge that Hamlet was really mad, by insisting on "the uniformity wherewith Hamlet *carried out his purpose* along certain given lines. Madness could not have done so in a manner so *systematic*. Hamlet *never once deviates from his determination.*" [3] And yet his active powers were completely paralyzed! What are we to make of Mr. Smeaton's two voices? The words of Stephano cry for quotation: "His forward voice now is to speak well of his friend; his backward voice is to utter foul speeches and to detract."

Tempest II ii 82.

One cannot but feel that such contradictions spring from the fact that Mr. Smeaton is repeating tradition, and not suffering his mind to play freshly upon the problem before him. Granted that Hamlet is introspective (while flatly denying that there is any justification for the prefix "ultra"), I would venture to inquire whether in Mr. Smeaton's own observation of life he has found that the tendency to introspection is really accompanied by paralysis — complete or otherwise — of the active powers. Undoubtedly there was this combination in Cole-

---

[2] Oliphant Smeaton, *Shakespeare: His Life and Work*, in Everyman Series, p. 338. (Italics mine.)

[3] *Ibid.*, p. 358. (Italics mine.)

ridge. That great man's experience of himself, I verily believe, occasioned his strangely forced interpretation of Hamlet; — just as it led him unconsciously to put into an analysis of Shakespeare's poetic powers (in his *Biographia Literaria,* chap. xv) those very qualities, and no others, by which his own poetry is distinguished. But Coleridge, in this as in much else, was a rare exception, and ordinary experience leads to a precisely contrary conclusion. The ablest men of action I have known in real life were introspective to a highly unusual degree. Indeed, I have sometimes suspected that their exceptional power of self-analysis was in part responsible for their skill in judging the character of others, and consequently for their efficiency in active life.

The root of the Coleridgean theory is the fact that Hamlet defers to the end of the play the vengeance to which he is sworn in the first act, and which apparently he might have executed at almost any moment of the intervening period. This long postponement occasions him frequent self-reproach. It is assumed by the critics that a man who finds occasion to rebuke himself for procrastination cannot possibly be a man of action; as if it were not precisely the man who achieves most who finds the most constant necessity for urging himself to uninterrupted activity! The real procrastinator never thinks of himself as such; and, if charged with his fault, instead of pleading guilty, he excuses himself.

Genesis of the ineffectual philosopher theory.

In the light of what precedes, we might well be content to hold that Shakespeare did not trouble himself about any reason for deferring Hamlet's vengeance, other than the obvious one that if it were not deferred there would be no play. But, while it is true that Homer nods, yet he is still

Homer; and carelessness of structure and inconsistency of conception in Shakespeare are the exception and not the rule. The conventional criticism, I submit, makes him guilty of far worse self-contradictions than he has actually perpetrated.

How long is Hamlet's vengeance deferred?

The question of the duration of the action has a most important, but, so far as I am aware, a hitherto unrecognized bearing on that of the character of the hero. If Mr. Richard Grant White could have maintained the extraordinary statement which he made in his preface to the play — that "into five acts Shakespeare seems to have compressed, as his manner was, the incidents of not less than *from eight to ten years*" — his case would be materially strengthened. But this assertion appears to be as baseless as the theory which it is intended to support. What evidence is there that the action of *Hamlet* is protracted beyond a few months at most? There is not a particle. Fortunately, we can here set Mr. Smeaton to catch Mr. White. The former gentleman, while admitting that the time-analysis affords "no very certain results" regarding the duration of the action, goes on to say (oblivious of the import of the admission) that "the complete space of time supposed to elapse is from two to three months, but only portions of seven days are really represented."

" Eight to ten years " (White).

" Two to three months " (Smeaton).

Now, is Mr. Smeaton right in his time-analysis? There seems to be no ground for doubting that he is. The play opens in cold, wintry weather — a detail which we glean from the remarks of Hamlet and the sentries upon the platform. The death of Ophelia takes place about the end of May or the beginning of June. This is established by the erudite researches of Professor Hall Griffin on

Evidence for the latter view.

Ophelia's flowers. He points out that "the violets are withered, while fennel, columbines, daisies, and pansies are in bloom; the willow-trees are in leaf, and Ophelia can make garlands of crowflowers, nettles and long purples." There is no trace of a suggestion that Ophelia did not die and the tragedy close in the same year in which it had begun. The longest interval which it supposes is not necessarily above a month or two in duration. Time has to be allowed for the journey of the ambassadors from Denmark to Norway and back, for the simultaneous trip of Laertes to France and his return, and for the shadowy expedition of Fortinbras against "the Polack." This last is a point upon which Shakespeare's customary vagueness in regard to chronology is even more obscure than usual. Hamlet's sea-voyage is by his own statement limited to a few days. The affray with the pirates takes place "ere we were two days old at sea," and the implication is that he was immediately brought back, since in the letter to Claudius he speaks of "my *sudden* and more strange return." Upon his return, the action proceeds in breathless haste to its climax. The fencing-bout with Laertes cannot be more than a day or two after Ophelia's funeral, for in the same scene in which it occurs Hamlet recounts his sea-adventures to Horatio and apologizes to Laertes for his behaviour at the graveside.

Concluding, then, that the events of the play occupy not more than two or three months at most, I would point out that within that time Hamlet learns the truth concerning his father's death, plans his course for obtaining the necessary evidence in confirmation of the Ghost's allegation, and proceeds to the consummation of his vengeance. The crowd of episodes which he plans or utilizes all take place within that brief period. Is it not a somewhat startling commentary on Mr. Smeaton's thesis to find that the man whose active powers are "completely paralyzed" achieves so much in so short a time?

The clue to Hamlet's conduct:

Coleridge and his followers have overlooked one all-sufficient reason for Hamlet's delay, of which Shakespeare has given us plenty of hints. It is true that Hamlet might have slain Claudius at any moment after his weird night-watch with Marcellus and Horatio; but what decisive *evidence* had he,

The need for evidence of Claudius's guilt.

until after his return from the interrupted trip to England, that his uncle was really guilty of murder and usurpation? I do not ask what evidence there was to establish subjective certainty in Hamlet's own mind. That, of course, he had, after (though *not* before) the episode of the play. By the behaviour of Claudius on that occasion he and Horatio were convinced that the Ghost's tale was a true one. But if Hamlet that night had slain his uncle in cold blood, he would have been unable to *demonstrate to the world* that his action was justified.

Now this it is that he wishes to do. The play is a detective story. Hamlet had suspected Claudius from the first, and the Ghost's revelation only confirmed the dark speculations of his own prophetic soul. Like a sane man, however, he would not take the Ghost's word for it, even though the supernatural disclosure chimed with his previous suspicions:

II ii 568-70.

> The spirit that I have seen
> May be the devil; and the devil hath power
> T' assume a pleasing shape.

Possibly, as he remarks to Horatio,

> It is a damnèd ghost that we have seen,   III ii 75 ff.
> And my imaginations are as foul
> As Vulcan's stithy —

thus repeating a misgiving which had occurred to   I iv 40-42.
him when he first saw the spectre.

The new king was to outward seeming dignified
and efficient, and was clearly popular. People who,
while the former king was living, would "make
mows" at Claudius, were now ready, as Hamlet
himself informs us, to "give twenty, forty, fifty,   II ii 343 f.
an hundred ducats apiece for his picture in little."
What, then, would be the position of any man who
should slay him, and afterwards offer as justification of the deed an unsupported allegation that a
ghost had declared Claudius the murderer of his
predecessor? Least of all could the heir-apparent
have done this thing without incurring suspicion as
to his motive. Hamlet alone knew what the Ghost
had said. Even the other men who had seen it had
heard no word from it. So how could Hamlet have
vindicated himself?

To be sure, the whole situation is complicated,   Why did not
because, although we are told that the monarchy was   Hamlet
elective, Hamlet was his father's immediate heir,   succeed his
and seems to have stood higher than Claudius in   father
the public estimation. In Saxo Grammaticus this   directly?
fact is taken account of, and the usurper is kept in
his position only by the support of an armed party.
Shakespeare, although he makes the murderer's
guilt secret, still leaves unexplained the acceptance
of Claudius by the nation as the successor of his
brother. This aspect of the matter, however, we
are not called upon to discuss. Our task is to reply
to those interpreters who represent Hamlet as a

morbid philosopher, lapped in abstract dreaming and unable to take decisive action. These critics have to account for the fact that Hamlet, at point after point of the play, shows himself capable of sudden decisions and of the most effective sort of action to carry them out. Hamlet conceives his policy at the beginning of the play, and carries it through, against all obstacles, to a triumphant consummation. If then he is really a man of Laputan detachment, what unthinkable inconsistency must we attribute to his creator!

Hamlet is a man of inflexible resolution,

I shall ask the reader to follow me through a survey of the play, in so far only as this is necessary to sustain my argument that Hamlet is in fact a man of inflexible resolution, perfectly fitted for the grim and terrible duty that is laid upon him. It cannot be pretended that he delights in discovering that his father had been murdered by Claudius, or that he is in love with the task of visiting retribution upon the usurper's guilty head. He is a gentleman of rare refinement, not a bloodthirsty barbarian. I

and a successful man of action.

do argue, however, that he has all the qualities of a successful man of action, and that this is evidenced by the fact that, against apparently insuperable difficulties, he attains his object, which is not merely to kill Claudius, but also — nay, chiefly — to ensure the world's approval of the justice of his course. I contend that Shakespeare so thought of his hero, and did not consciously envisage the weak, procrastinating creature of Coleridge's and Goethe's imagination. Fortinbras, to whom Hamlet gives his dying voice, declares that had Hamlet become king of Denmark, he was likely "to have proved most royally." Hamlet was certainly a scholar; but that did not mean, as it so often means in modern times, a cloistered and incapable recluse. Scholars in Shakespeare's day were quite likely to be men like Sir Walter Raleigh, author of poems and of a *History of the World,* but also a brilliant soldier, sailor and statesman, explorer of unknown seas, and founder of colonies in the Virginian wilderness; or like Philip Sidney, poet, statesman and soldier; or like Francis Bacon, a rare blend of the thinker and the man of action. There is no contradiction, then, between my interpretation and Ophelia's account of the "noble mind" of Hamlet:—

> The courtier's, scholar's, soldier's, eye, tongue, sword; III i 148 ff.
> The expectancy and rose of the fair state,
> The glass of fashion and the mould of form,
> The observ'd of all observers.

Such a characterization (which agrees with the general opinion of the Court and the populace) would never in the Elizabethan period have been given to an introspective dilettante, who only "unpacked his heart with words" when confronted by circumstances that demanded deeds. Nor is there any suggestion that King Claudius had so little respect for his enemy as to interpret him in the Coleridgean fashion. He recognizes that what Hamlet spoke, "though it lacked form a little, was not like madness." His entire conduct is prompted by ever-growing terror of the determinate vengeance of the Prince.

But let us glance through the play, and see the course that Hamlet actually takes. The clue to his entire conduct is given, I submit, in his dying words to Horatio:

Hamlet's dying requests to Horatio explain his whole course. V i 319 f.

> Horatio, I am dead;
> Thou liv'st; *report me and my cause aright*
> *To the unsatisfied.*

Upon Horatio's declining to do this, and offering, like an antique Roman, to die with his friend, Hamlet imperiously forbids him; and for what reason?—

Ibid. 325 ff.   O good Horatio, *what a wounded name,*
    Things standing thus unknown, shall live behind me!
    If thou didst ever hold me in thy heart,
    Absent thee from felicity awhile,
    And in this harsh world draw thy breath in pain,
    To tell my story.

   The words of a dying man are presumably to be taken seriously; and even those of a dying *dramatis persona* (to revert to Poe's distinction) must be assumed to indicate his creator's conception of him. Hamlet is anxious that his most intimate friend shall devote himself to the task of justifying Hamlet's cause to the unsatisfied. He urges it upon him to live solely for that purpose. This being the case, it seems justifiable to infer that Hamlet's own conduct in life had also been dictated by the desire to have the truth of his deadly secrets revealed upon incontestable evidence, in order that the world at large might judge him equitably. Now, when we scan his entire course of action, from the moment of his interview with the Ghost to that in which, with the thought of public vindication still uppermost in his mind, he dies, we find that this clue completely destroys the charge against him of being an ineffectual dreamer. It makes his acts consistent; it accounts for his delays; and in his conduct in unforeseen exigencies it shows the clear evidence of an effective man,—namely, that he is able to transform what, to ordinary people, would be insurmountable obstacles into instruments for the advancement of his cause.

When Hamlet first appears he is overwhelmed with grief for the recent loss of a beloved father, and racked in soul by the unimaginable vulgarity, not to say indecency, of his mother's conduct in marrying, hastily and illegally, her first husband's brother and successor. He already suspects that there has been foul play on the part of Claudius, but he has no evidence, save his general impression of Claudius's character, to justify the suspicion. Not being able to foresee that such evidence will ever be forthcoming, he contemplates withdrawing himself from a scene so distasteful to a man of refined spirit. His "aunt-mother" and his "uncle-father" are unable to understand the nature of his sorrow. They think it is simply grief for the loss of his father, and so they attempt to console him with platitudes about the commonness of bereavement, and urge him to throw to earth his unprevailing woe. His mother, coarse-grained as her conduct proves her to be, provokes Hamlet's first outburst by asking why the loss *seems* so particular with him. Confronted with the not uncommon difficulty of being unable to explain his position, Hamlet merely remarks that he has "that within which passeth show."

The initial situation.

I ii 87 ff.

Under these circumstances, it is not unnatural that upon being left alone he should pour out the grief, which "saps the mind" in any case, and all the more if it goes unexpressed. The first soliloquy is therefore not an evidence of brooding ineffectuality on Hamlet's part; it is rather a revelation of the state of a mind which, though for the moment thrown inward upon itself, for lack of a concrete situation upon which its energies may grip, gives promise of intense and effective action so soon as

The "Too, too solid flesh" soliloquy.

I ii 129 ff.

such a situation shall arise. The lament about the "too, too solid flesh" and the hankering after suicide express the sense of frustration which an *active* mind feels when denied outlet for its insurgent impulses. Such reflections do not occur to a lazy or irresolute mind. Hyper-intellectual people, whose chief delight is in meditation upon remote questions, do not feel that friction between the impulse to action and the environing conditions that obstruct action, which, when the latter constitute an impassable barrier, flames up into the desire for death.

Hamlet's outlook. The father for whom Hamlet would have given his life, and under whom he would have had a career that would have given scope to his best energies, is suddenly withdrawn. This means that the son's chance of self-realization and of usefulness to the State is likely to be abridged. Worse than this, his mother has displayed a most repellent aspect of her character, which before had been concealed. In less than two months from the death of the man who presumably deserved Hamlet's incomparable eulogy, she had married that man's brother, who was no more like to him than Hamlet to Hercules. Under such circumstances, what was there for Hamlet to do? It is not the disposition or the capacity for action that he lacks. Were it that, the situation would present no difficulties to him. But he is deprived of the material upon which to act, and of the authority for action; and this, added to the horror of his mother's conduct, is why he concludes, "Break, my heart; for I must hold my tongue."

The news about the Ghost. At this juncture Hamlet receives from Horatio and the two sentinels the disclosure that the spirit of his father has returned to haunt the scenes of his

life. He seizes with alacrity upon the opportunity
for action, and decides that, at all hazard to his
person, he will encounter and challenge the apparition. His mood is not that of one who dreads
the necessity to be up and doing, but quite the contrary. It is expressed in the impatient exclamation,
"Would the night were come!" Prompt as light-
ning he lays his plans and pledges his informants
to secrecy. At his next appearance, while watching
with his companions on the platform, he explains to
Horatio the customs of his country, in a fashion
that shows how keenly he is concerned for the
honour of his native land. It is true that he ascends
into the region of generalization; but it is no such
rare thing to find good men of action who are also
capable of discursive thinking. It is to be remarked
that in the first quarto and in the Folio Hamlet's
reply to Horatio's question, "Is it a custom?" consists only of the lines:—

> Ay, marry, is't: I iv 13 ff.
> But to my mind, tho' I am native here,
> And to the manner born, it is a custom
> More honour'd in the breach than the observance.

The ensuing twenty-two lines, the construction of
which is very confused, appear only in the second
quarto (1604). When Hamlet's harangue is interrupted by the appearance of the Ghost, he instantly
expresses his intention of following and speaking
with it.

Now, in the prosaic world in which we live,
ghosts no longer appear. But there yet remains
enough of the tradition of more credulous times to
convince us that a spectre was not considered an
altogether desirable companion, or one that most
people would have hastened to encounter and talk

with. The narratives of these eerie visitations generally represent those to whom they came as anxious to run away with all the speed possible, though usually inhibited from doing so by a sudden flaccidity of the knees, coupled with a stiffening of the hair. In fact, the Ghost's description of the effect which his tale, if unfolded, would produce on Hamlet, is a statement of what his mere appearance would have done to most people. Many of us are in the position of the dear old lady who with rare honesty confessed that she was afraid of ghosts, though she did not believe in them. The fact of a man's going out on a midwinter night deliberately to encounter such an apparition would seem to stamp him as a person of exceptional fortitude and determination.

Hamlet's encounter with the Ghost.

When the spectre beckons Hamlet, Horatio and Marcellus strongly urge him by no means to follow; but the "ineffectual philosopher" replies that he cares nothing for his life, and that the Ghost cannot injure his soul, which is as immortal as itself. His friends still urge him to remain, but, finding their dissuasions ineffectual, they seek by force to detain him. Upon this he breaks away, declaring with an oath that he will "make a ghost" of the man who hinders him.

In his interview with the unearthly visitant, he betrays no lack of readiness to receive the tragic revelation. On the contrary, the spectre remarks, "I find thee apt." As soon as the interview is ended, Hamlet solemnly pledges himself to remove all other interests from his mind, and devote himself to retribution. His conduct when his friends rejoin him (and, as we shall see, throughout the play) is consistent with this determination. No

word can they extract from him of what has transpired, but instead he swears them solemnly to
silence as to what they have seen. Already his plan
for feigning madness has taken shape in his mind,
and these men are enjoined from giving any hint,
when they see him put on an antic disposition, that
they could throw light upon his mystery if they
would.

He concludes his adjuration to them, it is true,
with the words,

> The time is out of joint: O cursèd spite,   I v 188 f.
> That ever I was born to set it right!

—a not unnatural exclamation to follow upon such
a preternatural and horrifying disclosure as that
which he has just heard. When a young man finds
that upon him alone is laid the responsibility of
effecting a revolution in the State, a task that demands the abjuration of love and of all the interests
of refined and luxurious life, may he not be permitted to express a sense of the cursèd spite of fate,
without being written down as an irresolute
dreamer?

I have admitted that by retaining the device of
feigned madness, while removing its motive, Shakespeare has perpetrated an inconsistency. But this
is no more a difficulty for my own interpretation of
Hamlet's character than it is for that of the school
of Coleridge. Their thesis is that Hamlet is incapable of action. Now the elaborate feigning of madness is itself a very difficult action, and one that
requires a good real of resolution to conceive and
carry through. It is not the sort of device that
would suggest itself naturally to an irresolute and
ineffective person. Shakespeare has not here shown

Shamming madness is a continuous action, demanding extraordinary alertness and resourcefulness.

his hero a speculative philosopher. His inconsistency lies in the fact that he has depicted an
extremely complex action, and one demanding
great resources and unrelaxing mental alertness;
but, while doing this, he has left the action without
an intelligible motive.[4]

II i 74 ff.

That Hamlet proceeds promptly to carry out the
plan he had hinted to Horatio and Marcellus is testified by the interview which Ophelia reports to
Polonius, who thereupon informs Claudius that he
has found " the very cause of Hamlet's lunacy."

Hamlet
versus Po-
lonius, Ros-
encrantz &
Guildenstern
II i 168 ff.

The kind of madness which Hamlet manifests at
his first interview with Polonius impresses even that
garrulous counsellor with the fact that there is
method in it. There is also a combination of deception with merciless chaff and irony, which, while
imperceptible to the worthy Lord Chamberlain, is
for the reader or spectator evidence of a particularly acute degree of sanity. What, further, could
be more skilful than the way in which Hamlet sees

Ibid. 213 ff.

through the purpose of his old school-fellows Rosencrantz and Guildenstern, and, while preserving absolute secrecy as to his own affairs, extorts from their
unwillingness a most significant disclosure of theirs?
And when, by the skilful chess-playing of an alert
and resourceful man, he has dragged from them the
acknowledgment that they were sent for to question
him, he proceeds to show them up to themselves:
" So shall my anticipation prevent your discovery,
and your secrecy to the King and Queen moult no
feather."

---

[4] Professor Bradley's explanation (that Hamlet's pretence
is a safety-valve to preserve himself from going insane in
earnest) is one of the points in his case that seem to err by
excess of subtlety.

Hard upon this passage of arms follows the entrance of the Players, and Hamlet instantly grasps at this fortuitous incident and makes of it a means towards the attainment of his object. He is still in the difficulty, be it remembered, that the evidence he possesses as to the guilt of his uncle is not merely worthless from the point of view of the world at large, but is not even to be trusted by himself, without confirmation from within the land of the living. At once, therefore, he makes up his mind that he will have acted in the usurper's presence something like the murder of his father, in order to make the " occulted guilt" of Claudius " unkennel itself."

His utilization of the Players.

In much of the conversation with Rosencrantz regarding the Players, and with the First Player on the principles of dramatic expression and criticism, Shakespeare is, to be sure, stepping out of his character and expressing himself; but again I would remind the reader that these conversations are no more inconsistent with my interpretation of the play than with that which I am seeking to refute. Indeed, in the fact that Hamlet wants to use the troupe for a serious purpose of his own, without betraying that purpose to them, they come nearer finding a reason than they do upon any other supposition. Their actual motive, however, has nothing to do with *Hamlet* on any interpretation. They are to be explained by the conditions in the London theatrical world at the time when the play was produced.

The irrelevant and anachronistic discussion of theatrical conditions.

The extent to which the conventional interpretation makes men overlook Hamlet's real motives is curiously illustrated by the remark of one critic,[5]

The motive of the sub-play.

[5] The author of an anonymous pamphlet entitled *The Upshot of Hamlet,* published in London in 1885.

who declares the entire incident of the sub-play to be "one of the most purposeless things in the action." This same critic remarks that Hamlet only *pretends* to disbelieve the statements of the Ghost. The writer to whom I refer makes a great parade of being scientifically inductive. It seems strange that an inductive critic, who assumes to proceed only upon the evidence actually before him, should be so ready to deny that Hamlet means what he says, and should so overlook the motive revealed in his dying words, which is, as I have said, the clue to his whole conduct. The murder has been committed with such secrecy and skill that no trustworthy proof of it can possibly come except from the guilty person. The son of the murdered man, despite his most violent suspicions, has been able to get nothing in the way of evidence except the unsubstantiated disclosure of the Ghost. Mr. Justice Stareleigh delivered the dictum that "what the soldier said is not evidence." Any judge would certainly have ruled that what the Ghost said is not evidence. Hamlet, therefore, devises a trick by which to make the guilty person betray himself. The device is so cunningly arranged that if it fails to produce the expected disclosure, it will achieve the alternative object of proving the Ghost a liar. The extraordinary ingenuity and effectiveness of such a scheme commands our admiration. It is an evidence of intense activity of mind, and of most daring resolution, on Hamlet's part. For not only is it calculated to procure him what he wants in the way of evidence, but, by succeeding in this, it is certain to confirm the suspicions of Claudius against him. It is difficult to imagine what more convincing thing Shakespeare could have done to show us that he thought of Hamlet as a man of stern purpose and indefeasible resourcefulness. Hamlet wants evidence; he cannot get it; he cannot trust the Ghost's word; and so he devises this brilliant plan for obtaining "grounds more relative."

Meantime, it is true, Hamlet has delivered himself of the "Rogue-and-peasant-slave" soliloquy, one of the chief strongholds of the conventional interpretation. He alleges against himself that the actor's pallor and tears over a fictitious situation are a rebuke to his own inactivity in face of "the motive and the cue for passion" that he has. In the act of reproaching himself for procrastination, he breaks off to revile himself for letting his passion evaporate in words. And so we are told that by his own confession he stands disclosed as a "dull and muddy-mettled rascal."

The "Rogue-and-peasant-slave" soliloquy. II ii 517 ff.

I have already remarked on the absurdity of taking a man's private self-condemnations as conclusive evidence against him. In the case of Hamlet, such procedure becomes doubly absurd when we realize that this soliloquy is uttered at the very moment when, with diabolical skill, he is spreading his net in the usurper's path. Had he been the speculative procrastinator, he never could have evolved this masterly trick. What the "peasant-slave" soliloquy really betrays is the same impatience revealed by the exclamation, "Would the night were come!" which he utters when he first learns about the Ghost. It is the state of mind not of an idle man to whom action is repellent, but of one who longs for action and is forced unwillingly to abstain from it. Hamlet is like a man who has climbed half-way up a mountain, and who, instead of giving himself credit for what he has achieved, looks only to the heights

No procrastinator would have so judged himself.

beyond. He blames himself for the slowness of his progress, and lashes his nerves into still stronger resolution to overcome the difficulties that yet lie before him. Your true procrastinator would either have relinquished the task, or would have been betrayed into hasty action, inconsistent with a statesmanlike purpose. Would it really have been the deed of a capable man to have killed Claudius, and then stood in the eyes of the world only as an ambitious murderer, caught *in flagrante delicto?* Any fool could have done this: but Hamlet is not a fool.

The truth is that the art of knowing how to wait is the most difficult acquisition of the great man of action. He who stands alone against an indifferent or hostile world, and cherishes a purpose which cannot be achieved save by converting the world to sympathy with himself, shows the very highest competence for his task if he knows how to bide his time. When we remember that Hamlet's mission was to prove the guilt of Claudius, in such a way that no man could possibly doubt it, we see that there is no ground at all for the idea that he was a "weak, imperfect, morbid, procrastinating creature"—to borrow a selection from Mr. White's choice "derangement of epitaphs."

The psychic accompaniments of enforced inactivity. The interval of waiting, however, is necessarily occupied by reflection and punctuated by outbursts of impatience. It has this further psychological peculiarity,—that though the man is doing the one thing which can gain his end, he is still prone to suspect himself of dereliction of duty. Action would be easy, and, to common judgments, natural. It is the highest discipline to hold oneself in leash, when the foe that one longs to spring upon is within one's grasp. Hamlet, moreover, being a scholar and a gentleman, finds no delight in the thought of vengeance. He feels that for him personally it would be better to die, but he has embraced the very duty which at the end he urges upon Horatio. He too will "absent him from felicity awhile," in order that he may restore the disjointed time and bring estranged and banished justice back to Denmark. Nevertheless, the interval of waiting is full of inward conflict, as it needs must be. Hamlet, at this juncture, illustrates that profoundly true psychological generalization which his creator has elsewhere uttered through the lips of Brutus: —

> Between the acting of a dreadful thing
> And the first motion, all the interim is
> Like a phantasma, or a hideous dream:
> The Genius and the mortal instruments
> Are then in council; and the state of man,
> Like to a little kingdom, suffers then
> The nature of an insurrection.

Julius Caesar II i 63 ff.

Hence the "To be" soliloquy, in which, however, as we have admitted, Shakespeare once more steps out of the character and falls into an inconsistency. The first sentence is the only one that is really appropriate to Hamlet's position; the further reflections are those of a disappointed plebeian. The statement about the dread of what may happen after death is inconsistent not only, as we have observed, with the fact of Hamlet's prior interview with the Ghost, but also with his declaration upon that occasion that he neither valued his life nor feared what could happen to his immortal soul. The meditation in this soliloquy on the motives that restrain men from suicide is the reflection of a coward; and, whatever else Hamlet may have been, nobody has thus far suggested that he was a coward.

The "To be" soliloquy. III i 56 ff.

Hamlet's
love for
Ophelia.

Upon the heels of these unquiet lucubrations comes the crucial interview between Hamlet and Ophelia, of which the only explanation that covers all the facts is that Hamlet was truly in love with her, but had decided (in accordance with his compact with himself after his interview with the Ghost) that he must break off his intercourse with her. For him life is to be a battle, which seems all too likely to culminate, as it actually did, in his early death. A man upon whom such a burden has been laid may not give himself up to the satisfactions of the life of peace. Laertes and Polonius insinuate to Ophelia that Hamlet's purpose is to play her false. She, however, has received no such impression, and the Queen has obviously looked forward to the marriage of her "too-much changèd son" with Ophelia. Amid the anger and the ranting of the Graveyard scene, there is no reason to doubt Hamlet's earnestness when he exclaims: —

V i 251 ff.

> I lov'd Ophelia; forty thousand brothers
> Could not, with all their quantity of love,
> Make up my sum.

There is thus the bitterness of real sorrow in his breaking off from her. This is clearly expressed in the somewhat "wild and whirling" words that he III i 90 ff. addresses to her in the espied interview. His anguish is intensified by the discovery — or at least the strong suspicion — that Ophelia, like Polonius, Rosencrantz, and Guildenstern, is being used as a tool by Claudius to pluck his secret from him. What is bitterer than such treachery from one so loved? And how must it have reinforced the deep revulsion against womanhood in general occasioned in Hamlet by his mother's conduct!

It is inferable that after he bids Ophelia "Get

thee to a nunnery," and before he asks, "Where's your father?" he detects the presence of Polonius behind the arras. That is the most feasible explanation of his sudden breaking off into insulting remarks about Polonius—"Let the doors be shut upon him, that he may play the fool nowhere but in's own house,"—and reviling women in general for making "monsters" of men.

Ibid. 120 : 128.

The King, too, as we have before remarked, entertains towards Hamlet the respect which a man feels for an alert and efficient enemy. He recognizes that Hamlet is neither enslaved by love nor genuinely mad, but that there is a "something-settled matter in his heart," which bodes no good to the usurper who has doubly wronged him. Hence his decision to send Hamlet to England. Throughout the play we can see the terror of Claudius growing; whereas, if Hamlet had really been a weak creature who grasped at every excuse for escaping his responsibility, Claudius would have come to look upon him with contempt, and to feel his own position growing ever more secure.

Effect of this interview upon Claudius.

A further evidence of Hamlet's character is given in his confidential speech to Horatio immediately before the Play scene. He there declares that he has chosen Horatio from all the world as his most intimate friend, on account of qualities in Horatio that would commend themselves only to a person of resolution and of action. It is worth while observing that a man's judgment of other people's characters always furnishes a useful clue to his own. His experience, and his volitional reaction upon his experience, dictate his preferences and antipathies in appraising other minds. An ineffectual, procrastinating person does not become capable of such a

Hamlet's judgment of Horatio as a clue to his own character.

psychological analysis as Hamlet makes in this speech. Such an one would not be led to say:—

III ii 61 ff.

> Blest are those
> Whose blood and judgment are so well commingled
> That they are not a pipe for fortune's finger
> To sound what stop she please. Give me that man
> That is not passion's slave, and I will wear him
> In my heart's core, ay, in my heart of heart;
> As I do thee.

Here, too, it seems appropriate to point out that Hamlet has to be held back by his friends from enterprises which to them seem rash, hazardous and precipitate. It is the Stoic Horatio, who has never been and could not be accused of timidity or irresolution, who begs Hamlet not to follow the Ghost, for fear it should tempt him toward the flood, and assume a shape that would destroy his reason. The contrast in this respect between Hamlet and Macbeth is an instructive one; and it is, as by now we might expect, the precise opposite of that which Coleridge alleged it to be. Macbeth figures in conventional judgments as a typical man of action; yet at every important step in his evil career he has to be stimulated and thrust on by his wife. He even proposes to abandon the enterprise which he has undertaken, and would do so were he not goaded to reluctant action by Lady Macbeth's reproaches. Then, in the very moment of action, he betrays his incapacity for self-disciplined efficiency. He brings away the evidence that was to have transferred his guilt to the sleeping grooms, and his wife is obliged to go back and repair the effects of his timid incapacity. If there were any evidence of failures of this kind on Hamlet's part, the Coleridgean theory would have a great deal more verisimilitude than it has. But I

Contrast between Hamlet and Macbeth.

Macbeth I vii (the whole scene).

Macbeth II i 47 ff.

find it difficult to understand how any impartial reader of these two plays can accept Macbeth as a man of action, and at the same time pass judgment on Hamlet as a flaccid and ineffectual dreamer; — on Hamlet, who, standing alone, succeeds in thwarting and mystifying the entire Court-full of lynx-eyed spies set on by the usurping King.

After the Play incident, Hamlet's danger is increased by as much as his certainty is intensified. He has betrayed himself to Claudius, just as Claudius has betrayed himself to him. Henceforth the combat between them must be open and *à outrance*. On the one side is the King, with the forces of the realm at his disposal; on the other are Hamlet and Horatio, inwardly convinced that Claudius is a murderer, but still with no evidence that they can offer to the world.

Stage of open enmity between Hamlet and Claudius.

This point must be dwelt upon for a moment, by way of anticipating the next objection from the Coleridgean school. Why, they will ask, did Hamlet allow himself to be packed off to England? Here, if nowhere else, we have the proof of his feebleness and ineffectuality. He has been sworn to vengeance by the Ghost. Not only does duty (as understood in those days, and accepted by him) urge him to slay his father's slayer, but his interest in life points in the same direction. Success will mean that he shall wear the crown and rule the State. Yet, in face of this twofold prompting to action, he tamely submits to being sent out of the country.

Why does Hamlet sail for England?

This contention may be met by simply pointing to the position in which Hamlet at this juncture finds himself. The fact of the indispensableness of convincing objective evidence as to the character and methods of Claudius cannot be too strongly insisted

For two reasons: (1) To get evidence,

upon; and by going off to England in the company of Rosencrantz and Guildenstern Hamlet has the best chance of obtaining it. That he realized this, and had planned his sea-*coup* beforehand, is plainly hinted in his words to his mother:—

III iv 202 ff.

My two schoolfellows,
Whom I will trust as I will adders fang'd,
They bear the mandate; they must sweep my way,
And marshal me *to knavery*. Let it work;
For 'tis the sport to have the enginer
Hoist with his own petar: and *'t shall go hard*
But I will delve one yard below their mines,
And blow them at the moon: Oh, 'tis most sweet,
When in one line two crafts directly meet.

It is further evidenced by his proceeding, as soon as the ship is at sea, to investigate the commissions which the two worthies carry with them. Had he not suspected that he would here find what he wanted, why should he have played the Sherlock Holmes? The discovery of Claudius's treachery *in a written document,* which could be produced at need before a court of inquiry, is the justification both of his detective enterprise and of the suspicion which prompted it.

which he succeeds in obtaining;

On the other hand, a refusal to undertake this voyage would now certainly have meant (as we see by the hints of Claudius, and earlier of Polonius) the imprisonment of Hamlet under pretext of insanity, to be followed speedily by his surreptitious murder. There would have been no inquiry into the fate of a lunatic, even a royal one, after he had been a short while removed from the public eye; and Hamlet is fully aware of the unscrupulousness of the man with whom he has to deal.

(2) Because refusal would have meant confinement as a lunatic.

Before he leaves, however, we are clearly shown the state of open conflict which now subsists between him and Claudius. Hamlet no longer keeps up the pretence of friendship with the King's tools, Rosencrantz and Guildenstern. He angrily denounces them for thinking him such a fool or a child that he is more easy to be played upon than a pipe, though with Polonius he contemptuously retains his mask of insanity.

The speech of Hamlet when he finds the King at prayer is, as has already been indicated, inconsistent with all the rest of the play. I admit that it does not support my interpretation of his character, but I contend that it is in equally violent conflict with the idea that Hamlet is a vacillating philosopher, whose will is "sicklied o'er with the pale cast of thought." Upon that view, while he is incapable of careful planning and the gradual carrying out of a deliberate scheme of vengeance, he *is* capable of sudden spasms of inconsiderate activity. But if so, why should he not at this point slay the King, as ruthlessly as in the very next scene he goes about to do it, slaying Polonius by mistake? He has now no doubt of the guilt of Claudius: the disclosure at the play has verified for him the allegation of the Ghost. Here, then, was just the turn of circumstance at which a moody procrastinator, inflamed with anger, might be expected to wreak his belated vengeance. There is but one reason which adequately explains his abstention. It is the reason I have urged throughout: that still his cause could never be explained aright "to the unsatisfied" if he were thus to kill the King. The fact that Claudius had risen in confusion from the play was susceptible of many other explanations than that which Hamlet naturally applied to it. By the uninitiated it would never have been taken as conclusive proof that he was guilty of

The "Now might I do it" speech, III iii 73 ff.

precisely such a murder as had been enacted before him.

But Hamlet's speech on this occasion is neither that of a resolute man, who for valid reasons decides to defer the fatal act, nor yet that of a perplexed philosopher given to overmuch brooding on the riddle of the painful earth. It is that of a superstitious barbarian. It is out of key, in style as well as in thought, with the rest of the play. It is incomparably inferior to the soliloquy of the King, which immediately precedes it. I find it much more suggestive of *Titus Andronicus* than of the general run of Shakespeare's work at the period of the great tragedies; and for this reason I incline to the conjecture that the passage is a survival from the old play, and is not Shakespeare's work at all. Its retention is one more evidence of his carelessness, or else an extreme concession to the taste of the groundlings;—unless, indeed, it is due to the fact of bad editing in the Folio, and the absence of Shakespeare's supervision when his works were prepared for the press.

The slaying of the concealed spy.

The mistaken slaying of Polonius, however, is in a different category as regards both its policy and its motive. Hamlet supposed that the man behind the arras was the King: "I took thee for thy betters." Had it really been the King, he could have set up a passable defence, since no man had a right to play the spy upon him. The catching of the King in such an act, coupled with the testimony of the sentries as to the appearance of the Ghost and of Horatio as to the behaviour of Claudius at the play, would have been circumstantial evidence enough to justify Hamlet to the world. For what more probable motive could have been assigned for the spying of Claudius than his apprehension that Hamlet had discovered his guilt?

The next pivot of the conventional interpretation is the appearance of the Ghost during Hamlet's conversation with his mother, and especially the words, "Thy almost blunted purpose."

> This visitation
> Is but to whet thy almost blunted purpose.

III iv 110-11.

Between this appearance, however, and the earlier one, there is a very significant difference. In the first act the Ghost is visible to everybody into whose presence it comes, whereas in this scene it is invisible save to Hamlet. Even the Queen is unaware of the presence of her dead husband's spirit. She asks Hamlet,

> How is't with you,
> That you do bend your eye on vacancy,
> And with th' incorporal air do hold discourse?

Ibid. 116-18.

And, again, upon Hamlet's addressing the Ghost, she asks, "To whom do you speak this?" When he in return inquires, "Do you see nothing there?" she answers, "Nothing at all; yet all that is I see." Hamlet's insistence on the presence of his father "in his habit as he lived" is repelled by her with the statement,

Ibid. 131 ff.

> This is the very coinage of your brain;
> This bodiless creation ecstasy
> Is very cunning in.

Disclaiming the charge, Hamlet declares,

> My pulse, as yours, doth temperately keep time,
> And makes as healthful music.

It would be not a little surprising under the circumstances if either his pulse or hers did "temperately keep time." After the killing of Polonius, and after such an interview, in which he had bluntly charged her with the incestuous nature of her union, and declared Claudius the murderer of her husband (an accusation which she now hears for the first time), they must both have been somewhat overwrought. I assume it to be Shakespeare's idea that in this place the vision is only a subjective fantasy of Hamlet's mind. No other explanation will account for the fact that the Ghost, which before was visible to everybody, can now be seen by him alone; and the words, "thy almost blunted purpose," while they are not at all true to the facts of the case, *are* true to the impatience of Hamlet's active mind, yearning to see completed the vengeance which yet he must defer to compass. In support of this view, I may point to the fact that the Ghost's words are little more than a repetition of those with which Hamlet greets its appearance before it speaks : —

III iv 107 ff.   Do you not come your tardy son to chide,
That, laps'd in time and passion, lets go by
The important acting of your dread command?

And, in reply to his mother's inquiry, he reiterates the same idea : —

Ibid. 126-7.   His form and cause conjoin'd, preaching to stones,
Would make them capable.

Now, a subjective vision is in itself by no means a proof of insanity, or even of serious derangement short of insanity. It is rather the proof of an intense, abnormal, and long-continued concentration of mind and will. Hamlet here precipitates the strength of his purpose and the anguish of its incompletion into the semblance of a presence visible to no eye but his.

The soliloquy about Fortinbras.   The explanation above suggested for the "Rogue-and-peasant-slave" soliloquy holds equally of the one beginning, "How all occasions do inform against me!" in which Hamlet indulges after meeting the Captain of Fortinbras's army. A sluggard or a coward would not have taken the point as Hamlet takes it. The slow walker always protests that he is going as fast as can be expected of him; it is the man of rapid strides who accuses himself for not making better speed. Just as John Bunyan, while a sinner, is scarcely conscious of his sins, but accuses himself of them with violent exaggeration after he has given them up, so Hamlet's conscience charges him with "letting all sleep," amid the very rush of the action by which he is preparing the execution of his vengeance.

Hamlet's conduct at sea, as related first in his letter to Horatio and afterwards in the conversation with him, cannot be accused of indolence or inefficiency even by the most thorough-going follower of Coleridge. Accordingly, it has been made an instance of the opposite vice — the headstrong, precipitate rashness which is assumed to alternate with his long spells of moody inactivity. Because Hamlet himself uses the terms "rashness" and "indiscretion" in describing the burglary of his schoolfellows' cabin (determined on by him before he sailed, as we have already seen), critics determined to impale him either on the one horn or the other, take these expressions at their face value. They forget that one must allow for modesty and self-depreciation in a man's own versions of his deeds. The simple fact is that Hamlet, at terrible risk, purloined the commission in which Claudius desired the English to assassinate him. If "rashness" can explain this, it can scarcely account for the calm efficiency with which he sits down and forges a substitute document, sealing it with his father's signet; and all this, be it ob-

Incidents at sea: The commission and the pirates.

served, on the *first day* of the voyage. Next day comes the fight with the pirates, in which Hamlet is the *only* man to board the hostile vessel. Is not this another curious commentary on his irresolution? Being made prisoner by the corsairs, he is diplomatic enough to induce them to return and set him on the coast of Denmark. The entire transaction is evidence of that unusual degree of mental activity which enables the man with a genius for action to transform every obstacle into an instrument for the furtherance of his cause.

" Meditations among the tombs." Some critics have sneered at Hamlet for being, upon his return from sea, "much more ready to meditate among the tombs than to carry out the purpose he still proclaims to Horatio of killing Claudius." [6] Now the conversation of the two Grave-Diggers is an exceptionally bold and striking instance of Shakespeare's frequent practice of alternating comedy with tragedy for the relief of the spectators' feelings. There is not a more daring use of this device anywhere in his plays, with the possible exception of the Porter's soliloquy in *Macbeth*. We have just witnessed the heartrending scene of Ophelia's madness; and then, after the conspiracy between Laertes and Claudius, we have heard from the Queen the woeful news that Ophelia is drowned. By these episodes our sympathies have been sorely lacerated. It is one of Shakespeare's sovereign defiances of the classic tradition to introduce comic relief at such a point, and to do it not by a departure from the theme, but by setting the two clowns to discuss the tragedy which has just been reported. The gibe about Hamlet "meditating among the tombs" would have some point were it not that he and Horatio obviously wan-

6 The anonymous writer cited above, p. 129.

der upon this scene by accident. As to Hamlet's reflections over the skulls, they are platitudinous enough, and make little point either for the thesis that he is a philosopher or against the thesis that he is a man of action. Any man is capable of detecting the ironical contrast between the swaggering self-sufficiency of men in life and the insignificance of their mortal fragments in death; though, to be sure, not every man can express it as Hamlet does.

Later in the scene, we are amazed to find Hamlet informing Horatio that "that is Laertes, a very noble youth." Again we have no alternative but to accuse Shakespeare of preposterous inconsistency. How could Horatio have failed to know Laertes? Had he not been constantly at the Court with him, from the time of the late King's funeral to that of Laertes' departure for France? This is as inexplicable as Hamlet's own doubt about the identity of Horatio at their first meeting, and his asking him, "What is your affair in Elsinore?" after he has been there two months.

Episodes at Ophelia's grave.

As to the unseemly rhodomontade in which Hamlet indulges over the grave of Ophelia, three motives on his part can be assigned: first, his love for Ophelia, which blazes into anger at the insulting language used about himself by Laertes; secondly, his disgust at the braggadocio of Laertes, which he expresses by out-ranting and satirizing him; thirdly, the instantaneous decision, when he finds himself in the presence of the King and courtiers, to resume the mask of mental derangement which he had worn prior to his departure.

Little remains, in outlining the character of Hamlet, save to rebut the criticism that the final catastrophe is brought about not by any determinate act

Causation of the final catastrophe.

of his, but by a chapter of accidents. Hamlet, after his return from sea, is in a position to take his vengeance whenever the hour favours, since he now has the objective proof that he has so long sought. He is in possession of Claudius's commission to Rosencrantz and Guildenstern, which is a clear proof that the King had treacherously sought to bring about the assassination of his nephew and step-son. Whenever Hamlet may kill him, he will only need to produce this document, and it will be a justification which in that age no man would dream of questioning. The two tools of the usurper's conspiracy he has sent to a doom which costs him no remorse:—

V ii 58 ff.

> Their defeat
> Does by their own insinuation grow:
> 'Tis dangerous when the baser nature comes
> Between the pass and fell incensèd points
> Of mighty opposites.

Nothing now remains but for him to "take his fair hour" to get rid of Claudius. The only "accident" there is in the matter is the disclosure and failure of the still deeper-dyed treachery by which Claudius has planned to ensure Hamlet's death in case the springe of Laertes should fail to ensnare him.

Thus, by a simple enumeration of the things that Hamlet does, and by an examination of his words in the light of everyday experience of the way men accuse and excuse themselves, I have sought to show that Shakespeare's notion of the stupendous character he creates is radically different from the construction commonly placed upon the text.

In Browning's *Bishop Blougram's Apology,* the hypocritical prelate chaffs his young interlocutor with having found "two points in Hamlet's soul unseized by the Germans yet — which view you'll print." But it would seem to be too late in the day for such discoveries. German scholarship, German thoroughness and German pedantry have done their admirable best and their villainous worst[7] in the endless commentaries they have piled up on this play. While the great mass of their critics have followed Goethe and Schlegel as slavishly as the English followed Coleridge, some few of them have taken independent ground, and reached a conclusion identical in principle with that set forth in the preceding pages, — namely, that the two chief points in Hamlet's soul are his inflexible resolution and his alert efficiency. The most elaborate discussion in this sense is that of Karl Werder, who, in his *Vorlesungen über Shakespeare's Hamlet* (1875), readily seizes upon the essential point: —

> As things stand, truth and justice can be known only from one mouth, the mouth of the crowned criminal, or at least from the King's party [*sic*], else they remain hidden and buried till the last day. . . . The encoffined secrecy of the *unprovable* crime: this is the subterranean spring, whence flows its [the tragedy's] power to awaken fear and sympathy.

Werder is an incorrigible idolater, but he follows this clue out consistently, though with insufficient fulness of detail. The only vital point he misses is the untrustworthiness of the Ghost's testimony. Before Werder's day, the hint for the true interpretation had been given by Klein (1846), but not worked out.

I remarked at the outset that *Hamlet* is not the greatest of Shakespeare's plays. The evidences of haste, and the palpable inconsistencies, to some only

[7] See above, pp. 112–13, *note*.

of which I have drawn attention, may be offered in support of this judgment. Such incidents as Hamlet's speech over the praying criminal, and the very unpleasant episode at the grave of Ophelia, are further obvious blemishes which cannot easily escape the most indulgent critic. Yet, withal, its universal popularity is richly deserved. Such closeness of speech, such insight into character, such masterly manipulation of incidents, are nowhere to be paralleled outside the volume of Shakespeare himself. Idolatry is no true reverence, and one shows deeper respect for the master by pointing out what he would himself have admitted as defects, than by accepting and praising indiscriminately all that is labelled with his name. Yet every reader of *Hamlet* must end by bowing his head in silent wonderment before the man who thus can "shake our dispositions with thoughts beyond the reaches of our souls."

CHAPTER VI

" MACBETH ": THE WORKING OF THE INWARD JUDGE

THE question as to which is the greatest individual play of Shakespeare is insoluble. You
cannot set the unfallen angels by the ears in competi-
tive strife. It is idle to attempt to decide between the
respective merits of a series of perfect sunsets or
sunrises. But we pass beyond the region of possible
dispute when we affirm that the three tragedies of
Macbeth, King Lear and *Othello* together form the
mightiest trilogy in human literature. Nowhere else
do we find such preternatural depth of penetration
into the volcanic forces in character that determine
conduct; nowhere else is the reality of the natural
nemesis, by which vice courts its own doom, so un-
erringly and relentlessly exhibited. The three sins
of inordinate ambition, ingratitude and jealousy are
traced through all their hateful cruelty to the innocent, and, still more, through their inevitable recoil
upon the guilty.

The crowning Trilogy: Macbeth, Lear, Othello.

The poet, being a creator, has no need to preach
at us; he makes his doctrine live. He is here exposing to our view what he conceives to be the moral
order of the universe in its tragic aspect. Here may
we see the price that men must needs pay for certain
ends. They are free; "none leads them, and none
ever led." Their freedom is not a gift from without,
but an inherently necessitated goal of their nature.

Shake-speare's view of the moral order of the world.

If it were given, it could not be freedom. If God "gave" us freedom, that would be to force us to accept it—and thus the gift would destroy itself. Hence springs the wondrous subtlety of the spiritual economy,—that we are our own creators. Freedom can only be self-achieved; and life is the decisive action by which we either realize it or relinquish it and enslave ourselves. According to Shakespeare, the moral order of the world is such that men reap what they have sown: not, however, in outward success or failure, good and evil hap,—not in the sense of so-called "poetical justice,"—but in the inner realm of the spirit's quality. Men become what they have willed to be; but that willing carries with it certain necessary consequences, which, as a rule, the wrong-doer realizes only when his self-entailed fate is upon him. The end *necessitates* the means; whence springs the deep ethical truth, not that the end justifies the means—that it can never do—but that only those ends are right, the means to which can be disinterestedly approved. The test of the rightness or wrongness of Macbeth's ambition is not the goal at which he aims, but the steps that he must inevitably take in order to reach it. These being spontaneously condemned by any fair moral judgment, the end is therefore to be stamped as wrong, irrespective of any good to which, once attained, it might lead.

Causative interaction between conduct and character.

But we are anticipating. Let us revert to the safer path of induction; and, to begin at the beginning, let us see what are the elements in this tragedy which first commended it to Shakespeare from the business point of view. What would the groundlings like in it? What is there on which the most successful playwright of his time could safely count

Macbeth from the box-office standpoint.

to ensure the first end of play-making,— namely, the winning of an audience?

These elements are not far to seek. The ever-darkening atmosphere of blood and thunder, with its poetic suggestion of a secret sympathy between the moral and the material world, would have its charm for an audience that could not detect its inner meaning. The Witches could be counted upon to impart a thrill that would vibrate in the box-office. The murder of Duncan, even without the magic vesture of poesy in which Shakespeare has dressed it, would appeal at once to that primal mental instinct which in our own time secures the sale of detective stories and of the sanguineous literature in which boyhood surreptitiously delights. The errant ghost of Banquo would fill more seats than Macbeth's, and the Sleep-Walking scene would be a precious novelty in horror. The simultaneous fulfilment and falsification of the ambiguous prophecy to Macbeth, which gives rise to the trick of bringing the boughs of Birnam Wood to Dunsinane, and to the disclosure of Macduff's abnormal advent into the world, was a certain draw. And, to crown all, the splendid clash of arms, in which Macbeth, after laying about him like a Titan, is slain by the deeply wronged Macduff, who later brings his bloody head upon the stage, make up such a pennyworth as the Jacobean Londoner could not fail to applaud to the echo.

The melodramatic material.

In this play, too, we find Shakespeare making concessions not only to the vulgar Philistines in the pit, but to the snobbish Philistine at Court. The comparison of *Macbeth* with its crude ore in Holinshed shows us with what judicious dexterity Shakespeare has incidentally turned his tragedy into a compliment to King James and a flattery of that pedantic

Baits for King James.

Solomon's regal egoism and his superstitions and fads.

The very choice of the theme was not improbably dictated by this consideration. Never during Elizabeth's reign had Shakespeare selected a subject from Scottish history; and *Macbeth* comes within two or three years of the accession of the first Stuart to the English throne. The representation of Banquo as a noble and gallant gentleman has no foundation in history—not even in history according to Holinshed. Banquo, as portrayed by that authority, is Macbeth's accomplice in the murder of King Duncan. He is, indeed, as inveterate a savage as any of the bloodthirsty mob of bandits whose adventures, according to the chronicler's conception of things, made up the history of Scotland. But the tradition had it that Banquo was King James's ancestor. He is to "get kings, though he be none"; and so, in the vision that horrifies Macbeth, the last disclosure is of Banquo's royal descendants carrying "twofold balls and treble sceptres"—a prophecy safely uttered after the event, which was the union of the sovereignty of England, Scotland and Ireland in the person of the son of Mary Stuart.

James, too, as is well known, was a deep student of witchcraft and demonology, and zealous in the extirpation of those who had purchased these maleficent powers from the devil. Hence the introduction of the Witches, with infinitely more of circumstance than is accorded to them in the chronicle. Another of James's amiable peculiarities was his belief in his own miraculous power of curing the scrofula, otherwise known as the "king's evil." His researches in science and divinity had led him to believe that one of the attributes of an anointed king (bestowed by

the divine grace only on legitimate monarchs) was
this therapeutic power, with which, of course, he
held himself to be endued. To this we owe that
irrelevant passage, which Shakespeare drags in by
the scruff of the neck, exhibiting Edward the Con-
fessor as exercising the holy virtue transmitted to
his illustrious seventeenth-century representative: —

Malcolm: Well; more anon. — Comes the King forth, I IV iii 139 ff.
  pray you?
Doctor: Ay, sir; there are a crew of wretched souls
  That stay his cure: their malady convinces
  The great assay of art; but at his touch —
  Such sanctity hath heaven given his hand —
  They presently amend. . . .
Macduff: What's the disease he means?
Malcolm: 'Tis call'd the evil:
  A most miraculous work in this good king;
  Which often, since my here-remain in England,
  I have seen him do. How he solicits heaven,
  Himself best knows: but strangely-visited people,
  All swoll'n and ulcerous, pitiful to the eye,
  The mere despair of surgery, he cures,
  Hanging a golden stamp about their necks,
  Put on with holy prayers: and 'tis spoken,
  To the succeeding royalty he leaves
  The healing benediction.

It is interesting to note that for this touch of loyal
flattery Shakespeare hunted up a different volume of
his authority from that in which he found the story
of Macbeth. The veracious Holinshed thus describes the saintly Edward's gifts: —

> As hath beene thought, he was inspired with the Holinshed's
> gift of prophesie, and also to haue had the gift of *Historie of*
> healing infirmities and diseases. He vsed to helpe *England*
> those that were vexed with the disease, commonlie (edition of
> called the kings euill, and left that vertue as it were 1587), p. 195.
> a portion of inheritance vnto his successors the kings
> of this realme.

The ana-
chronism, as
before: well
shaken be-
fore taken.

The events connected with the usurpation of Macbeth and his subsequent defeat covered a period of
some seventeen years in the eleventh century. But
Shakespeare (who, as we have seen on many occasions, was entirely aware of the difference between
poetry and history) really dated them in the year
1606, when he wrote the tragedy. Hence to quote
all the minor anachronisms he has perpetrated would
practically necessitate reprinting the play, since they
occur in almost every line. In the third scene of the
first act we read of "cannons" and "dollars"; in
the first of Act II, and elsewhere, we hear of a striking clock. But these are trifles. In every line we
get the mentality, the standard of moral judgment,
and the social tone and general civilization of Shakespeare's own day; and in this consists the peculiarity
which may be called either anachronism or creative
licence — as you like it.

The Porter's
soliloquy a
résumé of
XVII-cen-
tury occur-
rences.
II iii 1 ff.

It comes quite congenially to Shakespeare to make
his soliloquizing Porter, in a Scottish castle in the
eleventh century, discourse on affairs that happened
in London in the seventeenth century. The first of
the imaginary knockers at the gate whom that startling humorist enumerates is "a farmer, that hang'd
himself on the expectation of plenty" — an allusion,
so the wise tell us, to the abnormally abundant har-
vest of 1606. The second is "an equivocator, that
could swear in both the scales against either scale;
who committed treason enough for God's sake, yet
could not equivocate to heaven." The original of
this description was a Jesuit, by name Henry Garnet,
who was executed early in 1606 for participation in
the Gunpowder Plot, and who created a sensation by
making a fearless defence of equivocation at his trial.
Such wilful violations of historic or even legendary

consistency are indefensible; and yet is there not something the matter with a mind that could feel them to need defence?

Apart from these characteristic and habitual defiances of place and time, Shakespeare in this play has followed his authority with more closeness than usual; though it need scarcely be added that he finds in Holinshed only the barest scaffolding of the majestic edifice he has reared for us. And even this framework he has not hesitated to alter freely, in accordance with his own sense of poetic propriety and dramatic convincingness. For example, to deepen the heinousness of Macbeth's crime, he has made of Duncan something little short of a saint; whereas, according to the chronicler, that monarch was a vicious and incapable person, of whom his people were by no means displeased to be rid. Macbeth, despite the crime by which he usurped the crown, was, for more than ten of the seventeen years of his reign, an unusually satisfactory sovereign, who originated many righteous laws, and was a particularly good friend to the poor and to the Church.[1] In the chronicle the murder of Duncan is

> [1] " Makbeth [was] a valiant gentleman, & one that if he had not beene somewhat cruell of nature, might haue beene thought most woorthie the gouernement of a realme. On the other part, Duncane was so soft & gentle of nature, that the people wished the inclinations and maners of these two cousins to haue beene so tempered and interchangeablie bestowed betwixt them, that where the one had too much of clemencie, & the other of crueltie, the meane vertue betwixt these two extremities might haue reigned by indifferent partition in them both; so should Duncane haue proued a woorthie king, & Makbeth an excellent capteine."— Holinshed, *Historie of Scotland*, ed. 1587, p. 168.
>
> " Mackbeth shewing himselfe thus a most diligent punisher of all iniuries and wrongs attempted by anie disordered persons within his realme, was accounted the sure defense and

Side notes:

Shakespeare's use of his source:

(1) The whitewashing of Duncan;

(2) The blackwashing of Macbeth;

(3) The transplantation of the murder episode;

barely alluded to; and so Shakespeare has calmly annexed the description of the assassination of another king by another man, and made it the basis of his elaborate picture of the nocturnal crime. Lady Macbeth, too, is in Holinshed nothing but a name,—

(4) The synthesizing of Lady Macbeth.

nay, she is not even that; yet because the other murderer's wife is represented not only as exerting great influence over her husband, but as initiating his plots and ensuring their efficient carrying out, Shakespeare in his own fashion has transferred *her* attributes to the wife of his villainous hero. He loves to follow his authority only so far as it is convenient to do so. As soon as it seems otherwise, he becomes a law to himself;—a law which we may perhaps venture to formulate in some such terms as these: "If thine authority offend thee, pluck him out and cast him from thee; for it is better for thee to enter into dramatic success having no authority, than having an authority to be hissed into the hell of failure."

Text and editions.

With the exception of *The Comedy of Errors*, *Macbeth* is the shortest of Shakespeare's plays. *Hamlet* is almost twice as long. No quarto editions have been preserved, and it is virtually certain that none ever existed. Hence our only authority is the

buckler of innocent people; and hereto he also applied his whole indeuor, to cause yoong men to exercise themselues in vertuous maners, and men of the church to attend their diuine seruice according to their vocations. . . .

"To be briefe, such were the woorthie dooings and princelie acts of this Mackbeth in the administration of the realme, that if he had atteined therevnto by rightfull means, and continued in vprightnesse of iustice as he began, till the end of his reigne, he might well haue beene numbred amongest the most noble princes that anie where had reigned. He made manie holesome laws and statutes for the publike weale of his subiects. . . ."—*Ibid.*, p. 171.

text of the Folio, and there are various indications that what we find there is a version abbreviated for stage purposes. It has been maintained by some critics that the second scene of Act I, describing King Duncan's interview with the wounded Sergeant, is so inferior to the rest of the play that it cannot be from Shakespeare's hand. Others have alleged that the fifth scene of Act III, consisting almost entirely of the speech of Hecate, is also from another hand. Such decisions of the higher intuition may be saluted with respect, but they are too inscrutable for less inspired minds to endorse. I am quite unable to detect the alleged inferiority, still less to accept Mr. White's jaunty ascription of the Hecate scene to Middleton. While the latter is perfectly possible, yet it is a mere guess. And when one speaks of inferiority, it must be remembered that the comparison is not with Shakespeare's best work, but with the poorest that he is admitted to have done at this period.

Alleged interpolations: I ii and III v.

The intuitional method of criticism finds its *reductio ad absurdum* in that wonderful contention of Coleridge, that the Porter's soliloquy is ungenuine except only the single great sentence, "I'll devil-porter it no further: I had thought to have let in some of all professions that go the primrose way to the everlasting bonfire." This is too good to be given away; and so Shakespeare, forsooth, must be credited with having thrust it into the margin of a colleague's page![2]

[2] " . . . the disgusting passage of the Porter (Act II, sc. 3), which I dare pledge myself to *demonstrate* to be an interpolation of the actors. . . .

"This low soliloquy of the Porter and his few speeches afterwards, I believe to have been written for the mob by some other hand, perhaps with Shakespeare's consent; and that find-

The character of Macbeth as compared with Hamlet.

The true contrast between Macbeth and Hamlet is, as I have elsewhere urged,[3] the very opposite of that which it is conventionally assumed to be. Hamlet is the successful man of action, who always finds or makes his inward and outward resources adequate to the purpose he seeks to attain. Macbeth is the irresolute man of impulse, strongly drawn to deep designs, but perpetually inhibited by his recoil from the only means that could compass them. His character is dissected with literal truth in Lady Macbeth's first account of him:—

I v 11 ff.

Glamis thou art, and Cawdor; and shalt be
What thou art promis'd: yet do I fear thy nature;
It is too full o' th' milk of human kindness
To catch the nearest way: thou wouldst be great,
Art not without ambition, but without
The illness should attend it: what thou wouldst highly,
That wouldst thou holily; wouldst not play false,
And yet wouldst wrongly win: thou'ldst have, great Glamis,
That which cries "Thus thou must do, if thou have it";
And that which rather thou dost fear to do
Than wishest should be undone.

Not moral judgment but moral cowardice makes him shrink.

In this analysis, the deepest note of insight is the perception that Macbeth's hesitation at crime is due not so much to moral repugnance as to fear of consequences. When he lets "'I dare not' wait upon 'I would,'" it is cowardice that prompts him, not the sense of justice. His soliloquies are much fuller of irresolution and vacillation than any of Hamlet's;

ing it take, he with the remaining ink of a pen otherwise employed, just interpolated the words, 'I'll devil-porter it' [&c., as quoted above]. Of the rest, not one syllable has the ever-present being of Shakespeare."—"Notes on *Macbeth*," in Coleridge's *Essays & Lectures on Shakespeare*, Everyman series, pp. 156, 163–4.

[3] *Ante*, p. 136.

and his actions, quite unlike Hamlet's, are half-baked, premature, unthought-out. He suffers himself to be evaded by the men upon whose destruction his success depends. One cannot imagine Hamlet letting Fleance, Malcolm, Donalbain and Macduff slip through his fingers as Macbeth does. Nor can one think of the so-called "moody Dane" being bamboozled by the Witches, or by the prophecies of the apparitions in Macbeth's vision. Hamlet will not accept the testimony of his father's Ghost until he has verified it by proof drawn from the world of the living. Macbeth, on the other hand, believes the ambiguous oracle about the wood coming to Dunsinane, and about "none of woman born" being able to harm him, without even suspecting that the juggling fiends are paltering with him in a double sense. His credulity is as gross as that of the village maidens who swallowed the yarns of Autolycus. His courage, too, has to be screwed up by his wife at the crisis, whereas Hamlet cannot be held back by his friends. Until the closing acts, the murderous usurper is a quaking jelly of irresolution, but the woman has a will of steel.

His credulity.

The contrast between these two characters, and the difference in their development, is one of the rarest evidences of Shakespeare's insight. Macbeth at the outset is a man of dauntless physical courage, a gallant and oft-approved warrior. The invasion and the insurrection he has put down with a mighty hand, and his feats of valour in the stricken field merit all the praise they receive from the Sergeant and from Duncan. Hitherto, however, he has not periled his soul by exposing it to violence in the moral world, as he is accustomed to peril his body by

Two forms of strength and weakness: Macbeth & his wife.

exposure to the shocks and chances of the field. Though the evil he is to do originates in his own will, its first inward suggestion almost paralyzes his whole " state of man." The thought of playing false is new and unfamiliar, and its birth in his own mind steeps him in perplexity:—

I iii 134 ff.

> Why do I yield to that suggestion
> Whose horrid image doth unfix my hair,
> And make my seated heart knock at my ribs,
> Against the use of nature? Present fears
> Are less than horrible imaginings:
> My thought, whose murther yet is but fantastical,
> Shakes so my single state of man that function
> Is smother'd in surmise, and nothing is
> But what is not.

" Present fears are less than horrible imaginings" —that is the perfect summary of the man's state of mind; and it is in this that he is diametrically opposed to his wife. To her, horrible imaginings have been long familiar. The ambition that in Macbeth is but now waking to consciousness has from of old been her daily companion. Of present fears—that is, of immediate physical danger,— she has known nothing and thought but little. They are the man's affair. Hers must be the courage to plan: his the bodily valour to execute.

The two form a perfect partnership.

This contrast of the two forms of courage, both of which are equally necessary to the accomplishment of the feat, makes a perfect harmony between these partners in gigantic crime. When the hour draws near for its achievement, the two types become still more definitely silhouetted before us. The present horror so enervates Macbeth that he is ready to abandon the enterprise. The perturbation of his seated heart gives him a blinding flash of insight into the gulfs of terror that open beneath him; and, when he finds himself alone, he puts into words the whole philosophy of natural nemesis, the entire basis of experience on which reposes that belief in moral law which the greatest seers of mankind have proclaimed: —

> If it were done when 'tis done, then 'twere well
> It were done quickly. If th' assassination
> Could trammel up the consequence, and catch
> With his surcease success; that but this blow
> Might be the be-all and the end-all — here,
> But here, upon this bank and shoal of time,—
> We'ld jump the life to come. But in these cases
> We still have judgment here; that we but teach
> Bloody instructions, which, being taught, return
> To plague the inventor: this even-handed justice
> Commends th' ingredients of our poison'd chalice
> To our own lips.

I vii 1-12.

Thus does he justify all his wife's misgivings as to his infirmity of purpose. "We will proceed," he says, "no further in this business"; and it needs the sharpest goading of her shrewish tongue to make him repent of his repentance. The explanation is that what to him are novel horrors are to her accustomed mental companions, from whom familiarity has taken all dreadfulness; whereas the mere physical counterpart of these terrors, the presence of death and the sight of blood, which to Macbeth are as nothing, prove to her so overwhelming that they become the cause of her spiritual collapse and self-betrayal.

Psychological consistency of the two characters

Such being the opening situation, the development of the two characters is in strict accordance with psychological probability. Treachery, conspiracy and assassination become in time as familiar companions to Macbeth's mind as they have been to hers,

and of their development: Macbeth grows stronger

and he ceases to find in them the terror which their first birth in his mind produced. Hence he goes on from strength to strength, and, like the Satan of Milton, is most magnificent when encompassed by all the terrors of avenging justice. By the time he III i 19 to end. has to deal with Banquo he is so far graduated in wickedness that he is able to conceive the deed alone, and to withhold the disclosure of it from his wife until it has been accomplished. Instantly after his dangerous collapse at the sight of Banquo's ghost he is ready to plot fresh infamies. Already the purpose of slaying Macduff is born in his will, and he is resolved to go next day to consult the Weird Sisters, and learn from them the worst that may await him in the dark womb of time. He is at his strongest at the very end, after he has "supp'd full with horrors."

as his wife weakens. Lady Macbeth, on the contrary, is strongest at the outset, when he is feeble; and, step by step with the increase of his resolution, her powers weaken towards their collapse. Her strength of soul, that could conceive the murderous path to the crown, has no correlative strength of body that can endure the horror of the translation of these thoughts into action. When her senses are confronted with the deeds of blood to which her plans have led, her "tenement of clay" grows ever more recalcitrant to the fiendish will that o'er-informs it. When their stage is set with that accumulation of enmities which heightens the grandeur of Macbeth's soul in the very measure in which it threatens him with destruction, her reservoir of inward strength runs dry. The visions of her head upon her bed now trouble her, and in her somnambulism she betrays those thoughts which, had they lain quite unex-

pressed, must have shattered her sanity. At the last
(as we are led by Malcolm's closing speech to suppose) she dies by her own hand.

The analysis of Macbeth's character leads us directly to consider the part played in the tragedy by
occult or supernatural influences. Shakespeare, in
making use of these, is in the first place taking the
line of least resistance. They are in his authority.
Holinshed describes in some detail the excessive
credulity of Macbeth, and both the interviews with
the Witches — first that of Macbeth and Banquo,
and afterwards that of Macbeth alone — reveal a
close following of the chronicler's hints.[4]

In the second place, Shakespeare, as we have noted
above, is here making a characteristic concession to
popular taste in general, and to that of King James
I in particular. His use, however, of the supernatural machinery is noticeably different from
and superior to that of any contemporary writer.

*The preter-
natural ma-
chinery.*

[4] "It fortuned as Makbeth and Banquho iournied towards
Fores, where the king then laie, they went sporting by the
waie togither without other companie, saue onelie themselues,
passing through the woods and fields, when suddenlie in the
middest of a laund, there met them three women in strange
and wild apparell, resembling creatures of elder world, whome
when they attentiuelie beheld, woondering much at the sight,
the first of them spake and said: 'All haile, Makbeth, thane
'of Glammis!' (for he had latelie entered into that dignitie
and office by the death of his father Sinell). The second of
them said: 'Haile, Makbeth, thane of Cawder!' But the
third said: 'All haile, Makbeth, that heereafter shalt be king
'of Scotland.'

"Then Banquho: 'What manner of women' (saith he)
'are you, that seeme so little fauourable vnto me, whereas to
'my fellow heere, besides high offices, ye assigne also the
'kingdome, appointing foorth nothing for me at all?' 'Yes'
(saith the first of them) 'we promise greater benefits vnto
'thee, than vnto him, for he shall reigne in deed, but with an
'vnluckie end: neither shall he leaue anie issue behind him to

Others made such scenes grotesque: he makes them to the last degree weird and awe-inspiring; so that we have to turn to the Bible, to the story of the Witch of Endor, for a parallel to his achievement.

If issues are fore-known, what be-comes of freedom

It may be urged, however, that a supernatural scheme of prophecy and revelation through visions, if it means anything at all, means that the fate of men is determined not from within by their own character, but by uncontrollable external influences. How then can this be reconciled with my contention that, according to Shakespeare, men are free; that Macbeth's doom is self-originated; and that it is the inward judge, identical with his own deepest being and with the universal conscience of humanity, which condemns and punishes him? The prophecy of the Witches and the revelation of the apparitions implies that Macbeth's fate is foreknown; and fore-knowledge is equivalent to predestination. Whoever asserts that future human actions form part of the

'succeed in his place, where contrarilie thou in deed shalt not 'reigne at all, but of thee those shall be borne which shall gou-'erne the Scotish kingdome by long order of continuall de-'scent.' Herewith the foresaid women vanished immediatlie out of their sight. This was reputed at the first but some vaine fantasticall illusion by Makbeth and Banquho, insomuch that Banquho would call Makbeth in iest, king of Scotland; and Mackbeth againe would call him in sport likewise, the father of manie kings."— Holinshed, *Historie of Scotland,* ed. 1587, p. 170.

"He [Macbeth] had learned of certeine wizzards, in whose words he put great confidence, (for that the prophesie had happened so right, which the three faries or weird sisters had declared vnto him,) how that he ought to take heed of Mak-duffe, who in time to come should seeke to destroie him.

"And suerlie herevpon had he put Makduffe to death, but that a certeine witch, whome hee had in great trust, had told that he should neuer be slaine with man borne of anie woman, nor vanquished till the wood of Bernane came to the castell of Dunsinane."— *Ibid.,* p. 174.

knowledge of any consciousness whatsoever,— God's or demon's, it matters not,— thereby denies that those actions are in any sense contingent; denies, too, that the men whose deeds they seem to be, can justly be held in the full sense responsible for them.

I wish to state this objection as strongly as it can be put, because the right appreciation of these facts is crucial to the understanding of Shakespeare's conception of the moral world. The first point in my answer is this: that the entire action of Macbeth, all his crimes and all their consequences, would have been precisely what they were, even though no occult disclosures had ever been made to him. Herein, I suspect, Shakespeare is indulging the fine irony which we have traced in an analogous situation in *The Merchant of Venice:* he is dealing with a vulgar superstition, of which it would have been imprudent to make his private opinion too explicit. He humours the childish fantasies of the King, and at the same time he pours secret contempt upon them. These scenes are penned, let us remember, by the same mind that voiced in *Lear* the deep scorn of astrology and portent-hunting. Witchcraft, soothsaying, the consultation of oracles, the forced finding of a causal nexus in coincidences between human events and unusual phenomena of outward nature — all these are parts of " the excellent foppery of the world."

Shakespeare, in like manner, distinctly leaves open the question whether these preternatural appearances are not in fact subjective visions; that is to say, externalizations of the half-formed thoughts and half-buried desires of those who see them. After the first interview, Banquo asks his companion,

I iii 83 ff.

> Were such things here as we do speak about?
> Or have we eaten on the insane root,
> That takes the reason prisoner?

Further, the ghost of Banquo is seen by Macbeth *alone*.

Physical and psychic facts.

Now, this is the poetic device by which folklore, and pre-scientific thought generally, intimate to us that an apparition is only an imaginative bodying-forth of the state of mind of its beholder. If among a dozen people, all possessing normal organs of sense, one sees a form which remains invisible to all the others, we rightly conclude that the thing seen is not an objective presence, not an item in the phenomenal series; not truly " there," as we say. Visions thus lose their value as testimony to historic events, but gain a most important value as testimony to psychological conditions. If the voices heard by St. Paul and by Joan of Arc did not correspond to anything in the outward order of the universe, to the hearers they were reality itself,— because they were the immediate objectifications of their own deepest consciousness.

The ghost of Banquo is Macbeth's conscience.

Nothing could be finer or clearer than Shakespeare's indication of such a state of things by the first words Macbeth uses when he sees Banquo's ghost. The news of his half-successful plot has just been brought to him by the murderers. Full of the thought, he goes to take his seat at the table, but sees before him what nobody else can see: the pallid and bloodstained form of his assassinated comrade. At once he reveals the workings of his mind and the origin of his vision by the exclamation,

III iv 50 f.

> Thou canst not say I did it! never shake
> Thy gory locks at me!

thus potent with him, how strongly is his soul moved by the illusion provoked by the actual sight of Duncan's blood upon his hand! When he sees this, his torpedoed soul explodes in the most bewildering burst of imagery in our language:—

> What hands are here? ha! They pluck out mine eyes.
> Will all great Neptune's ocean wash this blood
> Clean from my hand? No, this my hand will rather
> The multitudinous seas incarnadine,
> Making the green, one red.

II ii 59 ff.

His fantasy being thus habitually creative, why should it not engender the vision on the blasted heath?—a vision, be it remembered, which revealed nothing to him save what had already passed through his mind.

It is this tendency to concrete visualizing which makes him at the outset so reluctant an instrument of his own and his wife's purpose. The sensitiveness, which makes his "fell of hair" rouse at a dismal treatise, causes him to suffer acutely at the contemplation of the horrors which his vaulting ambition must needs occasion. On the other hand, it is the absence of this kind of anticipatory representation which makes his wife strong when he is weak; though afterwards the realization of unanticipated horrors breaks her down, when familiarity with what he had foreseen has made Macbeth strong. Hence the tragic reversal of the opening situation, to which we have alluded. At the outset, we pity Macbeth, and look upon his wife with mingled hate and admiration; at the last, we must perforce pity her, whereas for him our admiration grows so great as almost to forget hatred.

This is the cause of his weakness.

V v 11.

Its absence is the cause of Lady Macbeth's strength.

Even apart from the unearthly scope and precision of Macbeth's language in his later speeches, the fig-

The magnificence of Macbeth at the close.

ure of the man himself grows so horrent and gigantic that its dimensions seem almost superhuman.
Ruined inwardly and outwardly, bereft of the prize
for which he had cast away his soul, and of the
deeply loved wife who had been his solace and his
strength; deceived by the juggling fiends to whom
he had trusted, he is forced inward upon himself.
There he finds no comfort, no happiness, no hope,
but the iron strength of utter despair. He will not
surrender;—not to himself, any more than to the
enemies at his gate. No suicide for him; he will play
the game out to the end:—

V iii 32.

I'll fight till from my bones my flesh be hack'd.
Give me my armour.

. . . .

V viii 1 ff.

Why should I play the Roman fool, and die
On mine own sword? Whiles I see lives, the gashes
Do better upon them.

Already he has been undeceived by the coming of
the wood to Dunsinane, and put to the last test by
the news of the death of his wife. His speech upon
receiving this intelligence is such a revelation of the
indefeasible strength of despair that, with all our
familiarity with Shakespeare, we read it for the
thousandth time with ever new amazement:—

V v 17 ff.

She should have died hereafter;
There would have been a time for such a word.
To-morrow, and to-morrow, and to-morrow,
Creeps in this petty pace from day to day
To the last syllable of recorded time;
And all our yesterdays have lighted fools
The way to dusty death. Out, out, brief candle!
Life's but a walking shadow, a poor player
That struts and frets his hour upon the stage,
And then is heard no more: it is a tale
Told by an idiot, full of sound and fury,
Signifying nothing.

I have already hinted at a resemblance between Macbeth and the Satan of Milton. The fancy is prompted chiefly by the bearing and language of Macbeth through the terrific trials of the fifth act. It comes from contemplating how with each new disaster he grows stronger and grander. Hitherto he has relied upon his wife; but, when that crutch fails him, the arm that had grasped it is freed and strengthened. Or he had trusted to the vaticinations of the "midnight hags." Ere this as yet had played him false, he had resigned himself to the fact that he can hold his position only by the sword. He knows that one crime begets a hundred: and he has whetted the temper of his will by accepting this, with all the terrors that it prophesies:—

> Now I am bent to know, III iv 134 ff.
> By the worst means, the worst. For mine own good
> All causes shall give way: I am in blood
> Stepp'd in so far that, should I wade no more,
> Returning were as tedious as go o'er:
> Strange things I have in head, that will to hand;
> Which must be acted ere they may be scann'd.

Having chosen his course, he must even dree his weird. He scents the battle afar off, and knows that the justice he has violated and the hatred he has deliberately provoked will surround his stronghold with ten thousand foes. Worse than this, he has forfeited the happiness he sought, by his very manner of seeking it:—

> I have liv'd long enough: my way of life V iii 22 ff.
> Is fall'n into the sere, the yellow leaf;
> And that which should accompany old age,
> As honour, love, obedience, troops of friends,
> I must not look to have; but, in their stead,
> Curses, not loud but deep, mouth-honour, breath,
> Which the poor heart would fain deny, and dare not.

But, just as adversity brings out the nobility of a good man, so self-evoked disaster reveals all that is great and heroic in the villain. Macbeth is never so splendid as when he rises above all outward aid, and embraces the utter ruin of his lot. Then it is that he is like Satan, when he, surrounded by the hostile cohorts,

Paradise Lost, IV.

> Collecting all his might, dilated stood,
> Like Teneriffe or Atlas unremov'd;
> His stature reach'd the sky, and on his crest
> Sat Horror plum'd.

The minor characters:

The concentration of interest in the two colossal characters of Macbeth and his wife recalls that earlier manner which Shakespeare learned from Marlowe. There is no such definite delineation of the minor personages as we find in *Hamlet* and *Othello.* Yet in the mature mastery of Shakespeare's present style he is able by a very few suggestive strokes to give a vivid impression, even of the least of his creatures. Duncan and Banquo are exquisitely individualized. For poetic effect, as we have seen, Shakespeare has departed from the account of Duncan which he found in Holinshed, and made of him a virtuous and amiable monarch. He has also, to heighten the crime, changed Duncan's age. The original victim was murdered early in life; Shakespeare's character is advanced in years. "Who would have thought *the old man* to have had so much blood in him?" says the dreaming Lady Macbeth, who at the time of the assassination had remarked that he resembled her father as he slept. The poet has also taken care to emphasize as strongly as possible the extreme kindliness with which Duncan had treated the Macbeths. The last we hear of him be-

(1) Duncan.

V i 35.

fore the murder is the message that he sends by
Banquo: —

> The King's abed: II i 12 ff.
> He hath been in unusual pleasure, and
> Sent forth great largess to your offices.
> This diamond he greets your wife withal,
> By the name of most kind hostess.

Before this, he has loaded his treacherous cousin
with honours, in return for services which, by the
standards of every age, it was Macbeth's clear duty
to render. The heinousness of the offence is further
emphasized by the fact that it takes place when Duncan is a guest in Macbeth's house. In order that the
crime may seem " most foul, strange and unnatural,"
these considerations are rehearsed by Macbeth himself an hour or two before the deed is done: —

> He's here in double trust; I vii 12 ff.
> First, as I am his kinsman and his subject,
> Strong both against the deed; then, as his host,
> Who should against his murtherer shut the door,
> Not bear the knife myself. Besides, this Duncan
> Hath borne his faculties so meek, hath been
> So clear in his great office, that his virtues
> Will plead like angels, trumpet-tongu'd, against
> The deep damnation of his taking-off;
> And pity, like a naked new-born babe,
> Striding the blast, or heaven's cherubin, hors'd
> Upon the sightless couriers of the air,
> Shall blow the horrid deed in every eye,
> That tears shall drown the wind.

For the same poetic purpose, Shakespeare has (2) Banquo.
transformed Banquo into a man of incorruptible
loyalty and integrity. In the chronicle, he is an ac-
cessory to the assassination of his king, though afterwards he is slain by the fiend whom he had aided. In

the play, we find him warning Macbeth piously against the prediction of the Witches:—

I iii 123 ff.

> Oftentimes, to win us to our harm,
> The instruments of darkness tell us truths,
> Win us with honest trifles, to betray us
> In deepest consequence.

And later, when Macbeth drops a hint to him that he may profit by joining the party of his companion-in-arms, he thrusts aside the unspoken condition by which he may increase his "honour":—

II i 26 ff.

> So I lose none
> In seeking to augment it, but still keep
> My bosom franchised and allegiance clear,
> I shall be counsell'd.

By the same art, Shakespeare represents Macbeth's reason for turning against Banquo not—as Holinshed implies—from fear of betrayal by a partner in crime, but because he apprehends Banquo's suspicions of his own procedure, and is daunted by the man's wisdom and virtue:—

III i 49 ff.

> Our fears in Banquo
> Stick deep; and in his royalty of nature
> Reigns that which would be feared: 'tis much he
> dares;
> And, to that dauntless temper of his mind,
> He hath a wisdom that doth guide his valour
> To act in safety. There is none but he
> Whose being I do fear.

And not only for these reasons, but he hates Banquo also from jealousy. Have not the "imperfect speakers" declared that Banquo's issue shall be kings of Scotland? Macbeth has no children, and expects none; but this absence of motive and interest is perhaps the very cause why jealousy, the most irrational of all the sentiments, should flame up into hatred against Banquo.

Thus does Shakespeare effect the double purpose of contributing to the dramatic development of Macbeth's character by intensifying his crime in every possible way, and also of portraying, in large part through the hero-villain's lips, the characters of his companions and enemies.

All that we hear from Shakespeare of Macduff makes us wish that we could hear more. He is a type of purest patriotism, weeping for his suffering country, but not sitting down in idleness to bemoan its fate. The scene in which we get our most vivid impression of him is that of his long interview with Malcolm in London, upon which Ross breaks in to tell the news of the sacking of Macduff's castle and the slaughter of his wife and children by Macbeth. The conversation with Malcolm is the one point in the play in which Shakespeare seems to be somewhat burdened by the history that he is following. It is simply a versified paraphrase of the tedious interview recorded by Holinshed, and we seem to feel the poet turning with relief to the conversation that ensues upon the entrance of Ross, in which his inventive faculty has freer scope.

One of the most interesting aspects of this tragedy is the study in marriage which the two chief characters present. Macbeth and his wife are a perfect partnership, in the sense that each has the qualities needed to supplement those of the other. Devils to the rest of the world, to one another they are angels. Mischance between them twain never comes; nor jealousy, nor distrust. Lady Macbeth spurs him on to the bloody courses that may lead to the fulfilment of his ambitions, but we feel that she is ambitious vicariously — for him, not for herself. Her murderous cruelty is no part of her true nature, but

(3) Macduff.

IV iii.

The play as a study in marriage.

is assumed by a violent effort, in order that she may be instrumental to those ends of his which, in loyalty to him, she has made her own. There is no pettiness in either of them, and neither is egoistic as against the other. Moreover, the effect of their joint crimes is to bring them closer together and enhance their mutual dependence, just as misfortune does in the case of innocent partners. The last thought of Lady Macbeth in the Sleep-Walking scene is for her husband; and his greatest outburst of black despair is provoked by the news of her death. Shakespeare is well aware that good qualities, though turned awry and denatured by a voluntary embracing of evil, are yet not destroyed. The mutual fidelity of the Macbeths is deepened by the wickedness that brings upon them the just hatred of all the world. Milton has remarked that there is firm concord among devils.

The doom of the assassins.

Yet this devoted couple, having chosen the way of treachery and blood, are self-doomed to a perpetual descent, through crime after crime, to the deepest hell of disappointment and remorse. The happiness they seek is slain in the very moment that they determine to seek it by foul means; and, once they have set out upon that road, nothing can draw them back, or give them again the serenity of innocence. Already while Macbeth is at his devil's work in Duncan's chamber, the misgivings which at last are to destroy her awaken in Lady Macbeth's mind: "The attempt, and not the deed, confounds us." When they have got the empty prize they have so foully played for, she forthwith finds what Dead-Sea fruit she has plucked:—

III ii 5 ff.

> Nought's had, all's spent,
> Where our desire is got without content:

> 'Tis safer to be that which we destroy
> Than by destruction dwell in doubtful joy.

But, though she makes this confession to herself, she puts a bolder face on the matter in trying to raise the drooping spirits of her husband. It is in vain, however; for, like every murderer, he has instantly learned that his victim is to be envied, while himself is pitiable. From the moment that he plans to slay Duncan, he is himself destroyed. Henceforth his life is like a tale told by an idiot. He can sleep no more, save with the affliction of terrible dreams that shake him nightly. And the irony of his fate is that he needs must go on planning crimes that revolt himself and drag him deeper into the pit of horror, to maintain a life that he feels to be worse than worthless: —

> Better be with the dead,
> Whom we, to gain our place, have sent to peace,
> Than on the torture of the mind to lie
> In restless ecstasy. Duncan is in his grave;
> After life's fitful fever he sleeps well;
> Treason has done his worst: nor steel, nor poison,
> Malice domestic, foreign levy, nothing,
> Can touch him further.

Ibid. 19 ff.

Macbeth, indeed, presents a startling contrast to the picture of the perfectly unjust man drawn in Plato's *Republic* by Glaucon and Adeimantus. These sophistic controversialists maintain that if a man were entirely untroubled by any scruple about what is commonly called righteousness, he would have all the advantages which the hypocritical assumption of integrity can bring, together with the profit of perfect unscrupulousness from his treatment of others. Even Socrates anticipates for such an one not the inward inferno of remorse, but the calm of

The fate of the perfectly unjust man.

an atrophied conscience. The wrongdoer, indeed, loses what is best in himself; but (so runs the Platonic argument) he is unaware of his loss. Shakespeare's insight pierces deeper. Macbeth follows the steps of the perfectly unjust man, but they do not lead him to the calm of a seared conscience. He has the exquisite agony of learning more and more of what happiness and virtue are, in the very measure in which he loses them irrecoverably.

Shakespeare's feats of sympathetic imagination.

A great structure of inference as to Shakespeare's biography has been raised by many students upon his picture of guilty love and betrayal in the Sonnets. One is therefore tempted to ask whether, from the terrific vividness with which he realizes the experience of Macbeth's soul under the stress of the impulse to murder, and under the horror generated by the guilty deed, it must be inferred that Shakespeare in his time had slain his man, and awoke to find himself in such a hell. Or, if it be admitted that without direct experience, but through the force of sympathetic imagination, he could so limn the psychology of guilt in regard to murder, why, one is moved to ask, could he not equally have lived imaginatively through the experiences depicted in the Sonnets? In view of his power of conceiving and conveying the feelings of men and women in situations entirely alien to his own experience, we are tempted to look with deep suspicion upon the theories which make of the Sonnets an autobiography.

CHAPTER VII

"KING LEAR": THE TRAGEDY OF FOLLY AND FATE

UNLESS one have in mind some special dramatic or poetic quality, it is idle, as we have
said elsewhere, to ask which is the greatest of
Shakespeare's plays. One may attempt to determine
which of his tragedies is most tragical, or which of
his comedies is most truly comic; one may seek to
decide which of his plays manifests any specific
kind of poetry in the most perfect form. If the
question is taken to mean, Which of Shakespeare's
works has appealed most universally to the human
heart? we pass into a different field of inquiry. But
if the problem is raised irrespective of any particular characteristic, the answers to it can only be
arbitrary.

Shakespeare's best play?

In the case of *King Lear,* we find this illustrated
by the surprising verdict of Hazlitt, who declares
this tragedy to be "the best of all Shakespeare's
plays, for it is the one in which he was the most
in earnest." It would be difficult indeed to determine what this judgment is based upon. Does the
critic mean that Shakespeare is here most earnestly
answering the question as to the worth of life? or
that he is more earnest in depicting in *Lear* the
results of ingratitude than in showing the outcome
of jealousy in *Othello* or of ambition in *Macbeth?*
Or is the earnestness exhibited in the condemnation

Hazlitt's reason for thinking it so.

of Lear's incredible folly? Assuming that *King Lear* is intended as one picture of human life and *The Winter's Tale* as another, are we to suppose that Shakespeare believed the former to be a truer picture than the latter?

The unity of Shakespeare's work.

These questions, being unanswerable, are unprofitable. We cannot determine Shakespeare's subjective judgment of the issue. It is scarcely wise to ask whether a heaven-splitting hurricane is more magnificent than a peaceful sunset: the two things are incommensurable. Life includes both, and must be interpreted not exclusively in terms of either, but in terms of a philosophy that takes account of both. Nor is it wise to assume that Shakespeare's verdict upon existence can be inferred from anything less than his work as a whole. We find it convenient to divide his product into three periods, by means of various tests of craftsmanship and degrees of skill and perfection. The man himself would not have so divided it; and if a contemporary had undertaken to formulate his general philosophy or religion from an examination of the work of any one of these periods, he would justly have protested that the formulation was inadequate. His life was a unity; and so, in the strict sense, is

He is neither an optimist nor a pessimist.

his work. To write him down as a gigantic pessimist on the strength of an examination, say, of *Hamlet, King Lear, Othello, Macbeth, Antony and Cleopatra, Timon,* and *Troilus and Cressida,* is really as arbitrary as it would be to declare him a headlong optimist on the strength of a survey of *Much Ado About Nothing, As You Like It, The Comedy of Errors,* and *A Midsummer Night's Dream.*

It cannot be too strongly insisted that the moral

order of the universe, as Shakespeare intuitively apprehended it, includes both "tragic" and "comic" aspects. The world we live in is one in which such folly as Lear's may lead to such a fate as Lear's; but it is also a world in which the analogous folly of Leontes may be atoned for, and the man's soul redeemed. Macbeth's crimes hurl him to destruction; but those of Sebastian and Antonio are forgiven. It is a world in which an accident, like the dropping of Desdemona's handkerchief, may lead to irretrievable horror and disaster; and, again, it is a world wherein the chance resemblance of the twins of Syracuse and Ephesus may give rise only to laughter and to happiness at the last. The critic who judges Shakespeare by either aspect alone, inevitably misunderstands him. And (may we not add?) the man who judges life by either aspect alone becomes a sectarian — a mere optimist or pessimist: the exponent of a view wholly inadequate to the subtlety of God.

Hazlitt may of course be right as to Shakespeare's earnestness, though he draws a wrong conclusion from it. Let us try to see for ourselves.

As regards the materials of *King Lear,* and the initial demand that it makes upon the credulity of the reader, there is obviously as generous a concession to the taste of the "groundlings" as in any of the other works. Shakespeare, here as elsewhere, has simply snatched up a tale which was popular in literary form, and had already been successfully exploited upon the stage. Of these materials, he has woven a tragedy that cannot be spoken of save with bated breath. Yet into it he has inserted one episode which grossly outrages every conceivable standard of propriety and good taste. That he

Barbarism in *King Lear*.

should cause the eyes of Gloucester to be hacked
out on the stage, rather than have the incident
reported, as he might with perfect ease have done,
is a bewildering proof of the lengths to which he
was willing to go in pleasing the populace. This is
perhaps the most horrible incident in the entire
range of Shakespeare's authentic work. How such
a situation might have been handled without violating good taste is exquisitely shown in the scene be-

tween Hubert and Arthur in *King John,* where the
threat, with all that it entrains of sympathetic dread,
is carried to the edge of fulfilment and then repented
of. In the case of Gloucester, some such treatment
might have been given, without the repentance.
Then the actual crime could have been pretended
behind the scenes, and for the remainder of the
play the groping victim could have been introduced
precisely as he is. Were it but for this one incident,
I could not find it in my heart to endorse Hazlitt's
verdict. Nothing is added to the tragic power of
the play by this episode; rather, its excess detracts
from the general effect, just as the mutilations in
Titus Andronicus nauseate us without awakening
the genuine emotion of tragedy. "Men are as
the time is," to be sure; and Shakespeare could not
well make Lear's generation models of Christian
courtesy and heroism. But, without a trace of violence to his conception of his characters, he could
have spared us this outrage.

In other concessions to the tastes of the mob
Shakespeare finds the opportunity for some of those
miracles which he alone could work. The use of
the Fool, and the device of disguising Edgar as
Tom o' Bedlam, are two most daring experiments,
which are overwhelmingly justified by their success.

There is this difference between the Fool in *Lear* and all Shakespeare's other fools, that he is introduced *not* to give comic relief, but rather to heighten, by his bitter commentaries, the terror and pity of situations already tragic. Everywhere else the fool is used for contrast and assuagement. Even the Porter in *Macbeth* is there to bring a shock of relief to emotions previously strained to the height, and destined to be strained so again in what immediately follows. But the Fool in *Lear* wears throughout the grin of a death's-head. His barbed words bring no comfort either to Lear or to the onlooker. They intensify his master's pain, and thereby accentuate the sympathetic pain of the beholder. When the Fool's words are wittiest and wisest, the light they throw upon the situation adds but so much to its horror. It is such a light as that whereby the fallen angels of Milton discerned the terrors of that "universe of death" into which they had been hurled.

The Fool intensifies the tragedy, not relieves it.

The tragedy of *King Lear* is the most terrible crescendo of agony in the wide range of human literature; and its highest terror consists in this, that goodness itself is the means by which evil triumphs. It is the sheer incorruptibility of Cordelia, and that dignity of principle in her which inhibits any concession to her father's folly, that gives rise to all the ensuing sorrow. It is the outspoken manliness of Kent that, by provoking his banishment, robs him of the power of effective service to the master he loves.

The essential horror: evil springing from goodness.

In no other play is there such decisive evidence of one peculiar difficulty which, as Sir Walter Raleigh has brilliantly proved, Shakespeare often encountered. He chooses a familiar story, and a set of puppets designed to go through a predetermined series of actions and episodes; but in the handling of these puppets, he cannot help breathing into them the breath of independent life. They take on character and personality of their own, and proceed to pull and strain the poor story in all sorts of directions other than the original one. The legend of King Lear which Shakespeare found in the authorities becomes altogether different under his hands,— not, apparently, because he had so designed, but simply because the characters, when they come to life before him, cannot be forced into the primitive framework.

The popularity of the Lear legend in Shakespeare's time is abundantly evidenced. Holinshed, we know, was favourite reading; and this tale (which Holinshed had found in Geoffrey of Monmouth's *British History*) was retold at some length by Spenser in *The Faerie Queene*,[1] and by half-a-dozen other writers. It was also the subject of a successful play, produced in 1594.

There is no more interesting instance of the transmutations effected by Shakespeare than the use he makes of this legendary material. The anonymous play of 1594, *The True Chronicle History of King Leir and His Three Daughters,* is an asinine production. It is more freakishly anachronistic than even Shakespeare ever permits himself to be, since its ancient pagan characters talk undisguisedly the language of Christianity, and there is no attempt whatever to produce the illusion of antiquity in the *mise-en-scène*. That which in Shakespeare becomes the heartrending tragedy of living men and women is here the farcical savagery of the puppets of Puncinello. Cordelia is a simpering sniveller, and

[1] Book II, canto x, verses xxvii-xxxii.

Goneril and Regan are as ludicrously incredible as the two ugly sisters of Cinderella. Leir and Perillus (the prototype of Kent), in their wanderings in Britain and Gallia, talk and behave like escaped inmates from an asylum for the feeble-minded. The blank verse is the flattest and most pedestrian prose. The author's sole conception of verse is that each line must contain ten syllables — though he cannot conform regularly even to that simple arithmetical rule.

The story as it stands in Geoffrey (which Holinshed follows substantially) is similarly dull and colourless. The speeches of the two elder daughters in reply to Lear's childish question are prosy and stilted; — as thus: —

(2) Geoffrey of Monmouth, *via* Holinshed.

> The question being proposed, Gonorilla, the eldest, made answer, " That she called heaven to witness, she loved him more than her own soul. . . . Then Regau, the second daughter, willing, after the example of her sister, to prevail upon her father's good nature, answered with an oath, " That she could not otherwise express her thoughts, but that she loved him above all creatures."

Cordelia, instead of the magical "Love and be silent" of Shakespeare, lectures her progenitor to the following tune: —

> My father, is there any daughter that can love her father more than duty requires? In my opinion, whoever pretends to it, must disguise her real sentiments under the veil of flattery. I have always loved you as a father, nor do I yet depart from my purposed duty; and if you insist to have something more extorted from me, hear now the greatness of my affection, which I always bear you, and take this for a short answer to all your questions: look how much you have, so much is your value, and so much do I love you.

Her banishment ensues, and the ingratitude of the elder sisters is speedily manifested; whereupon Lear takes ship for Gaul and complains to Cordelia, and she and her husband invade Britain and restore the old man to the kingdom which he had resigned. The elder daughters and the sons-in-law are routed, and the story ends happily. Lear survives for three years, after which Cordelia has the government of the kingdom in her own hands.

The originals end happily.

Out of these two or three pages of dull fiction Shakespeare has created the tragic world of that drama for the sake of which alone its sources are now remembered. Into the texture of the story he has woven another (suggested to him by that of a certain king of Paphlagonia which he found in Sidney's *Arcadia*), which grows into the by-plot of Gloucester and his two sons. As the characters project themselves dramatically through Shakespeare's mind, it becomes obvious to him that any kind of happy ending on earth, after such griding torments, would be an irredeemable anti-climax. Raleigh has well said of Lear that "a deeper peace than that of a comfortable fireside is needed to heal such gigantic sorrow." We feel, with Kent, that the quietude of death is the best boon that can be wished for the shattered soul :—

(3) Sir Philip Sidney's Arcadia.

V iii 312 ff.

> Oh, let him pass! he hates him much
> That would upon the rack of this tough world
> Stretch him out longer.

It is superfluous to remind the reader that the source from which the story comes has no basis in fact. Geoffrey of Monmouth's *British History* purports to cover the period from the fall of Troy to the Saxon conquest of England. It represents that the original colonists of Britain were Trojan exiles,

Geoffrey's History purely fictitious,

under the leadership of one Brute, and that in the
pre-Roman times the Britons were a populous and
highly civilized nation. The book is a curious collection of tales, full of the highest dramatic possibilities, yet told so dully that the narrator himself
seems not to feel their force. The raw material
of the Arthurian saga is here,— the legends of
Merlin and Uther Pendragon, of the traitor Modred
and the wondrous feats of Arthur. Cymbeline, too,
with his sons Guiderius and Arviragus, is first heard
of in Geoffrey's veracious pages. But it must be *but mistak-*
remembered that the sixteenth century was unaware *en for his-*
of the character of Geoffrey's tales, and accepted *tory in XVI*
them uncritically as sober history,— just as, until *century.*
yesterday, the folklore of the Pentateuch was
accepted.

According to Geoffrey's account, Lear "flourished" in the days when Isaiah and Hosea were
prophesying in Israel, and Romulus and Remus
were founding Rome — that is, during the eighth
century B.C. Shakespeare's contempt for historical *Shake-*
consistency and verisimilitude needs no other proof *speare's play*
than a comparison of this date with the list of *one im-*
dramatis personae prefixed to the tragedy. He *chronism.*
represents Britain as divided up into dukedoms and
earldoms in the eighth century B.C., just as it was
in his own day. The counties already possess the
names which they did not acquire until long after
the Saxon Conquest. The feudal orders of nobility
and knighthood, and the institutions of heraldry,
are already established. The rivalry of the kings
of France and the dukes of Burgundy is anticipated
by two thousand years.

When from the list of persons of the drama we
turn to the drama itself, we find impossibility piled

upon impossibility, until, giving up the quest for consistency, we frankly accept the play for what it is — one vast and defiant anachronism. Repeating what I hinted in an earlier chapter, I would warn the reader not to go through this play with the idea that those incidental contradictions which " leap to the eyes " are exceptional. There is no background of historical, or even legendary, consistency, with which they may be contrasted. When Gloucester I ii 34. says that to read Edgar's letter he will not need spectacles, we must not assume that the poet has made a slip, as he would be doing if he put such an expression upon the lips of a man whom he had supposed to live in remote antiquity, ages before spectacles were invented. A little later in the same scene *Ibid.* 95. Gloucester refers to " eclipses in the sun and moon " which took place in 1605 A.D. Several times the prevalence of classical paganism is implied, and Christianity is nowhere directly referred to. Yet in the Storm scene Lear talks of " our steeples " and " their cocks " — a preposterous allusion to non-existent parish churches.

If a dramatist to-day were to introduce characters ostensibly contemporary with Romulus and Remus, and make them refer — let us say — to aeroplanes or the present war in Europe, we should rightly gibe at him for perpetrating such howling anachronisms. But Shakespeare is not to be judged by any such criterion. The real period of his play is not the date of Geoffrey of Monmouth's tale; it is the very year in which he writes it. His characters are his fellow-countrymen and contemporaries. Edgar in his Bedlamite disguise (itself a late mediaeval assumption) uses the names of a number of devils — Frateretto, Flibbertigibbet,

Edgar's devils: III iv & vi.

Mahu, Modo, &c. — who were first introduced to mankind in Harsnett's *Declaration of Popish Impostures,* published in the year 1603. Kent denounces Oswald, in a rich flood of Billingsgate that would excite the envy of any costermonger, as "a three-suited, hundred-pound, filthy, worsted-stocking knave; a lily-liver'd, *action-taking* knave" (*i. e.,* one who would "have the law of you" rather than fight); and, a moment later, as a "cullionly barber-monger." These choice epithets are as evidently limited to Shakespeare's own time as are the coins of Elizabeth and James I, which bear their dates upon them. Edmund's ridicule of astrological portents also dates itself. Such things are not inconsistencies but consistencies. There is nothing in this play which Shakespeare can possibly have believed to be of the eighth century B.C. except the names of King Lear and his three daughters. All the rest he has frankly made contemporaneous with himself.

Harsnett's book.

Kent's XVI century Billings-gate: II ii 14 ff.

The initial situation makes a severe demand upon our credulity, but not so great a one as might at first sight be supposed. We are not asked to believe that King Lear, having decided to relinquish his power and responsibility, asks his daughters how much they love him in order to determine their portions by their replies. This absurdity is indeed in the source, and in the pre-Shakespearean play; but the master-dramatist, though he must needs accept from his authorities a mass of nonsense, does what he can to minimize the improbability of the situation. He represents that Lear has made his decision and divided his realm before the play opens, reserving the third and fairest portion for his favourite youngest daughter. This is clearly

The opening situation: improb-abilities assumed, not created.

intimated by Gloucester's words in the first scene:—

> In the division of the kingdom, it appears not which of the dukes he values most; for equalities are so weigh'd, that curiosity in neither can make choice of either's moiety.

The King in his first speech also announces that "We have divided in three our kingdom." The test of his daughters' affections is made for his own satisfaction, and for confirmation of the decision

(1) Lear's abdication;

which he has come to in advance. Even at this, such an abdication and such a throwing of himself, without security, upon the gratitude of his daughters and sons-in-law, is unusual to the verge of incredibility; but, after all, so are a score of actual incidents in every day's newspaper! And Shakespeare cannot be held responsible for this improbability. He is simply taking what he finds in his authority. As Sir Walter Raleigh puts it, he does not ask us to *believe* that an old king divides up his kingdom among his children; he asks us to *assume* that this has happened. Given this situation, he says, I will show you what must necessarily follow.

(2) his credulity;

The King is "a very foolish, fond old man,"—so foolish that he is deceived by the openly mercenary pretences of his elder daughters, and cannot see the sterling worth of the youngest. Nor is Shakespeare to be held accountable for the tactlessly unconcilia-

(3) Cordelia's brusqueness.

tory tone of Cordelia in this explanatory scene. If it be urged that her behaviour here is inconsistent with the character she subsequently displays, the answer simply is that unless she behaved in this way there would be no play. The character she afterwards manifests is Shakespeare's creation. Her words and manner here are the datum, the indispensable episode, out of which the whole situation is to arise. Taking these things for granted, and assuming that Goneril and Regan, with their husbands and satellites, behave with perfect selfishness, Shakespeare proceeds to work out the consequences for us.

The result is that all these people become intensified in their individuality as the plot unfolds itself. Edmund, the traitor on principle, the man to whom injustice is a religion and evil a thing to be pursued for its own sake, is a combination of the qualities of Richard III with those of Iago. Like Richard, he has the giant strength of wickedness, which makes him irresistible and yet leads directly to his defeat and destruction. At the end of his days he seeks to do one good deed, or rather to undo one of his own bad deeds, by recalling the doom he had plotted for Cordelia. Only in this is he untrue to himself. When the hand of death is upon him, he weakens, exchanges charity with his wronged brother, and relaxes into humanity.

Development of character: Edmund, the criminal genius.

This stupendous character-study is at the outset an instance of the catholicity of Shakespeare's sympathy. Edmund is one of that class of unfortunates upon whom, from of old, mankind has relentlessly visited the sins of its fathers. His birth is illegitimate; and for the offence of his parents he is punished by exclusion from inheritance either of his father's lands or goods, or of his prestige and station in life. In Edmund's reflections upon this subject, we feel his creator's commiseration with him, and an implied censure upon the cruelty of the world. We feel also the touch of that popular superstition, or rather that uncritical assumption, which made men imagine that children begotten as Edmund was are likely to be finer and more stal-

Shakespeare's sympathy for the illegitimate.

I ii 1 ff.

wart men, to have "more composition and fierce quality," than their legitimate brethren. This assumption underlies the far more agreeable study of the valiant Faulconbridge, in *King John.* But Edmund, with his passionate love of crime and his total freedom from the restraints of ordinary humanity, seems to concentrate in himself all the bitterness and cruelty which have been inflicted upon his ill-starred tribe. He is determined to wreak it all upon mankind, so far as in the single lifetime of a genius for cruelty this can be done.

Edmund's betrayal of Edgar,

He first betrays his legitimate brother, who, by Edmund's own confession, is a noble spirit. By forgery and lies he creates in the mind of his father the belief that this generous brother is in intention a parricide. Therefore is Edgar disinherited and driven forth, branded with the murderer's stigma. With the like ingenious diabolism, Edmund next betrays his father to Cornwall, the result being that

Gloucester,

Gloucester is fiendishly blinded. Edmund's appetite for villainy is still unsated; nay, it waxes with indulgence. Having won his advancement from Cornwall by the charge against his father, he pro-

Cornwall and Albany.

ceeds to betray both Cornwall and Albany by his intrigues with Regan and Goneril. At last his double-dealing between the two villainous women releases the nemesis which his own deeds have progressively matured, and he is snared in the toils he had set for others.

The nemesis of Goneril and Regan.

The characters of Goneril and Regan are so much alike that it needs a discriminating analysis to decide which is the wickeder, or rather the more capable in wickedness. After such a study, the reader will probably award the palm to Goneril, as having more initiative than her worthy sister. The very quality which makes them faithless to their father makes them recreant to every other obligation of life. Whatever may be doubtful about Shakespeare's view of the universe, it is certain that he never wavered in his conviction that the law of man's moral nature executes itself with unfailing fidelity. To thine own self be false, and it shall follow, as the night the day, thou canst not then be true to any man. He does not need to invoke an external form of fate, such as was postulated by some of the tragic poets of Greece. The fate that each man carries within himself, and the natural causation which his own deeds set going, are potent enough to produce and to explain the tragedies of life. The sordid self-idolatry of such characters as Goneril and Regan saps their power of fidelity to anything but the successive objects of their own gross desires. It also destroys the judgment by which, in persons normally disciplined, the very run of desire is itself controlled. By the time they have disclosed their vile ingratitude to the father whom they had cajoled, they have become incapable of resisting the infatuation for Edmund which eventuates in their own ruin as well as his.

Shake-speare's conception of " fate."

This doctrine, that the nemesis of Lear and his enemies springs from within themselves, is one which it would have seemed superfluous to contend for, were it not that competent critics have overlooked it and proclaimed the contrary. One of these writers tells us that the characters in this play are "as men possessed." This critic seems to have taken as the clue to the tragedy that terrible utterance of the blinded Gloucester: —

As flies to wanton boys are we to the gods:
They kill us for their sport.

IV i 37-8.

The world looks thus to its victims, no doubt; but not to the instigators of the wrongs by which they suffer. It certainly did not look thus to Shakespeare, who seems to utter his personal conviction in the many passages in which he expresses the contrary doctrine. May we not say, for instance, that Edgar's words,—

V iii 169-70.

> The gods are just, and of our pleasant vices
> Make instruments to plague us,—

more truly convey the judgment of a poet who invariably shows us the fate of men determined by what they are and what they do, rather than by the blind play of outward circumstance? Taking the whole of Shakespeare's tragedies together, one may say that their spiritual philosophy is compacted into those few pregnant words of Helena in *All's Well:*—

All's Well I i 201 ff.

> Our remedies oft in ourselves do lie,
> Which we ascribe to heaven: the fated sky
> Gives us free scope; only doth backward pull
> Our slow designs when we ourselves are dull.

Gloucester's tragedy self-originated.

It is a long sweep from the sin of Gloucester, confessed on the first page of the play, to the visitation in which, through the treachery of his baseborn son, his eyes are plucked from his head. But that Shakespeare was conscious of the inexorable series of causes which bound this result to that act, is clearly shown in Edgar's words, and in the confession of Edmund: "the wheel is come full circle." Edmund himself is a Marlowesque atheist, and wholly free from all that he counts superstition. It is not unwarrantable to suppose that Shakespeare may sometimes have given us a confession of his

Edmund (and Shakespeare?) on astrological fatalism.

own belief through the mouth of a villain. In many other connections he has expressed a conviction similar to that which Edmund puts into such close and perfect-fitting phrases: —

> This is the excellent foppery of the world, that, when we are sick in fortune,— often the surfeit of our own behaviour,— we make guilty of our disasters the sun, the moon, and the stars: as if we were villains by necessity, fools by heavenly compulsion, knaves, thieves and treachers by spherical predominance, drunkards, liars and adulterers by an enforc'd obedience of planetary influence, and all that we are evil in, by a divine thrusting on: an admirable evasion of whoremaster man, to lay his goatish disposition to the charge of a star! My father compounded with my mother under the dragon's tail, and my nativity was under *Ursa major;* so that it follows, I am rough and lecherous. Tut! I should have been that I am, had the maidenliest star in the firmament twinkled on my bastardizing.

I ii 108 ff.

Man's search for scapegoats whereon to lay the burden of his own weakness and folly has led to plenty of wild thinking, and not only in astrology. Many religious and scientific theories are prompted by his readiness to place his own responsibilities anywhere but upon himself. He thinks that he alone is fated; he sees plenty of free agents in the universe, but they pursue him with mockery and frustration. It is he that is the slave and puppet. The stars in their courses predetermine his lot, or heredity entails upon him a debilitated constitution. Out of the deeds of his remote ancestors springs his weakness. For this *they* are culpable; but he will not charge himself for the sin and incapacity of his posterity! Shakespeare felt the irony of all this as deeply as did Matthew Arnold, who wrote in his

Empedocles on Etna a stinging indictment of the arbitrary folly of mankind:—

> Loath to suffer mute,
>   We, peopling the void air,
>   Make gods to whom to impute
>   The ills we ought to bear;
> With God and Fate to rail at, suffering easily!

True meaning of "fate."

Only in one sense can the term fate be sanely used; namely, that some word or act of the man's own, the natural outgrowth of his character, may carry with it consequences that extend over the whole course of his life and the lives of others, but that yet are unforeseen by him. Lear's folly is his fate. He madly seeks to resign duties that he has no right to surrender while he lives. He transfers them to others, who have no sense of them as duties and responsibilities, but think of them only as privileges and means of self-assertion and self-indulgence. Given this situation, the rest is inevitable; but the situation never need have arisen. Lear's folly, to be sure, has its own traceable source. It is the consequence of mistaking for true metal that pinchbeck divinity which doth hedge a king. Perpetual flattery and obedience have blinded him to the fact that he received them not from honest deference to his personal force, but in virtue of his office; and when he surrenders that, he must lose the reverence it had gained him.

Repellent characteristics of Lear.

Nothing, as Hallam says, could reconcile us to Lear, or win our sympathy for him, save the intense woe and the unnatural wrong which it is his doom to suffer. The petulant folly of his rejection of Cordelia is matched by the naïve astonishment which he expresses on discovering the ingratitude of his elder daughters. He is a spoiled child; as much so in his ignorance of human character as in the purblind wilfulness of his conduct. Nothing can redeem him save the discovery of himself. The terrific humiliation and heart-shattering grief which await him effect this too-belated discipline. It is revealed to him that the whole of his life has been a mockery, and that all the adulation heaped upon him has but spun the opaque texture of a cloud to hide himself and the world from him. Thus the evil chance that destroys his self-idolatry makes of him a man at last. His lunacy is saner than his sanity. It is more like the inspiration which the old Greeks held it to be. Before the end, Lear becomes as wise as his Fool is when the play opens.

The intuitive psychology of a great poet could not go farther than it has gone with Shakespeare in the conception of this character. He knew from the secret augury that madness in a hoodwinked king might mean the deepening of his mental powers, through the shock of self-discovery. The process that Lear undergoes is that of losing his life, as the only means whereby he may find it. We are now familiar with the truth that the madman is often the person who has lost everything except his reason. Thus it is with Lear. In the world of make-believe that he had always lived in, his reason was overborne by the self-will that at last drove him to his doom. Illusions mocked his sight at every turn. He was cased in a triple armour of flattery and self-deception, which made him proof against the shocks of truth and reality. Not till he stands bare-headed against the seven-bolted thunder does he find how poor a thing he is; and not till then is the childish wilfulness relaxed and subdued, so that the reason it had overlain might work in freedom.

Rational power enhanced by madness.

The " sane " Lear lapped in illusion;

As the ancient balance of his life is destroyed,—as his pride is smitten with a mortal wound, faith and hope die out, natural affection is blasted and his will racked,—we see his rational power developing, until at last he becomes, as it were, a naked intellect, functioning at random, without the restraints of purpose. So dominant becomes this disillusioned mentality that he ceases even to be subject to bodily conditions, and grows proof against the assaults of the elements. He is torn between condemnation of the monstrous children whose poisonous ingratitude he bewails, and yet sterner condemnation of the folly in himself which had exposed him to their merciless mercy. This makes him willing to bow his head before the blind forces of the world; for they have not wronged him, save in so far as they are the unconscious accessories of his man-like but more inhuman foes:—

the " mad-man " sees reality.

III ii 1 ff.

Blow, winds, and crack your cheeks! rage! blow!
You cataracts and hurricanoes, spout
Till you have drench'd our steeples, drown'd the cocks!
You sulphurous and thought-executing fires,
Vaunt-couriers to oak-cleaving thunderbolts,
Singe my white head! And thou, all-shaking thunder,
Smite flat the thick rotundity o' th' world!
.   .   .   .
                    Spit, fire! spout, rain!
Nor rain, wind, thunder, fire, are my daughters:
I tax not you, you elements, with unkindness;
I never gave you kingdom, call'd you children;
You owe me no subscription: then let fall
Your horrible pleasure; here I stand, your slave,
A poor, infirm, weak and despis'd old man:
But yet I call you servile ministers,
That have with two pernicious daughters join'd
Your high-engender'd battles 'gainst a head
So old and white as this. Oh! oh! 'tis foul!

His own insensitiveness to the storm does not blind him, however, to the needs of others; nay, it reveals them to him. He is infinitely gentle to his Fool, and to the disguised Kent and Edgar. With perfect rationality he explains to Kent his indifference to the tempest:—

Thou think'st 'tis much that this contentious storm   III iv 6 ff.
Invades us to the skin: so 'tis to thee;
But where the greater malady is fix'd,
The lesser is scarce felt. Thou'ldst shun a bear;
But if thy flight lay toward the raging sea,
Thou'ldst meet the bear i' th' mouth. When the mind's free,
The body's delicate: the tempest in my mind
Doth from my senses take all feeling else
Save what beats there.

The problem of insanity, as we are now learning, is far subtler than the world formerly imagined. That Lear is insane is not for a moment to be doubted; but in what sense is he insane? Chiefly in this, that the testimony of his senses regarding the outer world no longer tallies with the common experience; he sees what other men do not see, and cannot see what is present to them. His will, too, is disorganized, because all the valuations of his life have been destroyed, and the impulsions that from of old had actuated him are turned awry. But his emotions remain normal and sound; nay, they are clarified and purified by that greater strenuousness of intellection which we have noted as the strangest and most characteristic symptom of the change he has undergone. He praises and dispraises what the disinterested judgment of universal humanity approves and disapproves. His sense of justice is keener than ever. For the first time in his life he

Margin notes: Lear is "insane" only as regards (1) Sense-perception and (2) will. His emotions become saner,

realizes the lot of the houseless outcasts, to whom
the rain and the storm-wind are old companions : —

III iv 28 ff.

> Poor naked wretches, wheresoe'er you are,
> That bide the pelting of this pitiless storm,
> How shall your houseless heads and unfed sides,
> Your loop'd and window'd raggedness, defend you
> From seasons such as these? Oh, I have ta'en
> Too little care of this! Take physic, pomp!
> Expose thyself to feel what wretches feel,
> That thou mayst shake the superflux to them,
> And show the heavens more just!

and his
reasoning
power is
enhanced.
IV vi 169.

As for the intensification of his intellectual power,
what could be truer than Edgar's characterization
of one of his greatest outbursts: "O matter with
impertinency mix'd! reason in madness!" Never
before had he been aware, as now he is, of the difference between appearance and reality. Hitherto
the excellent foppery of the world has befooled him;
he has seen only what seems, not what is. He had
taken himself to be a little god, because they called
him so : —

IV vi 96 ff.

> They flattered me like a dog; . . . To say ay and
> no to everything that I said ay and no to was no good
> divinity. When the rain came to wet me once, and
> the wind to make me chatter; when the thunder would
> not peace at my bidding; there I found 'em, there I
> smelt 'em out. Go to, they are not men o' their words:
> they told me I was everything; 'tis a lie, I am not
> ague-proof.

Alas, where shall wisdom be found? What is
the sanity that could hide these palpable truths of
human littleness from the gilded folly that mistakes
itself for majesty? Only now has Lear learned the
alphabet of life. He has indeed been "mightily
abus'd"—but far more by the parents and courtiers, who had told him that he was a god, than even

by the inhuman daughters and the relentless elements which have shown him that he is only a man. There is reason reinforced in the wild words with which, imitating Tom o' Bedlam, he tears his garments from him. Never before had he experienced the utter helplessness and dependence of humanity:—

> Is man no more than this? Consider him well. Thou ow'st the worm no silk, the beast no hide, the sheep no wool, the cat no perfume. Ha! here's three on 's are sophisticated! Thou art the thing itself: unaccommodated man is no more but such a poor, bare, forked animal as thou art. Off, off, you lendings! Come, unbutton here!
>
> *[Tearing off his clothes.*

III iv 96 ff.

Though this be madness, yet there's reason in it. At this price must the abused idol learn what stern reality teaches to common men from their childhood. But the lesson, once begun, drives itself deeper into Lear's soul than into other men's, by reason of the shock through which it comes. He not only loses the illusions peculiar to a king, but cuts through many that befool other men to the end. And in the deepest utterance of his new perception of reality, he is won to that all-pardoning mercy which is godlike:—

How he unlearns the insanity taught to kings.

> *Lear:* What, art mad? A man may see how this world goes with no eyes. Look with thine ears: see how yond justice rails upon yond simple thief. Hark, in thine ear: change places; and, handy-dandy, which is the justice, which is the thief? Thou hast seen a farmer's dog bark at a beggar?
>
> *Gloucester:* Ay, sir.
>
> *Lear:* And the creature run from the cur? There thou mightest behold the great image of authority: a dog's obey'd in office. . . .
>
> . . . The usurer hangs the cozener.

IV vi 147 ff.

Through tatter'd clothes small vices do appear;
Robes and furr'd gowns hide all. Plate sin with gold,
And the strong lance of justice hurtless breaks;
Arm it in rags, a pigmy's straw does pierce it.
None does offend, none, I say, none; I'll able 'em:
Take that of me, my friend, who have the power
To seal the accuser's lips. Get thee glass eyes;
And, like a scurvy politician, seem
To see the thing thou dost not.

There are some few perfections of human achievement before which the voice of praise is dumb; and one of them is that scene in which Lear is won back to sanity by Cordelia's love. No words that we can use but would be too beggarly to characterize it. One may, however, be permitted to point out how, by means of his inspiration, Shakespeare seized upon a truth which our most modern specialists in mental science are now discovering: the truth, namely, that one of the first conditions for the restoration of an alienated mind is that the sufferer shall be brought to admit that he has been insane. Lear, awaking from his dream of torment, makes this acknowledgment; and by grace of that confession comes the recognition of his daughter and of the common world that is present to other minds: —

Lear's return to sanity.

IV vii 52 ff.

Where have I been? Where am I? Fair daylight?
I am mightily abus'd. I should e'en die with pity,
To see another thus. I know not what to say.
I will not swear these are my hands: let's see;
I feel this pin prick. Would I were assur'd
Of my condition! . . .
                    Pray, do not mock me:
I am a very foolish fond old man,
Fourscore and upward, not an hour more nor less;
And, to deal plainly,
I fear I am not in my perfect mind.
Methinks I should know you, and know this man;

Yet I am doubtful: for I am mainly ignorant
What place this is; and all the skill I have
Remembers not these garments; nor I know not
Where I did lodge last night. Do not laugh at me;
For, as I am a man, I think this lady
To be my child Cordelia.

One of the points of difference between this play and its near contemporary *Macbeth* is the extent to which in *King Lear* the minor characters are individualized. *Macbeth,* as we observed, is somewhat more in the Marlowe tradition, in the sense that one colossal figure fills the stage, and the rest, with few exceptions, are sketched only so far as is necessary for their function as foils to the evil Titan they subserve. In *Lear,* Edgar and Edmund, Gloucester and Albany, Kent and the Fool are limned to the life. They revolve upon their own axes, besides circling in their orbits around the central figure. The part of Edgar must be one of the most difficult to enact in the entire range of Shakespearean rôles. It demands a versatility such as only the most accomplished actors can compass. Hamlet's feigning of madness is child's play to the relentless realism with which the chivalrous Edgar transmutes himself into the loathsome Bedlamite. His "nothing's more than matter."

Contrast with Macbeth: definiteness of minor characters.

The outstanding characteristic of the Fool we have already noted. His function is to intensify our perception of the horrors of the situation, not to dull it or relieve our strain. As in war-time the memory of the days of peace deepens our sense of present horror, and any note from the old symphony reminds us how the bells are jangled; so jests, that in other days would add spice and sweetness to life, in such a context as the world of Lear only acidulate the

The Fool: the nadir of pessimism.

bitterness of death in life, and pile horror upon horror. Lear's motley follower is a master of irony. Were he to curse God and die, it would be more tolerable than the inhuman vividness, the merciless veracity, with which he paints the things of his world as they are. Koheleth's "vanity of vanities" sounds like a love-song beside the icy despair of this "bitter fool."

The " relief " comes from Kent and Edgar.

The real relief comes not from him, but from the faithful Kent. In this awful play, only Kent and Edgar safeguard our threatened sanity, by reminding us of that other real world, in which truth and manly fealty still exist. Though his loyalty is made excessive by its touch of superstition,— though he does not quite escape, as his master does, from the ironical illusion of divinity about a king,— yet Kent is by nature true as steel. Through his fidelity we are enabled to retain our faith in the worth of life. If it were a world made up of none but Gonerils and Regans, of Cornwalls and Edmunds, then the sun would be turned into darkness and the moon into blood, and the stars would fall from heaven, and we should beseech the mountains and the rocks to fall upon us and hide us. But through that hell of Mammon-greed and Moloch-homicide, where love is perverted into the lust of Beelzebub, and the fair face of the earth itself grows hideous in the sullen glare of Tartarean flames, the humanity of Kent and Edgar keeps alive our almost spent and gasping faith in the hidden heart of man. Kent it is who sees how merciful is death,— how far better than any more stretching on the rack of this tough world. Like the Stoic Horatio, he parts from us with the assurance that his loyalty is not bounded by the grave. He will follow after his departed leader, lest in the undis-

covered country there should still be need for fealty
like his: —

> I have a journey, sir, shortly to go; V iii 321 f.
> My master calls me; I must not say no.

To live by sympathetic imagination through the *The strain upon Shakespeare.*
experiences of Othello and Desdemona, Hamlet and
Ophelia, Gloucester and Edgar, Lear and Cordelia,
is terrific even for the reader. What these giant
creations, and, still more, what the limning of that
evil world in which they are entangled, cost the man
Shakespeare, their creator, is more than it hath entered into the heart of man to conceive. We feel,
with Professor Raleigh, that even Shakespeare's
mind is now in danger; even that noble and most
sovereign reason comes perilously near to being like
sweet bells jangled. The explanation of the poet's
years of darkness is holden from us; the tales of
despised love which so many students have read
into the Sonnets are all groundless, and, even
though they were not, they could not solve for us
this mystery.

There is much sound insight mingled with *Shaw's Dark Lady of the Sonnets, preface.*
the pert trifling of the essay in which Bernard Shaw
seeks to convince us that the creator of Lear was pre-
dominantly a happy man. Shakespeare, it is certain,
was too great to be a pessimist. He does not die of
a broken heart, and his last state is not one of moody
railing at the world. Always there is the joy peculiar to genius, the ecstasy of creation, which, as
Tasso has said, the poet alone shares with God.[2]
By grace of this, the man who passed through the
fiery hell of Macbeth and Lear overlived that awful,
and to any less man blasting, experience. The

[2] *Non merita nome di Creatore, se non Iddio ed il Poeta.*

The calm
after the
storm.

nausea with life, which we detect in Lear's creator, passes away, and the terrible strain is relaxed. He lives to be the Shakespeare of *The Winter's Tale* and *The Tempest;* to find, after his upward flight from hell, a paradise in which he is no intruder but a lawful occupant. Meantime, however, we tremble even for him. As in Swift's description of the Houyhnhnms we feel the approach of the insanity that afterwards laid low the master-satirist, so in *Lear* we dread lest Shakespeare may in like manner be overthrown. For here he paints a world in which the only blessing is the gift of death. One last inconceivable horror he has spared us: in *Lear* there are no children. Nothing childlike could breathe that blasted and polluting air. A denizen of that foul world must needs know the devilries that surround and await him, and so cannot be childlike; for, as Francis Thompson has reminded us, " To be childlike is to know not as yet that you are under sentence of life, nor petition that it be commuted into death."

The demand
for a happy
ending to
Lear.

Those critics who, after reading the tragedy of *King Lear,* can inquire why Shakespeare did not redress the balance by making Cordelia victorious, must be dismissed in silence. Only Mr. Swinburne could have commanded the words that might express their condemnation; and Mr. Swinburne, alas! is no longer with us. These writers have mistaken the sphere in which they are moving. They do not know hell when they see it. They cannot read the Dantean doom which is inscribed in characters of blood above the portals of Lear's world. They have not realized that this is a land "where peace and rest can never dwell, hope never comes, that comes to all."

The enigma of the soul of Shakespeare has here its most bewildering proof. The creator of this universe of torment passed among his fellows as "the *gentle* Shakespeare." With Lear's Gethsemane embodying itself in his mind, he sat in taverns and drank wine with mortal men. Is there not something of bathos in the search for a personal experience of his that could account for the mood in which he wrought this magnificence of terror? Not the lost love of fifty women could have revealed to him so much of bitterness. It was because his soul was perfectly balanced and attuned that he was able to body forth this form of horrors before unknown, to look upon it, depict it, and live. You may create such a world in your thought by taking the dark phases of human character, by eliminating all that redeems them, and veraciously projecting them to their logical and bitter end. But beware how you tread the burning marl whereon even Shakespeare was scorched nigh to blasting.

The miracle of Shakespeare's "gentleness."

In the great comedies, we have life simplified in one direction—namely, by the subordination of earnestly working evil. In the great tragedies, on the other hand, life is simplified by the virtual suspension of earnestly working good. Edmund and Goneril and Regan live in us all; there is, as Socrates said, a wild beast in our nature: but happily there dwells a Jekyll with the Hyde. Edgar, the legitimate man, sojourns always in the same soul with Edmund, his illegitimate brother. It is the strife, the mutual limiting, of the brute and the god that keeps them both in balance, and enables us to turn towards the world the face of a man. Such simplification of human character as the master-dramatist has presented upon the stage, if it were found in daily

The notes of the comic and tragic worlds.

life, would mean insanity. Even to be righteous overmuch is a danger: St. Francis may become St. Simeon Stylites. We have to cling to the precious **The balance** inconsistencies, the seeming weaknesses and foibles, **of normal** that keep us sane. It is better to eat with Pharisees **life.** and publicans, and to be called a winebibber, than to feed on locusts and wild honey in the inhuman solitude of the wilderness. Well was it for Shakespeare that his daily walk was among the kindly haunts of men; for so he was enabled to master the devil that tempted him in that lonely place where his soul fought out the struggle of Lear in the storm.

Dante, they said, was the man who had been in hell; and Dante never quite got out again, because they could always see it in his face. But the man Shakespeare did not reveal to his fellows what he had seen and known. His triumph was that after *Lear* he still could laugh.

CHAPTER VIII

"THE WINTER'S TALE": THE COMEDY OF FOLLY AND FATE

THE fourth and last of the periods into which we divide Shakespeare's literary life is represented by three plays, between which there is a family likeness, as marked as their difference from the productions of his earlier years. These three are *Cymbeline, The Winter's Tale* and *The Tempest.* In *Pericles* we have a drama only partially of Shakespeare's authorship, though in the portions which criticism is unanimous in ascribing to him we have foreshadowings of some of the rarest excellences of his final trilogy. *Pericles* dates back to the year 1608 or earlier; *Cymbeline* and *The Winter's Tale* are most probably ascribed to 1610, and *The Tempest* to 1611. We know with certainty that *The Winter's Tale* was being played at the Globe Theatre in May, 1611, and that it was acted at Court on November 5th of the same year. It was witnessed at the Globe in May by a certain Dr. Simon Forman, who preserved in a MS. diary (recovered some years since) an account of the performance he saw. The fairly complete outline of the plot jotted down by Forman leaves no doubt that what he witnessed was the extant play by Shakespeare. As in the case of *Cymbeline* and *The Tempest,* there are no quarto editions of this play. It was first published in the Folio of

Shakespeare's last period and its products.

Forman's Diary.

[209]

1623, where the text is in an exceptionally accurate condition.

Jonson's reference in *Bartholomew Fair.*

The popularity of *The Winter's Tale* and *The Tempest* is further attested by a satirical allusion in the Induction to Ben Jonson's *Bartholomew Fair,* which was first produced in 1614:—

> If there be never a servant-monster in the Fair, who can help it, he [*i. e.,* Jonson] says, nor a nest of antics? He is loth to make nature afraid in his plays, like those that beget Tales, Tempests, and such like drolleries, to mix his head with other men's heels; let the concupiscence of jigs and dances reign as strong as it will amongst you: yet if the puppets will please anybody, they shall be entreated to come in.

The reference here to Caliban and the harpies in *The Tempest,* and to the dance of satyrs in the Sheep-Shearing scene in *The Winter's Tale,* to say nothing of the titles, is unmistakable.

Contrast with earlier work.

Taking the three plays of this final period together, and comparing them with the productions of the years of inner storm that had preceded, we find a marked contrast. There is little or no return to the mood and manner of the 1590's, to which the great comedies belong. Comedy of the richest vintage there is, to be sure; never, even in the days of Bottom and Falstaff, had their creator's heart been more over-brimming with fun and with the unbought joy of life than when he poured out his soul in the rogueries of Autolycus and the Bacchic fooling of Stephano and Trinculo. There is tragedy, too: the woes of Posthumus and Imogen, the self-originated agony of Leontes and the sixteen years' death-in-life of Hermione; the life of Prospero, shipwrecked in a tempest which is over long before the play begins; the superfluous but none the less shattering sorrow of Alonzo for the son he counts as lost;—all this, while it lasts, is evil enough, though not to be compared with the doom of Macbeth and Lear. But we have passed into a new world from that earlier one of irresponsible jollity, where happy endings were ensured by undesigned coincidence; a new world, too, from that of inexorable doom and bloody revenge, where the death of the victims is their only possible approach to happiness. A new spiritual world

This new world is—may we not say?—one of romantic realism, where sins may be atoned for, injuries forgiven, and errors set right. No man here is saved by chance; but here salvation is not impossible, and in each of these plays it is attained before the end. Yet the endings are not "happy" in the sentimental sense. The characters live and grow and change before our eyes; they are mellowed by experience, made humaner by sorrow and repentance; and the end is peace. of romantic realism, where expiation of sin and error is possible.

Another noteworthy difference between these plays and those of fifteen years earlier is the fact that Shakespeare now looks with other eyes upon the creatures, young and old, of his imagination. Formerly he had presented the young lovers and frolickers as his contemporaries, or, more strictly (if the too pedantic term may be allowed), as his coetaneans. In *Love's Labour's Lost* he is of an age with Biron and Longaville, and looks with their eyes upon their lady-loves. In the *Two Gentlemen of Verona* he sees Sylvia as Valentine saw her, and the lights and shadows of the world betray the valuations of a young man's fancy. In his first tragedy, the undying tale of the star-crossed lovers, he weighs all issues in the balances of Romeo, and betrays the instinctive hostility of youth towards what youth needs must Shakespeare now writes as an older man.

think the heartless and ungenerous prudence of age. He is on the side of Juliet and her beloved — not upon principle, but instinctively. A detailed comparison of these early heroes and heroines with Posthumus and Imogen, Florizel and Perdita, and Ferdinand and Miranda, would make an interesting study. The hint for this has been given to us by Sir Walter Raleigh, who, speaking of the romantic dramas of Shakespeare's last period, makes these discriminating observations:—

Raleigh's *Shake-speare*, chap. ii, p. 60-61.

> A new type of character meets us in these plays; a girl, innocent, frank, dutiful, and wise, cherished and watched over by her devoted father, or restored to him after long separation. It is impossible to escape the thought that we are indebted to Judith Shakespeare for something of the beauty and simplicity which appear in Miranda and Perdita, and in the earlier sketch of Marina. In his will Shakespeare bequeaths to Judith a "broad silver-gilt bowl," — doubtless the bride-cup that was used at her wedding. There were many other girls within reach of his observation, but (such are the limitations of humanity) there were few so likely as his own daughter to exercise him in disinterested sympathy and insight, or to touch him with a sense of the pathos of youth.

Professor Raleigh is not oblivious of the danger of carrying such speculations too far — as some may think he has already done in the foregoing passage; but his verdict on the changed attitude in the latest plays is incontestable.

He now treats of parents as one of them, The other aspect of that new attitude is the fact that, whereas in the earlier plays the older people are viewed from the standpoint of rebellious youth, in the later ones Shakespeare identifies himself much more with the parents and guardians. You cannot read *Romeo and Juliet* without feeling that old Montague and Capulet are the natural enemies of the youthful poet, as well as of his hero and heroine and of each other. Despite his ripening judgment, moreover, he portrays the abduction of Jessica by Lorenzo in *The Merchant of Venice* as one of those glorious larks in which the spirit of youth, self-justified by its desires, triumphs over crabbèd age. In all the earlier works there is an elusive but unmistakable suggestion that age, merely as such, and irrespective of individual character, has about it something alien, repellent, and slightly ridiculous. But in *The Tempest* Shakespeare is obviously identified by sympathy with Prospero rather than with Ferdinand. He looks on Miranda with a father's, not with a lover's eye. In *The Winter's Tale,* despite the prominence of the young couple, the poet's heart is with the parents — with Polixenes and Hermione. To put the point briefly, the poet when young is primarily concerned that his lovers shall *attain* their happiness; in his maturer years, his first anxiety is that they shall *deserve* it. Had we none but internal evidence, we could not fail to date the final trilogy at the point where the existing external evidence confirms us in placing it. The general effect of the three plays is most happily summed up by Dowden in the following sentences: —

and looks on the young with a father's eye.

Over the beauty of youth and the love of youth there is shed, in these plays of Shakespeare's final period, a clear yet tender luminousness not elsewhere to be perceived in his writings. In his earlier plays, Shakespeare writes concerning young men and maidens, their loves, their mirth, their griefs, as one who is among them, who has a lively, personal interest in their concerns, who can make merry with them, treat them familiarly, and, if need be, can mock them into good sense. There is nothing in these early plays

Dowden's Shakespeare: His Mind and Art, 1876 ed., p. 406 ff.

wonderful, strangely beautiful, pathetic about youth and its joys and sorrows. . . . But in these latest plays the beautiful, pathetic light is always present. There are the sufferers, aged, experienced, tried — Queen Katherine, Prospero, Hermione. And over-against these there are the children, absorbed in their happy and exquisite egoism — Perdita and Miranda, Florizel and Ferdinand, and the boys of old Belarius. . . . In each of these plays we can see Shakespeare, as it were, bending tenderly over the joys and sorrows of youth. We recognize this rather through the total characterization, and through a feeling and a presence, than through definite incident or statement.

Two plays dealing with lost children.

The similarity of thesis between *Cymbeline* and *The Winter's Tale* is worthy of consideration. Both these romances are pivoted upon the adventures of lost children, who are brought up in obscurity. In the former play it is the tyrannous cruelty of King Cymbeline in banishing the worthy Belarius that robs him of his two boys. In *The Winter's Tale* it is the groundless jealousy of Leontes that causes the death of Mamillius, the concealment of Hermione and the loss of Perdita.

Source: Greene's novel.

As regards its subject-matter, *The Winter's Tale* is little more than a free dramatization of a novel by Shakespeare's quondam enemy, Robert Greene — the man who on his deathbed, in 1592, had launched against the unlearned "upstart" a jealous and vindictive denunciation, which, by one of the happiest of time's revenges, has come to serve as a precious datum for the study of the master-artist's career. It is, indeed, the earliest reference to Shakespeare in contemporary literature, and serves (by its malicious paraphrase of a line in the Third Part of *King Henry VI*) to prove that Shakespeare was then already known, at least to the inner theatrical circle, as an adapter of other men's plays for the stage, if not as a dramatic author in the full sense.[1]

Greene's novel, in the earliest known edition (1588), is thus described on its title-page, after the long-winded fashion of the period:—

> " Pandosto. The Triumph of Time. Wherein is discovered by a pleasant Historie, that although by the meanes of sinister fortune Truth may be concealed, yet by Time in spight of fortune it is most manifestly reuealed. Pleasant for age to auoyde drowsie thoughtes, profitable for youth to eschue other [*sic*] wanton pastimes, and bringing to both a desired content. Temporis filia veritas. *By Robert Greene* Maister of Artes in *Cambridge*," etc., etc.

This prosy and euphuistic production had a long and extensive popularity, and after a number of editions had appeared its title was changed to *Dorastus and Fawnia.* Pandosto is the original of Shakespeare's Leontes, Dorastus and Fawnia of Florizel and Perdita. Shakespeare has changed the names of all the characters, transposed the scenes from Bohemia to Sicily and *vice versâ,* altered the *dénouement* by keeping Hermione alive instead of letting her die, created the personages of Antigonus, Autolycus, Paulina and the shepherd's son, and re-created all the rest. He has preserved all the vagaries of Greene's impressionistic geography and haphazard chronology, and added a generous crop of anachron-

Vogue of Pandosto.

Shakespeare's innovations.

---

[1] " There is an vpstart Crow, beautified with oure feathers, that with his *Tygers heart wrapt in ᴊ Players hide* supposes he is as well able to bumbast out a blanke verse as the best of you; and being an absolute *Johannes factotum*, is in his owne conceit the onely Shake-scene in a countrie."— Greene's *Groatsworth of Wit bought with a Million of Repentance,* 1592. The line parodied is "O tiger's heart wrapt in a woman's hide," *King Henry VI,* Pt. III, I, iv, 137.

isms of his own. The life and vigour, the naturalness and dignity of the characters, are due to him.

In the novel, Franion (= Camillo), Bellaria
(= Hermione), Pandosto, Fawnia, Dorastus and
Porrus (= the Shepherd), all pour out their woes
in stilted and stupid soliloquies of precisely the same
character. One sample may well serve for all.
When Bellaria is imprisoned, she indulges in two
pages of rhetoric of the following order:—

> Alas, Bellaria, how unfortunate art thou, because
> fortunate! Better thou hadst been born a beggar than
> a prince, so shouldest thou have bridled fortune with
> want, where now she sporteth herself with thy plenty.
> Ah, happy life, where poor thoughts and mean desires
> live in secure content, not fearing fortune because too
> low for fortune! Thou seest now, Bellaria, that care
> is a companion to honour, not to poverty; that high
> cedars are crushed with tempests, when low shrubs
> are not touched with the wind; precious diamonds are
> cut with the file, when despised pebbles lie safe in the
> sand. Delphos is sought to by princes, not beggars,
> and Fortune's altars smoke with kings' presents, not
> with poor men's gifts. Happy are such, Bellaria, that
> curse fortune for contempt, not fear, and may wish
> they were, not sorrow they have been. Thou art a
> princess, Bellaria, and yet a prisoner; born to the one
> by descent, assigned to the other by despite; accused
> without cause, and therefore oughtest to die without
> care, for patience is a shield against fortune, and a
> guiltless mind yieldeth to sorrow.

And so on, and so forth. When her child is born,
she apostrophizes it in similar fashion. Were it not
that all the rest of Greene's puppets, including the
illiterate Shepherd, use precisely similar language
(save that, by a humorous stretch of absurdity, the
untutored Fawnia is rather stronger on erudite allusions than most of the others), we might think that

Bellaria's tongue gave a show of reason to her husband's rage — though, to be sure, it would leave his jealousy more inexplicable than ever.

In view of Shakespeare's radical change in the plot, his enrichment of the cast, and his metamorphosis of Greene's dry bones into living souls, the statement of White that "the novel is followed very closely, not only as to plot and personages, but as to thought, *tone,* and sometimes even *language,*" is beyond measure surprising. There are not more than half-a-dozen verbal echoes of Greene's phrases in the whole play, and even in these the resemblance is as that of a polished jewel to an uncut stone; and there are not two compositions in the world between which there is a greater contrast of tone than between *Pandosto* and *The Winter's Tale*. *R. G. White on the dependence of the W. T. on Greene.*

The abundance of prose, the emancipation from metrical restraints, and the heavy freightage of thought in the play, are further characteristic stigmata of Shakespeare's maturest style. The rush of ideas impatiently clamouring for utterance leads him to many violations of grammar and syntax. Yet in several places the poetry is rich almost beyond precedent, and nowhere has he more subtly adapted style and vocabulary to the revelation of varieties of individual character. The blending of the mellow calm of maturity with the spirit of youthfulness is inexpressibly charming. Read immediately after one of the great tragedies, *The Winter's Tale* deepens one's sense of the inexhaustible range of Shakespeare's versatility and his matchless mastery of the various music of the human soul. The Sheep-Shearing scene, evidently drawn from life, is full of zest and joy. The catholic soul of the poet lives through each shade of feeling in the *Stylistic qualities.*

simple spirits of his peasants and shepherds. He vibrates to the unique beauty of every flower that blows. His appreciation of the shrewd rogueries of Autolycus is as absolute and full as his delight in the magic harmonies of poetry and philosophy that he utters through the lips of Polixenes and Perdita.

The astonishing discovery, which I have recently made, that many good readers of Shakespeare are unfamiliar with *The Winter's Tale* makes it seem necessary to outline the plot before attempting a brief interpretation.

Plot of the *Winter's Tale*: I i-ii.

Leontes, King of Sicilia, is entertaining his boyhood friend Polixenes, King of Bohemia. The visitor announces that he must depart, but Leontes urges him to protract his stay. Failing in his persuasions, Leontes requests his wife, Hermione, to add her inducements to his. Polixenes at her entreaties consents to remain longer; whereupon Leontes at once becomes madly jealous, interpreting the solicitations of his wife (which he forgets — as some of the critics also seem to forget — were undertaken at his

Scene ii, 27.

own request), and the ready assent of Polixenes, as evidence of scandalous relations between them. He discloses his suspicions to his counsellor Camillo, whom he urges to poison Polixenes. The horrified courtier at first seeks to disabuse him of his mad belief; but, finding this impossible, and being given the choice between a reward for compassing the murder and death for refusing, he pretends to ac-

Ibid. 363 ff.

cept the task. Instead of prosecuting it, however, he discloses the situation to Polixenes, with whom in secret he flies to Bohemia.

II i.

The discovery of his departure strengthens the insane convictions of Leontes, who publicly accuses

line 64 ff.

his wife (though she is about to bear a second child)

of adultery, and hurries her to prison. Here she
gives birth to a daughter, which is taken to Leontes II iii.
by Paulina, who roundly denounces him for his
barbarous injustice. He at first declares that both
mother and babe shall be burnt, but decides instead *Ibid.* 170 ff.
to expose the child; and, for revenge upon Paulina,
he forces this odious task upon her husband, Antigonus. Messengers meantime have been sent to III i.
Delphi, to obtain Apollo's oracular verdict upon Hermione. At their return she is brought to trial, and
forced, though newly risen from childbed, to plead III ii.
her cause before the gaping crowd. The oracle,
being read, pronounces her innocent, but Leontes in- *Ibid.* 129 ff.
sanely declares it mere falsehood, and orders the
trial to proceed. It is interrupted, however, by news
that his little son Mamillius, sick with horror at the
treatment accorded to his mother, has died; whereupon Hermione swoons and is carried off as dead.
These shocks cure the tyrant of his insanity, and he
dedicates himself to a life of penitence.

Meantime Antigonus has conveyed the child by III iii.
sea to the coast of Bohemia (a place strongly resembling the coast of Iowa or Switzerland, but invented
by Greene, not Shakespeare), where he reluctantly
exposes it, leaving with it a rich garment, some
jewels and a purse of money. As he is returning to
his ship he is seized and devoured by a bear, and the
ship itself is wrecked in a gale and lost with all on
board. The child, however, is discovered by a
Shepherd, who, with his clownish son, takes it home;
and it is reared by the Shepherd as his daughter.

At this point there is a clumsy but inevitable gap IV i.
of sixteen years, bridged over by a speech from
"Time as Chorus," which is so dissimilar in style
to the rest of the play, and so inferior, that it is com-

monly assumed to be from a different hand. It may quite conceivably have been thrust in by another writer to soften the shock of the transition.

IV ii.

We now learn that Camillo is established as a counsellor to King Polixenes in Bohemia (whither the scene is transferred), and that the King's son Florizel is disturbing the royal complacency by bestowing his attentions upon a shepherd's daughter, with whom Polixenes and Camillo plot to discover him in disguise. Thus we are introduced to the pastoral scenes, which are the heart of the play, and in

IV iii & iv.

which Shakespeare pours out all the fullness of his joy and of his most perfect poetic power. Autolycus, the gipsy pedlar and "snapper-up of unconsidered trifles," discarded from Florizel's service and down

" When daffodils begin to peer," iii 1. Scene iv.

on his luck (though not too depressed to give us a song that will never die), overtakes the Clown, who is going to buy cates for the shearers' feast, and by dexterous "cozening" steals his purse. Then, for the first time, we meet Florizel and the strangely preserved Perdita, the two young people swearing eternal fidelity to each other, even though the Prince

Ibid. 55 ff.

have to sacrifice his royalty to his love. The festivities now begin, attended by Polixenes and Camillo *incog.*, and Perdita as hostess distributes flowers, accompanied by gems of poetic philosophy, to the assembled guests. A rural dance ensues, and is followed by the reappearance of Autolycus, freshly disguised as a pedlar, to pursue his light-fingered craft under pretence of selling ballads and fripperies to the lads and lasses. After a scene of exquisite fun, which gives place to the "dance of twelve Satyrs" that Jonson sneered at, we are about to witness the

Ibid. 403 ff.

troth-plighting of Florizel and Perdita; but this is interrupted by the enraged protest of Polixenes, who

throws off his disguise, denounces his son, and
breathes out threats of torture and death against the
unlucky Shepherd and his supposed daughter, for
beguiling the heir to the throne from the paths of
duty and prudence.

Polixenes having departed in fury, Florizel turns
to the more placable Camillo, and engages his aid in
a scheme for carrying Perdita off by sea — not, as
the youth had intended, "to unpath'd waters, un- *Ibid.* 553.
dream'd shores," but to Camillo's native Sicilia,
which the old man yearns to visit once more. He
provides them with commendations to the penitent
Leontes, and they go down disguised to the shore,
to embark. The Shepherd and his son meantime,
to exculpate themselves with Polixenes, set out to
carry to that monarch the proof that Perdita is not
of kin to them, but (as testified by the things found
with her) of noble lineage. Autolycus, however,
overtakes them; and, wishing to ingratiate himself
with Florizel, induces them to go to the ship. They
are thrust aboard, and with their testimony and their
treasure trove accompany the eloping couple to
Sicilia.

No sooner has Florizel, with his bride-elect, ar- V i 124 ff.
rived there and told Leontes a cock-and-bull story of
his adventures, than Polixenes and Camillo land
upon his heels,— Camillo having informed Polixenes
of the flight, for the double purpose of befriending
the fugitives and of enabling himself to return to
Sicily. They discover the identity of Perdita by in-
terviewing the old Shepherd, and turn up at Leontes'
Court for a purple moment of romantic revelation
and reconciliation, which the dramatist, very wisely,
causes to be narrated, not enacted. The royal party
then adjourns to the house of Paulina, to see the

statue of Queen Hermione, "now newly performed by that rare Italian master, Giulio Romano" (and a precious rare master he must have been, to have worked in pagan times, two thousand years before he was born). Whilst they are gazing in wonderment at this prodigy of the sculptor's art, it comes to life before them; and they learn that the Queen had not really died, but had gone into religious retirement, until (as hinted in Apollo's oracle) the lost child should be found.

So ends *The Winter's Tale,* with all the ravelled strands spliced up anew, and everybody's winter made glorious summer.

The character of Leontes.

Though sketched more slightly and with less fullness of detail, the character of Leontes is scarcely less interesting than that of Othello, with which, indeed, it forms an instructive contrast. No Iago comes to poison Leontes' mind with hellish suspicions. His madness is self-engendered and self-begotten. He has lived long happy years with Hermione, who had the world to choose from, and kept him waiting three months before consenting to marry him. He has neither found nor even imagined the faintest provocation to suspicion in her conduct through the years of their union. It is at his own specific request that she urges his oldest friend to prolong his visit in their Court. When, despite his solicitations, Polixenes remains determined to depart, Leontes turns to Hermione with the words,

I ii 27.

"Tongue-tied, our Queen? Speak you."

This fact quite destroys the basis of Hartley Coleridge's estimate of him. "I am not sure," says Coleridge, "that the ready soliciting of Hermione, and the easy compliance of Polixenes, might not produce in a better mind a momentary cloud, a wish that the request had not been made, an impatience for Polixenes' departure." To say this, overlooking the terse but clear request of Leontes to Hermione to do the very thing which he is afterwards infuriated with her for doing, is to miss the subtlety of Shakespeare's portrayal of the character. The point is that Leontes' jealousy is throughout of the nature of insanity; and first of all in this, that it has no objective cause, no justifying motive. Its origin is that abnormal egoism which, more often than any divinity, doth hedge the spoiled children who are called kings. Self-worship is a root of many kinds of madness. By inducing self-blindness, it renders its victim a prey to every flatterer and proof against all wholesome counsel. Leontes is so predisposed that the moment he has "eaten on the insane root that takes the reason prisoner," his ears are closed against the respectful remonstrances of Camillo and Antigonus, and the somewhat shrewish common sense of Paulina, and open only to the sycophants who indulge his disastrous whim. The result is that he speedily develops that unmistakable symptom of insanity, the belief that all around him are conspiring against him, and that everything which happens is part of the plot. Camillo is the first to incur his fury for offering a most reasonable protest: —

The root of his jealousy.

> Good my lord, be cur'd
> Of this diseas'd opinion, and betimes;
> For 'tis most dangerous.

I ii 296 f.

But Leontes insists that, even so, it is true: wherein being contradicted, he retorts: —

> It is; you lie, you lie:
> I say thou liest, Camillo, and I hate thee,
> Pronounce thee a gross lout, a mindless slave,
> Or else a hovering temporizer, that

Ibid. 299 ff.

> Canst with thine eyes at once see good and evil,
> Inclining to them both.

And in like manner, when he finds that his counsellor has fled with Polixenes, he instantly concludes that Camillo has been privy to his friend's misdoings with his wife:—

II i 46 ff.

> Camillo was his help in this, his pander:
> There is a plot against my life, my crown.
> All's true that is mistrusted: that false villain
> Whom I employ'd was pre-employ'd by him:
> He has discover'd my design, and I
> Remain a pinch'd thing; yea, a very trick
> For them to play at will.

His cure must be the uprooting of self-worship.

The root of the disease being his overgrown self-love, only such a shock as will eradicate this can restore his sanity. He persists in his delusion until his tyranny has killed his son and (as he thinks) his wife, and robbed him of the daughter whom he had made the victim of Hermione's imaginary crime. Son and wife being gone, his pride is broken in the dust; and, with the cause, the effect—his insane self-delusion—is shattered. Not yet is Leontes saved; but he is now in the way of salvation. Sixteen years of penitence, and he will be fit to receive the forgiveness of his monstrously injured wife, and worthy of the love of the daughter whom his madness had in intention murdered.

Contrast between Pandosto and Leontes.

The difference between Greene's and Shakespeare's insight into human character is crucially illustrated by the final state of Leontes in *The Winter's Tale* as compared with that of Pandosto in the novel. Shakespeare has two or three lines in which Leontes, struck by Perdita's resemblance to his lost wife, expresses a momentary desire to make her his queen; but this, at Paulina's rebuke, he instantly relinquishes. This is because Shakespeare does not forget the spiritual discipline which for sixteen years his creature has been undergoing, and its purging effect upon his soul. Greene's Pandosto, on the contrary, is the same unregenerate savage after all his penitence as he was before. He imprisons Dorastus (= Florizel), and makes violent and dishonourable advances to the desolate girl whom chance has placed in his power.

Few even of Shakespeare's magnificent women are limned with more delicacy of insight than the sublime character of Hermione. Accustomed all her life to reverence and solicitude, loving her husband with a spotless love, and incapable of the scarce unsullied forethought which could teach her by precautions to avert suspicion from herself, she is suddenly exposed, at the moment of her greatest need of love and cherishing, to the foulest insult which can assail a woman. Yet her bearing, both when first accused and when forced to answer at her trial, has a serene dignity and a patient fortitude which stagger even the blustering lunatic who is torturing her. When he blurts out the words, "She's an adulteress," her answer is too perfect for praise:—

> Should a villain say so,
> The most replenish'd villain in the world,
> He were as much more villain: you, my lord,
> Do but mistake.

After a further tirade of calumny from Leontes, she answers, with the same strong gentleness,—

> How will this grieve you,
> When you shall come to clearer knowledge, that
> You thus have publish'd me! Gentle my lord,
> You scarce can right me throughly then to say
> You did mistake.

The placid strength of Hermione.

II i 78 f.

Ibid. 96 ff.

Her deep
qualities
manifested
through
adversity.

Robbed of her son, barbarously imprisoned, and by stress of "honourable grief" prematurely delivered of her ill-starred babe, she is haled out, ere yet her body has recovered its strength, and placed like any coarse criminal in the public court, a gazing-stock for men and devils. Yet all the brighter through this crucifixion-darkness shines the high courage of untainted integrity. She knows how little it can boot her to plead Not Guilty; yet she trusts that powers divine shall at last enable innocence to make falsehood blush and tyranny tremble. She appeals to her husband's knowledge of her past life, and movingly contrasts it with her present situation; but she cares for nothing save honour, and (like a true woman) only for that lest her children be tainted:—

III ii 34 ff.

> Behold me,
> . . . a great king's daughter,
> The mother to a hopeful prince, here standing
> To prate and talk for life and honour 'fore
> Who please to come and hear. For life, I prize it
> As I weigh grief, which I would spare: for honour,
> 'Tis a derivative from me to mine,
> And only that I stand for.

Has she loved Polixenes? Yes, but only

Ibid. 61 ff.

> With such a kind of love as might become
> A lady like me, with a love *even such,*
> So and no other, *as yourself commanded:*
> Which not to have done I think had been in me
> Both disobedience and ingratitude
> To you and toward your friend. . . .

(She here uses the term *love* in the secondary Elizabethan sense, which we to-day express by a feebler term—such as *like* or *esteem.*)

A speech that only purest innocence could have framed is powerless to move the seated malice of the madman; and so he answers it with further insult and a threat of death. With the calm scorn of one raised above hope and fear, she retorts that she rather seeks than fears to die; but since she still cares for her honour, though she values not her life, she appeals to the oracle: "Apollo be my judge!"

Losing hope, she loses fear, and longs for death.

Vindicated by the god, in the eyes of all save the spell-smitten Leontes, the heroic woman scarce has time to breathe ere fortune's next murderous blow is upon her: the news of the death of her boy. Tried beyond mortal endurance, she swoons, and is thought to have died; and so she passes into the silence of sixteen years, to pray for the day when the oracle, which has saved her honour, may be fulfilled by the recovery of her daughter; and when, after patience and penitence have achieved their perfect work, she may again be able to call "husband" the broken man who has marred her life.

The reappearance of Hermione at the end of the play, in the Statue scene, is one of those daring experiments only possible to the master at the zenith of his powers. It is interesting to observe how, from the very beginning of the play, each trait in Hermione's character is made to prepare the way for this climax. She is so depicted as to make it possible for us to believe, in advance, that she is the one woman among millions who could enact such a part without turning its breathless awfulness into absurdity or extravagance. She is an unrivalled combination of sensitiveness and self-restraint. From her own lips we learn that while she is not prone to weeping, yet she has "that honourable grief . . . which burns worse than tears drown." She is like

The Statue scene (V iii).

the centre of the cyclone, which is undisturbed. She has within her the very source of all the agonies which in natures less profound give rise, even through sympathy, to tumultuous lamentations.

The transcendent pride of Hermione.

Mrs. Jameson, in an admirable analysis, declared that, among her other qualities, Hermione had "dignity without pride." If it be not too rash to pit a man's judgment of a woman against another woman's, I would venture to say, on the contrary, that Hermione is full of pride,— but pride of the loftiest and worthiest kind, as of the yet unfallen Lucifer. She is in every detail a classical figure; and her creator, though utterly careless of historic consistency, is never careless of what may be termed the moral consistency of his creatures. Hermione illustrates that conception of ethics according to which *magnanimity* is the crowning virtue. Aristotle's idea of the good man is that of one who, being compact of all the admirable qualities, justly values and respects himself as possessing them. The quality of greatness of soul, or magnanimity, becomes a virtue — nay, becomes possible — only when all those characteristics are present for which a man could be disinterestedly admired by others.

She dies to self, but not to self-respect.

This, I venture to think, is the clue to Hermione's character. Her resignation has little in common with the debased ideal of humility which the Dark Ages substituted for the Christian ideal. She is not prostrate before the gods, nor does she think (as St. Augustine or Calvin would have thought) that the mountainous evil which overwhelms her expresses the divine will and the divine sense of her deserts. She is proud with the consciousness of rectitude, and her contempt of death is that of the strong soul which can raise itself above even hope.

She dies, indeed, to self, like any Christian; but this does not mean dying to self-respect, as in the degenerate form of the Christian ideal it has often been taken to mean.

The charm of Perdita's character has been so often praised that further eulogy would be impertinent. I find it interesting, however, to trace the resemblance between Perdita and her mother. All the lovely qualities of this girl are in bud what Hermione's are in flower. There is, to be sure, an initial inconsistency on Shakespeare's part. How comes Perdita by her culture, her knowledge, her refinement of manner? Inward grace is given by nature; but outward grace comes only by art, by training, by social heredity. Perdita is brought up motherless, by a kindly but illiterate old chawbacon. She has no schooling, and the standard of mind and manners in her environment is perfectly reflected in the characters of the Shepherd's son and of Mopsa and Dorcas. The improbability here is even grosser than in the case of the two princely sons of Cymbeline, for they at least had the counsel and example of the noble old Belarius. Miranda, too, finds in Prospero a teacher whose resources cannot be considered inadequate to account for the fineness she displays. But Perdita must be assumed to have created, from the unsupplemented resources of her native genius, all those graces of bearing, speech and demeanour — *les riens qui sont tout* — which command the reluctant admiration of Polixenes, and cause the consuming but by no means undiscriminating passion of Florizel.

Such oversights, however, must be freely pardoned to Shakespeare. Had he portrayed Perdita in terms of strict probability, — had he made her

Perdita's qualities a reflection of Hermione's.

But how comes she by her education?

such an epitome of her environment as in real life she must have been,— we should have had no *Winter's Tale.* We must take her as we find her, manifesting both in joy and grief the same stately *savoir faire,* the same serenity of surface, denoting soundless depths below, as we see in her mother.

Her passion is consistent with prudence.

She is wholly given to her lover; but the passionate affection she feels for him does not in the least blind her judgment. In this she contrasts completely with Florizel, who is swept off his feet by the tide which leaves her unshaken, though it submerges her. Shakespeare has shown in many characters how thoroughly he had observed the phenomena of the sex attraction. He knew that it is generally far more rationalized, and far more subject to volitional control, in women than it is in men.

IV iv 16-24 and 35-40.

Perdita has warned Florizel of the probable consequences of his constancy to her. She is by no means unwilling to accept the sacrifice, but she insists that he shall realize beforehand how great that sacrifice may have to be; and she will not accept him until he is completely ready to make it.

The impression she creates on others.

In Florizel's praises of her we may suspect the exaggeration of passionate love,— as when, for example, he declares that her hand is

Ibid. 349 f.

As soft as dove's down and as white as it,
Or Ethiopian's tooth, or the fann'd snow that's bolted
By the northern blasts twice o'er.

Scarcely less restrained is that earlier wonderful tribute of his to the grace and charm of her actions:—

Ibid. 135 ff.

What you do
Still betters what is done. When you speak, sweet,
I'ld have you do it ever: when you sing,
I'ld have you buy and sell so, so give alms,

Pray so; and for the ord'ring your affairs,
To sing them too: when you do dance, I wish you
Nothing but that; move still, still so,
And own no other function: each your doing,
So singular in each particular,
Crowns what you are doing in the present deed,
That all your acts are queens.

But if Florizel is an untrustworthy witness, there can be no suspicion of exaggeration in the tribute which the deeply displeased Polixenes pays her in a confidential aside to Camillo: —

This is the prettiest low-born lass that ever
Ran on the green-sward: nothing she does or seems
But smacks of something greater than herself,
Too noble for this place.

Ibid. 156 ff.

Such an estimate by the royal father, who, even while making it, intends to prohibit the fulfilment of his son's desire, leads us to suspect that the passion of Florizel is prompted by that wisdom of the instincts which sometimes serves us well when our deep plots do pall. His fancy is fired by the outward graces of the shepherdess; but her inner wealth of mind and spirit, of which these are the symbols, is such as to justify the seemingly extreme imprudence of his choice. Shakespeare makes Perdita a tower of strength, a well of purity; the incarnation of innocence without ignorance, and passion without illusion. Several even of her speeches are too plain for modern taste. The sophisticated pruriency of our age cannot understand how fullness of knowledge of the world's and nature's ways, unconcealed by any simpering hypocrisy of affected ignorance, can co-exist with perfect inward chastity. To Shakespeare, however, there was in this matter no contradiction and no difficulty. Perdita is here exactly like Imogen, Rosalind, Miranda and Portia, and his heroines generally.

The character of Florizel.

Prince Florizel is a gallant and rather headstrong youth, much like Ferdinand in *The Tempest,* and placed in similar circumstances. Greene, in his novel, has presented a situation which had a great attraction for him,— that of a prince falling in love with a country girl who turns out to be a princess. We have the same romance in the courtship of Prince Edward and Margaret in his play of *Friar Bacon and Friar Bungay.* Shakespeare's Florizel is as austerely honourable as Perdita herself, but, being a young man in love, and therefore in a hurry, he displays a headlong precipitancy which is markedly opposed to her prudence. He is ready to abandon his position and career for her sake, but one cannot quite escape the feeling that "for her sake" means for his own. He is acting upon a passionate impulse which may lose all its force when the passion has spent itself; whereas Perdita's impulses, though none less passionate than his, are perfectly controlled by rational foresight. We cannot be sure but that Florizel may repent of his decision if things turn out badly; whereas we are quite certain that, come what will, Perdita will remain not only outwardly loyal but inwardly contented with the lot which she has chosen.

Profound philosophy mingled with poetry in the Pastoral scene.

Many lovers of the supreme in poetry will concur with philosophic students in thinking the words of Polixenes, in reply to Perdita's objection to the "streak'd gillyvors," the deepest note of cosmic insight in the whole of Shakespeare's work. Perdita dislikes the "gillyvors" because they are not the handiwork of unaided nature. Herself a wildflower, owing nothing to art, she cannot love the blooms that art has favoured. But to this Polixenes replies:—

> Yet nature is made better by no mean   IV iv 89 ff.
> But nature makes that mean: so, over that art
> Which you say adds to nature, is an art
> That nature makes. You see, sweet maid, we marry
> A gentler scion to the wildest stock,
> And make conceive a bark of baser kind
> By bud of nobler race: this is an art
> Which does mend nature, change it rather; but
> The art itself is nature.

It has become the fashion for some modern critics to dispraise Shakespeare for lack of ideas, while admitting that as regards mere verbal felicity he is an unapproachable master. This I take to be the gist of Mr. Bernard Shaw's frequent criticism. Mr. Shaw has never perpetrated the tasteless absurdity, with which he is often charged, of pretending that he is a greater dramatist than Shakespeare. He does, however, plume himself upon the wealth of ideas which his plays contain, and he does think that Shakespeare is in this respect deficient. Mr. Shaw has few sincerer admirers than I may claim to be. Yet I cannot but find in this attitude of his a curious instance of the way in which men are prone to misinterpret themselves, and to value themselves for qualities or powers in which they are by no means conspicuously gifted. It is no disrespect to Mr. Shaw to say that, after reading with the closest care every play and every preface he has written, I cannot remember meeting in all of them with one single idea that had not been made current by previous writers. Why Mr. Shaw cannot be content with combining, as he does, the finest genius of Molière (not to mention Aristophanes) with the finest skill of Voltaire, is hard for his admirers to

(marginal notes:) Shakespeare's alleged paucity of " ideas."

Mr. G. B. Shaw's criticism.

understand. But it is more germane to my present theme to insist that Shakespeare is not at all deficient in ideas, and that whoever asserts him to be so perpetrates a dumfoundering misjudgment.

Instances of his power as a thinker.

Shakespeare, who in all probability had never read Plato, gives us in his tragic world a living dramatization of Plato's ethical philosophy. It is also probable that he had not studied with close attention the works of Nietzsche or of John Stuart Mill. Yet in *Richard III* his colossal villain utters in one pregnant sentence a thought[2] to which Nietzsche devoted elaborate volumes, and in which Nietzsche was so original that, to the best of my knowledge, he had been anticipated (apart from Shakespeare) only by Plato. And here, in these words of Polixenes in *The Winter's Tale,* we have summed up in unapproachable phrase the essential philosophy of nature worked out with such relentless logic by John Stuart Mill and the evolutionists, and indeed underlying, as a regulative principle, the entire philosophy of science, from Bacon to Karl Pearson. Yet it is the effortless vision of the poet, not the intellectual labour of the systematic thinker, which enables Shakespeare to overleap the centuries and anticipate the slow results of thought.

The Pastoral scene is contemporary Warwickshire.

In these pastoral scenes Shakespeare frankly abandons even the pretence of historical consistency. The mental world of all the characters becomes that of rural England in Elizabethan or early Jacobean days. Already in the earlier scenes we have heard of Russian emperors and Whitsun pastorals contemporary with the Delphic Oracle. The

---

[2] Conscience is but a word that cowards use,
Devis'd at first to keep the strong in awe.
        —*King Richard III,* V, iii, 309 f.

gentle boy Mamillius begins his pathetically unfinished tale with the words, "There was a man dwelt by a churchyard"; by which simple phrase he transports himself from the time and country in which he is supposed to live to the time and country in which he was born in Shakespeare's mind. And now comes Autolycus, drawing himself to the life as a clever rogue with "sixteenth century" stamped all over him. He "haunts wakes, fairs and bear-baitings," and goes about with a puppet-show of the Prodigal Son. He has been an ape-bearer, a process-server, and a bailiff. The authenticity of his wondrous ballad of the great fish is warranted by its having "five justices' hands at it." And the fashionable finery which he brings "for my lads to give their dears" is unblushingly Elizabethan. The scamp is as delightful as Falstaff, and the triumph of Shakespeare's genius is shown in making him so consummately attractive, without for a moment making his vices alluring. Falstaff is altogether too wonderful for this imperfect world, but one feels that Autolycus might turn up at any country fair. He is perhaps a shade too sophisticated, a thought too brilliant in his power of generalization and self-analysis; which is but saying that he takes too much after his creator. But all his desires and all his deeds are those of the gipsy stroller, who loves and appreciates the beauties of nature and has an unconquerable antipathy to honest work. Shakespeare not only renews his own youth, but gives voice to the unspoken spring fever of all the world, in the song of the jolly mountebank, ragged and hard-up but irrepressible: —

The modernity of Autolycus.

> When daffodils begin to peer,
> With heigh! the doxy over the dale!

Further dis-
crepancies:
(1) Hermi-
one after the
Trial.
The disappearance of Hermione after her trial is so discreetly veiled that its utter improbability is apt to sink out of our memory. How was it possible for Paulina to make Leontes believe that his wife was dead when she was not? The most ordinary common sense would seem to demand a genuine corpse and a real funeral; and assuredly not less so in the case of a queen than in that of a private person. Yet Paulina manages to work the deception, apparently without taking anybody into her confidence.

There is a minor discrepancy, which the mere exigencies of stagecraft would have seemed to make impossible. We are distinctly told (in sc. iv of Act IV) that Florizel is disguised in shepherd's attire; yet in that very same scene, when he changes clothes with Autolycus, it is *court* apparel that Autolycus puts on. And who told the old Shepherd (Act III, sc. iii) that Antigonus, whom he had not seen, was an old man?

(2) Flori-
zel's clothes.

(3) The
Shepherd
and Antig-
onus.

Another of the delightful innovations of Shakespeare occurs in the passionate outburst with which Polixenes disclaims to Camillo the accusation of Leontes. If he has done this thing, he says, then let his name be "yok'd with his that did betray the Best." This familiarity with the story of Judas Iscariot in the days of Apollo-worship would be startling, were it not so fully in accord with our poet's invariable practice.

I ii 419.

Shake-
speare's na-
ture-plays.
The best scenes in *The Winter's Tale* place it in the series of Shakespeare's nature-plays. They have the out-of-door atmosphere of *Love's Labour's Lost, A Midsummer Night's Dream, As You Like It* and *The Tempest*. They are set in an idyllic world,— one of

those happy climes that lie
Up in the broad fields of the sky. . . .
All amidst the gardens fair
Of Hesperus and his daughters three
That sing about the golden tree:
Along the crispèd shades and bowers
Revels the spruce and jocund Spring;
The Graces, and the rosy-bosom'd Hours,
Thither all their bounties bring;
There eternal Summer dwells. . . .

Milton's
Comus, Epilogue.

The splendour of the world is but a bodying forth of the creative power in the mind of man; and every great poet has enriched the visible universe, by enabling us to see with his eyes things before invisible to mortal sight.   Shakespeare's Wood near Athens and his Forest of Arden are a part of the adorable *Sylva Poetarum,* which has added to the charm of every forest glade in this lower world.   Whenever we see the summer sunshine glancing between hoary trunks and dappling the soft grass with its fairy gold, we think of King Oberon and his Titania, of Bottom and the freakish Puck, or of Touchstone and his bucolic companions.   Never a harvest-home again but shall be shot through with a richer happiness for the memory of Perdita's sheep-shearing and the droll rogueries of Autolycus.   Each flower in a Shakespeare garden becomes a talisman, calling up magic vistas of the scenes in which his deathless shadows dwell.   All the mystery of our race-memories, that reach back beyond our individual lives, is stirred by the cadences of Perdita's flower-offering speech.   We are taken into the inmost sanctuaries of feeling, where speech would be a profanation, by the sight of

daffodils   IV iv 118 ff.
That come before the swallow dares, and take
The winds of March with beauty; violets dim,

> But sweeter than the lids of Juno's eyes
> Or Cytherea's breath; pale primroses,
> That die unmarried, ere they can behold
> Bright Phoebus in his strength. . . .

There is perhaps more of the purely romantic spirit in the woodland scenes of *As You Like It* than in the pastoral ones of *The Winter's Tale,* and in the former Jaques and Touchstone have the fascinating uniqueness of Shakespeare's best-loved figures. But the charm of these scenes in *The Winter's Tale* is that here we feel the presence of the author, more even than in the greatest comedies of his second period. All that Shakespeare has learned of the wisdom of time and eternity presses for utterance through these conversations. Irony and satire are all fordone; nothing is left even of the gentle cynicism of Jaques. The man who has lived through the problems of Hamlet, the destroying ambition of Macbeth, and the shattering terrors of Lear, has emerged into a calm and bright land, where, understanding all, he can forgive all and find joy in all. The story is rooted in folly which begets its own fate; but the end is peace: not the quietness of death, but the quietness of life.

CHAPTER IX

"THE TEMPEST": SHAKESPEARE'S SWAN-SONG

THERE is fairly clear testimony that *The Tempest* was the last completed play that came from Shakespeare's hand. Its scene, the enchanted island, is suggested by some accounts of the Bermudas that were not issued till the end of the year 1610. The character of Caliban embodies many traits ascribed to the natives of various parts of America, in whom the British public was at that time strongly interested; and it is barely possible that Trinculo's satirical remarks about the gaping curiosity of the English over "monsters" may have been prompted by the exhibition of a North American Indian called Epenew, who, as we learn from Captain John Smith's *Historie of New England,* was taken to the Old Country in 1611, and, "being a man of so great a stature," was "showed up and down London for money as a monster." Date of composition and production. II ii 25 ff.

It is known from official records that *The Tempest* was produced at Court for the opening of the winter season of 1611–12, and that it achieved conspicuous success both there and at the public theatre. Ben Jonson's allusion to it (quoted above, p. 210) was written at some date between 1611 and 1614, in which latter year his *Bartholomew Fair* was produced.

[239]

Subsequent plays: the Shakespearean "apocrypha."

To be sure, tradition ascribes to Shakespeare at least a share in three plays that did not see the light till a later date: *Cardenio, The Two Noble Kinsmen* and *King Henry VIII*. The first of these is lost. The share of Shakespeare in the second, if he had any, can only have been slight; many, indeed, of the ablest critics maintain that he had no hand in it at all. The fact that his name appears with Fletcher's as joint author in the first printed edition (1634), eighteen years after his death and nine after Fletcher's, is of little significance. Contemporary publishers were extremely unscrupulous or inaccurate about such ascriptions, which can never be accepted unless supported by independent evidence. The omission of these two plays from the Folio, coupled with the internal evidence in the case of *The Two Noble Kinsmen,* justifies us in denying to them the honour of anything more than a slight revision by the master.

King Henry VIII.

With *King Henry VIII* the case stands differently. It is included in the Folio, and of its seventeen scenes there are at least six which all agree can only have been created by the genius of Shakespeare. The rest are in Fletcher's best manner, and include a number of passages which, while they have the earmarks of his style, rise so far above any of his other work as to compel the conclusion that they have been enriched by the magician of language. Yet the play as a whole is poorly constructed; its great moments come early, and are followed by scenes of flagging interest. Though it was not produced until 1613, we cannot be certain that Shakespeare's share in it was his latest work: he may have had it lying by him for several years. The much-discussed character of the father of

Queen Elizabeth could not well have been put upon the stage during her lifetime, but might have been at any date after her death in 1603; and was, in fact, in one very poor play in 1605. Shakespeare, then, would have felt free to treat the theme, if it commended itself to his judgment, at any time during the ensuing eight years.

It was the firing of ordnance during the performance of this drama on June 29th, 1613, that caused the destruction of the Globe Theatre. Some ignited paper from one of the cannons fell upon the thatch over the stage, and, being unnoticed, produced a conflagration that consumed the entire building. No lives were lost, but considerable property of the company, which probably included Shakespeare's original MSS., was destroyed. *The Globe Theatre fire.*

Sir Sidney Lee, whose knowledge of all the facts connected with Shakespeare's life and work, and with the life and work of his professional contemporaries, is so bewilderingly complete, is intolerant of anything that seems to him like a fanciful construction being placed on the personages, speeches or incidents of any of the plays. He will not have it that Shakespeare was thinking of himself in describing any one character or episode, more than in dealing with any other. The analogy between Prospero, wielder of a wondrous art which at the close of the play he voluntarily resigns, and the more gifted magician whose last completed effort was expended in creating Prospero and his fairy realm, suggests itself very naturally. Many have hazarded the guess, accordingly, that it was intentional on Shakespeare's part. It has been assumed that he consciously, or half-consciously, symbolized, by the noble speech in which Prospero takes leave of his *Prospero's farewell to his art.*

supernormal powers, the imminent renunciation of his own poetic labours. Such very pardonable speculations incur Sir Sidney's rebuke:—

Life, ed. 1916, chap. xix, p. 434.

> In Prospero, the guiding providence of the romance, who resigns his magic power in the closing scene, traces have been sought of the lineaments of the dramatist himself, who was approaching in this play the date of his farewell to the enchanted work of his life, although he was not yet to abandon it altogether. Prospero is in the story a scholar-prince of rare intellectual attainments, whose engrossing study of the mysteries of science has given him magical command of the forces of Nature. His magnanimous renunciation of his magical faculty as soon as by its exercise he has restored his shattered fortunes is in accord with the general conception of a just and philosophical temperament. Any other justification of his final act is superfluous.

Possibility that Shakespeare consciously pronounced his own valediction.

With the deepest deference to the encyclopaedic biographer, whose fruitful labours in every field of Shakespearean research have laid us all under an inexhaustible debt of gratitude, I would venture to suggest that his reasoning here is somewhat less convincing than usual. He has scarcely accounted for Prospero's renunciation of his magical faculty. One is tempted to suspect that Sir Sidney Lee here forgets the poet, or confuses him for the moment with the logician. But, even so, it is not quite strictly "in accord with the general conception of a just and philosophical temperament" that a man should part with tremendous powers the moment he has attained the particular end for the sake of which he has been employing them. Such a man usually proceeds to seek fresh worlds to conquer — new fields for the exercise of powers, the use of which has become a joy in itself. Nor is the view which Lee repudiates prompted solely by the desire to find a *justification* for Prospero's course. The question is whether in describing his hero's "final act" Shakespeare may not also have been thinking of his own long years of sway, by virtue of an art peculiar to himself, over the minds and hearts of other men; — a sway which, with the enormous labour it entailed, he had certainly bargained with himself to resign before old age should take the charm from the other satisfactions of life.

Now, so far as external evidence goes, nobody can pretend to settle this question; and there is no room and no occasion for dogmatizing about it. The biographer, moreover, is right in insisting that the utmost economy should be exercised in applying to Shakespeare himself the words of his characters. But, *pace* Sir Sidney, the analogy is poetically so perfect that the great mass of non-specialist readers will continue to please themselves by seeing it. Shakespeare certainly could not have framed a more appropriate valediction to his twenty years of creative work than is conveyed in those lines wherewith Prospero takes leave of the tools of his wizardry: —

> Ye elves of hills, brooks, standing lakes and groves,   V i 33 ff.
> And ye that on the sands with printless foot
> Do chase the ebbing Neptune and do fly him
> When he comes back; you demi-puppets that
> By moonshine do the green sour ringlets make,
> Whereof the ewe not bites, and you whose pastime
> Is to make midnight mushrooms, that rejoice
> To hear the solemn curfew: by whose aid,
> Weak masters though ye be, I have bedimm'd
> The noontide sun, call'd forth the mutinous winds,
> And 'twixt the green sea and the azur'd vault
> Set roaring war:[1] to the dread rattling thunder

[1] We have here, of course, the kind of break in the structure of the sentence which the grammarians call "anacoluthon."

Have I given fire, and rifted Jove's stout oak
With his own bolt; the strong-bas'd promontory
Have I made shake, and by the spurs pluck'd up
The pine and cedar: graves at my command
Have wak'd their sleepers, op'd, and let 'em forth
By my so potent art. But this rough magic
I here abjure; and, when I have requir'd
Some heavenly music (which even now I do)
To work mine end upon their senses that
This airy charm is for, I'll break my staff,
Bury it certain fathoms in the earth,
And deeper than did ever plummet sound
I'll drown my book.

Effects of
Shake-
speare's
magic.

O man of men, O wondrous prince of the enchanted isle of Britain! How in this age of shame-
faced reticence may we give voice to the pride and
joy and love that your immortalizing work enkindles
in us? You have waked sleepers from their graves,
but they die no more. You cannot lay again the
spirits that by your art you have called from their
confines to enact your fancies. Your staff is broken,
and buried certain fathoms in the earth, whence
none may disinter it; none may wield it again! But
never shall your book be drowned; never shall we
forget the visions you have shown us. The solid-
seeming things of sense pass like the spindrift: but
your words and your fantasies abide for ever. Ages
and generations come and go; monarchs and con-
querors arise and fall: many a regal garland since
your day has crowned the queenly head of sacred
England. And now again, with woe immeasurable,
she strives to uphold the holy heritage that you and

Such things are common in Shakespeare, and the literary
usage of his time was more tolerant of them than that of
to-day. But the best defence of Shakespeare's irregularities
is the fact that his lines were written to be *spoken* rather than
read, and in oratory such a violation of grammar is often a
help, not a hindrance to the conveying of the meaning.

Milton have bequeathed to her, against the fierce
might of envious hatred. The foe is embattled, and
our happier brethren are pouring out their lifeblood
to break his cruel onslaught. England, your England, has called, and from all the ends of the world
her children come, eager to die that Shakespeare's
land may live. O princely soul, we know not what
shall be the issue: but you have given us the victory,
let fall what will. Though the island home we love
were sunk in the oblivious sea, yet should it live in
men's memories and be blessed for ever for your
sake. Your glory has bedimmed the noontide sun,
and the shadows of your fancy are more real than
aught the sun looks down on. Hail, magician, who
may yet allay this last dread tempest! You at least
have conquered the foe with whom we wrestle: and
though he could destroy us it were nothing, for you
shall live serene above the whirlwind of destruction.
Look not down with sorrow from the realm where
your imperial spirit sits ensphered. The tempest
and the agony shall be spent, and earth shall breathe
again in peace and bind up her wounds in hope and
faith. Then shall fraternity, re-born, make us forget the heaviness that's past; and over the grave of
buried hatred shall rise anew the temple of the God
in man. England, that lives by you, through you
shall live for ever; and never shall wane our love
for you, or our pride and joy in you. Hail and
farewell!

In the preceding chapter, the general characteristics of the three plays of Shakespeare's final period
have been outlined. While *The Tempest* shares
these, it yet represents in a sense another new departure. "Tragi-comedy," the type of play in

Tone of the Shake-spearean tragi-come-dies.

which there is tragic action but no death,[2] and in which the ending must be happy, had become fashionable in the opening decade of the seventeenth century, and the success of such works by other writers may account in part for Shakespeare's turning his genius in this direction after his years of tragedy were over, instead of returning to comedy pure and simple. However deeply his inner life may have been perturbed, he always remained a true man of business, and never failed in transmuting the moods of his soul into plays that seemed sure of popularity. But this could not prevent his work from reflecting the feeling that dominated him at the time of doing it. The sunset calm, the peace after storm, which we see in *Cymbeline, The Winter's Tale* and *The Tempest,* is no subjective fancy of the reader's, and it is not accounted for by the nature of the medium in which the poet was working. We have here the record of a spirit which has drunk life to the lees, without dulling the zest of its palate for the various vintages. Such joy and sorrow as Shakespeare's comedies and tragedies communicate cannot have sprung from anything short of the reality of life in him. Plays may be written to order, but not such plays. Passion may be simulated; but the woes of Lear, the agony of Othello, the proud melancholy of Hamlet, could not have been created save by one who had lived through their spiritual trials.

In what sense the plays are autobiographical.

This is not to say, however, that some special personal experience underlies each of the great characters Shakespeare depicts, and every one of the

[2] A rule which, *more suo,* Shakespeare could not refrain from violating! He kills Cloten in *Cymbeline* and Antigonus in *The Winter's Tale.*

great problems about which his tragedies revolve. I do not believe that even a biography which faithfully reported the incidents of every day of his life would give us the genesis of the changes of spiritual tone to which his works bear witness. Only a diary of personal confessions could do this. When a man has the seeing eye, the moral problems of the world haunt his reason and rack his soul, whether he be called upon to bear a load of purely personal grief or not. The religious experience — the discovery within oneself of a thirst for perfection which condemns the outward order of things, and which the world of the senses and the transient can never wholly satisfy — comes to every man who is endowed by nature with the appropriate organ, as it were. Now, this was what Shakespeare underwent. For many years he was tortured by the contrast between what the world gives and what the soul demands: between "what is" and "what ought to be." It is banal to think that such a soul needed to wait for a disappointment in love, or for betrayal by a trusted friend, before he could describe, in imaginary characters, the effects of such experiences. His distinctive power is that of suffering vicariously. It is no petty personal sorrow or joy that he gives voice to, but the joy of all mankind, the burden of the whole world.

There is no truly tragic experience save where a man by sympathy can universalize what he has seen or felt. The child-mind pities the martyr solely for the nails in his hands and feet, and the thorngashes on his brow; but riper experience shows us that these things are as nothing. Christ was *no* sufferer, so far as actual physical pain, or the immediate spiritual assaults of false friendship or evil

Why and how the martyr suffers.

hap, were concerned. Thousands of men have en-
dured bodily agonies, to which his few hours of
crucifixion were child's play; thousands, too, have
suffered from the cruelty of the world, the anguish
of bereavement or betrayal, in ways to which his
short life offers no parallel. Yet men are right in
applying to him the prophetic designation of the
Man of Sorrows. He may truly be said to have
borne the sins and sufferings of the whole world,
because he had the unique gift of penetration and
feeling that forced him to know and bear them.
Because in his own breast he experienced whatever
happened or was done to the least of his brethren,
he was doomed to suffering and destined to joy
beyond what other men could even imagine. Thus
was it also, though in different manner, with Shakespeare.

The joy and sorrow of genius.

The Tempest, then, like the two plays that immediately preceded it, is to be explained as embodying
the mood of a spiritual Ulysses, who has reached
his Ithaca after voyaging through strange seas of
thought alone. Its peace is that deep peace which
comes as a positive experience only to those who
have known the contrast of war. "To have suffered
much," it has been said, "is like knowing many languages: thou hast learned to understand all and to
make thyself intelligible to all." This is a great
saying, but it omits half the truth. To understand
all, we must also have drunk deeply of the joy of
life: and the divinest gift of a saviour of mankind
is that he leaves his *joy* to be fulfilled in us. Shakespeare in these last plays says to us, in his own
fashion, "Be of good cheer: I have overcome the
world." That is why we turn to them with such
deep relief after dwelling long in the land of the

tragedies — a land that seems forsaken of God. It is here that the wheel comes full circle. Comedy and tragedy are broken arcs; here we find the perfect round. It matters not how romantic or fantastic the tale he tells may be; the poet's "criticism of life" is conveyed in its serene maturity only here. The actual incidents of the final trilogy may be remote from prosaic experience, but the music of humanity is brought to full symphonic perfection. Shakespeare gives us at the last

> a doubtful song,
> Its meaning faint or none, but mingled up
> Of all that nests and housekeeps in the heart,
> Or puts out in lone passion toward the vast,
> And cannot choose but go.[3]

The resemblance between *The Tempest* and the *Midsummer Night's Dream,* Shakespeare's only other fairy-tale, great as it appears on the surface, is in reality less striking than the difference. The two plays are separated by an interval of well-nigh twenty years. The earlier one is brimming over with youthful fun. Life in it is one gorgeous lark, and the delirious beauty of the language is an all-satisfying end in itself: it is the poetry of description and immediate sensation, not that of penetrating reflection and deep-delved thought. The spirit of Puck dominates the whole play; and that spirit is summed up in the phrase, "Lord, what fools these mortals be!" The poet has not yet been into the depths. He can laugh at everybody, because he has not detected the tragic shadow that stalks behind everybody. The *Midsummer Night's Dream* is one of the "dreams out of the ivory gate, and visions before midnight." But in the intervening years,

Contrast between The Tempest and the Midsummer Night's Dream.

M. N. D. III ii 115.

[3] W. V. Moody, *The Fire-Bringer,* Act I.

Shakespeare's soul has passed through the midnight hours, and his dreams have taken a more sober colouring. He has seen even the village hinds turn into figures of infinite pathos; and the young men and maidens have grown into the martyrs or murderers of his tragic years. He is no longer external to the joys and sufferings of his dream-children, but has become a part of all that he has met. He has discovered, as we all must do when the laughter of youth is put to silence by the grim earnestness of the spirit's warfare, that

> . . . Life is not as idle ore,
>
> But iron, dug from central gloom,
>   And heated hot with burning fears,
>   And dipped in baths of hissing tears,
> And battered with the shocks of doom
>
> To shape and use.[5]

At the *Midsummer Night's Dream* stage there are no characters to compare with Prospero or Alonzo, or even Gonzalo. The morning-prime of youth is an irresponsible revel, and age is alien, crabbed, and ridiculous. The poet is like his own Prince Hal, spending in fun the days of freedom, but nursing in secret the giant force that the serious tasks of life will call into play in their due hour. The magic is all new and delightful, and there is no thought of burying the staff or drowning the book. It is high spring-tide with Shakespeare and his rout of airy nothings. But now the harvests all are gathered in, and, in *The Tempest* as in *The Winter's Tale,* it is to autumnal revelries that we are bidden. Perdita's festivity is a sheep-shearing, and

[5] Tennyson, *In Memoriam.*

she laments that the flowers o' th' spring are gone. The entertainers of Ferdinand and Miranda are sunburned sicklemen, of August weary. The magician's project gathers to a head; his charms crack not, his spirits obey, and time goes upright with his carriage: but the day is on the sixth hour, at which time his work should cease; for the night cometh. . . .

In view of Shakespeare's lifelong practice, we should hardly expect to find the plot of *The Tempest* entirely original. Several contemporary treatments of the same fictitious situation, moreover, are extant; but whether they were known to Shakespeare we cannot ascertain. There is a German play, the *Comedia von der schönen Sidea* (traced back to 1595, but not printed at the time), in which a noble magician is exiled with an only daughter. He takes refuge in a forest, and is attended by a spirit somewhat akin to Ariel. By spells he brings the son of his enemy as a prisoner into his retreat, and forces him to carry logs, like Ferdinand. Finally the youth marries the daughter, and the parents are reconciled. It is conceivable that this story may have been reported to Shakespeare by some English actors who performed in Nuremberg in 1604 and 1606. The same theme had appeared in Spanish romance, particularly in a collection called "Winter Evenings" *(Noches de Invierno)*, by Antonio de Eslava, whose virtuous magician (a king of Bulgaria) builds for himself and his daughter a submarine retreat. Both these versions and Shakespeare's play may have been founded on an earlier rendering of the legend, now lost.

We are on firmer ground in tracing the source of other elements in *The Tempest*. Current sea-

Sources of The Tempest.

Jacob Ayrer's comedy.

The Spanish novelists.

stories, both written and oral, supplied the poet with numerous hints for the description of his island, and for the character of Caliban. The Bermudas, though they had been sighted and named by the Spaniards nearly a hundred years earlier, were really discovered in 1609, when an English fleet, bound for the new colony of Jamestown in Virginia, was scattered by a storm in those latitudes, and the ship carrying the admiral (Sir George Somers) was wrecked on one of the islands. After a ten months' sojourn there, the crew made their way to Virginia in a couple of boats they had constructed. The return of this expedition, with some of the survivors of the wreck, to England created a good deal of interest and excitement. Several accounts of the shipwreck and the mysterious island were published,—notably one by Sylvester Jourdain, entitled *A Discoverie of the Bermudas, otherwise called The Isle of Divells.* Another was issued by the Council of the Virginia Company, and a third by Sir Thomas Gates. Certain mysterious noises by which the shipwrecked crew were disturbed, and which led them to suppose their island infested with spirits or devils, are obviously responsible for one of the most pleasing peculiarities of Prospero's fairy realm.

Caliban (whose name is merely an anagram of "canibal," the contemporary spelling) is an imaginary composite, drawn from accounts of Virginian, Caribbean and Patagonian savages. His deformed shape (which corresponds to his perverted soul) is a device of Shakespeare's, though travellers' tales were current of whole tribes of distorted dwarfs dwelling in the unexplored forests of South America. His god Setebos is the name given by the Patagonian savages to the object of their primi-

Margin notes:

The discovery of the Bermudas.

Sylvester Jourdain's book.

The American aborigines and Caliban.

Setebos.

tive worship. His ascription of divine attributes to the drunken Stephano [6] is true to many accounts by American explorers of their reception by the natives. When he declares that he will make no more fish-dams for Prospero, he alludes to a very necessary service exacted from the Indians by the early colonists.

One of the most ludicrous discussions in the literature of Shakespearean criticism has raged about the locality of Prospero's island. As though it ever had one! Some have contended that it was an island in the Mediterranean, lying between Italy and Tunis; others have placed the scene in the Bermudas. Both these sets of wiseacres appeal for justification to the speech in which Ariel tells Prospero how he has disposed of the Neapolitan fleet:—

Where was Shakespeare's island?

> Safely in harbour
> Is the king's ship; in the deep nook, where once
> Thou call'dst me up at midnight to fetch dew
> From the still-vex'd Bermoothes, there she's hid:
> The mariners all under hatches stow'd;
> Who, with a charm join'd to their suffer'd labour,
> I have left asleep: and for the rest o' th' fleet,
> Which I dispers'd, they all have met again
> And are upon the Mediterranean flote,
> Bound sadly home for Naples. . . .

I ii 226 ff.

The only clear inference from these lines is that the magic island was neither in the Mediterranean nor among the Bermudas; and there is not a reference throughout the play to show that Shakespeare was thinking exclusively of any one quarter of the globe. To be sure, he embodies features from the descriptions he had read of the Bermudas. But are we to be such hopeless pedants as to tie him

[6] *Not* Trinculo, as Sir Sidney Lee obliviously writes, twice over. (*Life,* ed. 1916, p. 431 *note.*)

down, in such a matter, to any other authority than
his own imagination? His treatment of geography
is always as cavalier as his handling of history and
legend: in this very play it is implied that Prospero
was thrust on board a bark at the gates of Milan.
And what could be wilder than the notion of the
relative positions of Naples and Tunis disclosed by
Antonio? He reminds Sebastian that the present
heir to the Neapolitan throne is Alonzo's daughter
Claribel:—

II i 236 ff.

> She that is queen of Tunis; she that dwells
> *Ten leagues beyond man's life;* she that from Naples
> Can have no note, unless the sun were post—
> The man i' th' moon's too slow—till new-born chins
> Be rough and razorable.

It is wonderful to think that even commentators
on Shakespeare (some of whom are in other respects quite normal) could bear to waste their time
over such a discussion. They remind one of that
worthy man who, when *Gulliver's Travels* was
first published, got out his maps to look for Lilliput.
Prospero's island lies in the same latitude and longi-
tude with Erewhon, Altruria, Utopia and the New
Atlantis.

The para-
phrase upon
Montaigne.

One other literary datum for *The Tempest* is
interesting, because it introduces us to an author
who had a good deal of influence on Shakespeare,
and would have a good deal on us, if we read him
as he deserves: the wise and worldly-wise, the comfortable and sceptical old Michel de Montaigne.
John Florio had translated Montaigne's Essays into
an English almost as racy as the original French,
and his version had been published in 1603. Now,

II i 141 ff.

Gonzalo's account of the ideal commonwealth he
would like to establish in the island is a direct para-

phrase of a passage in Montaigne's essay on Cannibals, as rendered by Florio.

In the character of Caliban, Shakespeare surprises us, even after we have read all his earlier plays, by a new revelation of his power of sympathetic imagination. Prospero's swinish servant is primeval man — man as he was after reason had dawned, but before the moral nature was developed. The subtlety of intuitive perception is shown in Shakespeare's clear discrimination between these two things. There is no evidence but that men in the Stone ages were equal, so far as regards innate mental power, to men of the present day. The unrecorded inventors of the wheel, the uses of fire, and the arts of weaving and spinning; the domesticators of the horse and ox, and the discoverers of agriculture, must have possessed rational powers which, though unenlarged in scope as ours are by the traditions conveyed in speech and writing, were equal to those of the scientific wizards of the modern world. But, with no social heredity, with no experience to reveal to them the necessary solidarity of mankind; with nothing but the law of the jungle, faintly tempered by gregarious instinct, for their standard, their innate mentality must have been self-centred and self-assertive.

Caliban as a study in primitive psychology: mentality without morality.

By what secret augury Shakespeare, centuries before man's animal heredity was known, could divine these things, we cannot say. He listened to the promptings of his genius, and it told him truly. Caliban has a quick and capable mind. Like any modern child, he can overleap, in the few years of his intercourse with the garnered wealth of civilization, the million ages of the growth of the race. He can learn language, and learn it passing well.

Caliban's ability.

He can master all the tasks that his instructor needs
to put upon him. He has no small measure of primitive poetry in his soul: the poetry of vivid sensuous
impressions, of aesthetic response to the charm of
outward things. He shows this when he tries to
allay the superstitious terrors of his two besotted
companions:—

III ii 128 ff.

> The isle is full of noises,
> Sounds and sweet airs, that give delight and hurt not.
> Sometimes a thousand twangling instruments
> Will hum about mine ears, and sometime voices
> That, if I then had wak'd after long sleep,
> Will make me sleep again: and then, in dreaming,
> The clouds methought would open and show riches
> Ready to drop upon me, that, when I wak'd,
> I cried to dream again.

It is he who directs the conspiracy against Prospero, and it is the imbecility of the two civilized
men that deprives it of any chance of success. To
be sure, Prospero's forethought and Ariel's vigi-
lance would have defeated it in any case; but the
mental superiority of Caliban to his European associates is clearly manifested.

*His bestial-
ity.*

His moral or social nature, on the contrary, is
scarcely elevated above that of the gibbering ape.
The frustration of his bestial effort to violate
Miranda, in return for all Prospero's painstaking
kindness, awakens in him no touch of shame or
repentance. When Prospero reminds him that his
present servitude is the punishment for that crime,
he only answers:—

I ii 349 f.

> O ho, O ho! would 't had been done!
> Thou didst prevent me; I had peopled else
> This isle with Calibans.

Of respect for the generous intelligence that has

laboured to instruct him, of gratitude or reverence, he is quite incapable:—

> You taught me language; and my profit on't
> Is, I know how to curse. The red plague rid you
> For learning me your language!

Ibid. 363 f.

Nothing but terror will restrain his malice and make him serviceable:—

> I must obey: his art is of such power
> It would control my dam's god, Setebos,
> And make a vassal of him.

Ibid. 372 f.

When he is alone at his tasks, even this motive is incapable of restraining the fury of his hatred. Though he knows that Prospero's intelligencers will betray him, he still must fall a-cursing to unpack his heart:—

> All the infections that the sun sucks up
> From bogs, fens, flats, on Prosper fall, and make him
> By inch-meal a disease! His spirits hear me,
> And yet I needs must curse. But they'll nor pinch,
> Fright me with urchin-shows, pitch me i' th' mire,
> Nor lead me, like a firebrand, in the dark
> Out of my way, unless he bid 'em; but
> For every trifle are they set upon me;
> Sometime like apes that mow and chatter at me
> And after bite me, then like hedgehogs which
> Lie tumbling in my barefoot way, and mount
> Their pricks at my footfall; sometime am I
> All wound with adders, who with cloven tongues
> Do hiss me into madness.

II ii 1 ff.

Browning, with a sympathetic power scarcely inferior to Shakespeare's own, has imagined this poor, misshapen, brutal thing turning his reason, as primitive man everywhere so pathetically did, to find some answer to the eternal riddle of the universe;—that problem which formulates itself in the mind of the child, and only waxes in its haunting

Browning's study of Caliban's religion.

inscrutableness for the mightiest thinkers of civilized times. Browning's *Caliban upon Setebos* shows us Shakespeare's creature speculating upon the origin of things, and formulating a theology. His god, naturally and inevitably, he makes in his own image. He thinks that Setebos has created him and the other sentient creatures to amuse his godship by torturing them. Caliban knows that he loves to inflict suffering, and he infers that the maker of the sun and the isle (but not the stars!), who dwells in the cold o' the moon, must resemble him in that. Hence he concludes that his wisest course is to hide himself whenever he is happy, and, when he is not in his secret place, to put on a moping and dejected air, by way of deceiving his god.

The nature of Ariel. Ariel, the "ayrie spirit," as the Folio calls him, is best understood by comparing and contrasting his nature with that of Caliban. He is pure disembodied intelligence, the spirit of life untrammelled by matter, capable of applying universally that wonderful, unlearned power over the forces of nature which the instincts of animals apply to specific objects only. Stopford Brooke declared that Ariel is electricity. But, while many of his feats are such as in modern times are achieved by means of that mysterious energy, others of them — such as **His powers.** the reconstruction of the split ship, the power of raising and allaying the storm, the assumption of any form he chooses, and the production of illusions of the eye and ear — go beyond what the skill of electricians can as yet accomplish. The comparison, too, implies on Shakespeare's part a power of specific prevision which it would be fantastic to ascribe to him. Besides, Ariel is a self-conscious personality, with power of thought and will, and even

some power of feeling. He is very like one of the
angels of Jewish or Persian imagination, or the
djinns of the *Arabian Nights*. Time and space are
nothing to him, and the properties of matter oppose
no obstacles to his path. He can be visible and invisible at will; can fly or swim, or dive into the fire.
He can run upon the sharp wind of the north, and
do his master's business in the veins of the earth
when it is "baked with frost." When he is sent to
the haven to fetch the shipmaster and the boatswain,
he can "drink the air before him, and return or ere V i 102.
your pulse twice beat." Yet, withal, his powers are
strangely limited: he cannot oppose the will of Prospero, though his service is reluctantly rendered. He
is the very spirit of nature, serving perforce when
coerced by the mind of man, but longing to regain
its old independence and be a slave no more.

While Ariel's intellectual power is highly devel- Ariel has
oped,— far more than Caliban's, or indeed any no social
nature.
human creature's — yet his moral nature is almost
non-existent. This, however, is not from vicious-
ness, but because he is not human, even in poten-
tiality, and therefore has none of the "consciousness of kind" with other creatures, out of which
fellow-feeling and morality spring. He was too
delicate, indeed, to execute the abhorred commands
of Sycorax. The only feelings he displays, however, are a keen vanity (he always wants his feats
commended), and an impatience of his servitude.
To Prospero, who had rescued him from torment,
he seems to be neither grateful nor ungrateful. He
dreads offending him; not from affection, but because he knows that the magician has power to carry
out his threats. To secure his obedience, Prospero
has to remind him constantly of the torture from

which he had delivered him. Only once does Ariel betray a touch of kindliness; and even then it is but to say that *if* he were human, the sight of the spell-bound prisoners would stir his pity:—

V i 17 ff.

> *Ariel:* . . . Your charm so strongly works 'em
> That if you now beheld them, your affections
> Would become tender.
> *Prospero:* Dost thou think so, spirit?
> *Ariel:* Mine would, sir, were I human.

When the time for parting comes, he is all agog with joy to be going. His exquisite song implies that all his work with Prospero has been irksome, and he is happily rid of it:—

Ibid. 88 ff.

> Where the bee sucks, there suck I:
> In a cowslip's bell I lie;
> There I couch when owls do cry.
> On the bat's back I do fly
> After summer merrily.
> Merrily, merrily shall I live *now,*
> Under the blossom that hangs on the bough.

Prospero says, "Why, that's my dainty Ariel! I shall miss thee"; but Ariel never hints that he will miss Prospero.

Character of his songs.

The songs of Ariel have this marvellous peculiarity, that, while (with the exception of the one just quoted) they do not suggest any feeling on his part, they yet unlock in mortal auditors all the hidden gates of forgotten memories, and transport us through the golden vagueness of childhood's dreams to the inmost realms of faerie. Their words are talismanic, lifting us out of ourselves into unity and sympathy with all things. When Ariel announces the death of Alonzo to Ferdinand, the witchery of the language is simply indescribable:—

I ii 395 ff.

> Full fathom five thy father lies;
> Of his bones are corals made;

Those are pearls that were his eyes:
   Nothing of him that doth fade
But doth suffer a sea-change
Into something rich and strange.
Sea-nymphs hourly ring his knell. . . .

To analyze the nature of this spell is impossible. We can but say with Ferdinand, "This is no mortal business, nor no sound that the earth owes."

Prospero figures in the story so exclusively as a benignant providence to all concerned that we find it hard to think of him as a sinner, undergoing punishment for a heavy fault. Yet such he is. He plots for the happiness of Miranda and Ferdinand; he forgives Alonzo and the unnatural brother who has robbed him of his dukedom; he compels Antonio and Sebastian to repentance and amendment of life. But all this is now possible only because he has done his penance and been absolved from his sin. That sin was the very offence of Lear: the shirking of his responsibilities, and the putting first of his own satisfactions in life. Being the Duke of Milan and a prince of power, his duty was to administer the affairs of his state, not to neglect them and absorb himself in the luxury of study. The guilt of the usurper Antonio, to be sure, is to the full as great as it would have been if Prospero had punctiliously discharged all his responsibilities; but Prospero's neglect of them makes the usurpation, so far as he is concerned, a just infliction. All this, however, he has atoned for by his twelve years' exile with the little daughter, whose love and whose needs have kept alive the humanity in him, and supplied a motive for his working, when the fair hour comes, for the confusion of his enemies and the regaining of his heritage.

The sin and repentance of Prospero.

Effects of
his exile:
(1) his mag-
ical powers
developed;

The years of exile, moreover, owing to the generosity of Gonzalo in furnishing him with his beloved
books, have given him the opportunity to develop
his studies in occult lore to the stage of complete
mastery. Prospero is a man of science, as his times
understood that term. The conception our mediæval forefathers had of a man of science was that
of one who had acquired magical power over the
airy spirits, and who (without himself understanding or being able directly to control the laws and
forces of nature) could gain his ends by extorting
miraculous aid from the spirits. Such was the art
supposed to have been mastered, or purchased from
the devil with their souls, by men like Roger Bacon,
Paracelsus, and Doctor Faustus. And so we find
that Prospero can now cast his spells upon earth
and sky and sea, as well as upon men. The spirits
will come from the vasty deep when he does call
for them. He can control the winds, and have tem-
pests come and go at his bidding. He can bedim
the noontide sun, set tables in the wilderness, and
even, as he alleges, raise the dead. Nay, he can
command the presence of the very gods, and con-
strain them to bestow their benison upon Ferdinand
and Miranda at their troth-plighting.

(2) his moral
nature per-
fected.

But it is not for this that we admire Prospero.
Power, even though it were infinite, would constitute no claim upon our respect unless it were allied
with the will to serve. The personal devil of the old
theology was believed to be possessed of power only
less than God's;—power to which human imagination could set no bounds;—yet nobody ever thought
him on that account worthy of reverence. What is
worshipped in God is not omnipotence but goodness.
Prospero wins our love and admiration because in

his twelve years' solitude he has learned nobler lessons than those of the art that secures him the services of Ariel. He has learned to forgive them that trespass against him. The king's ship being in his hands, he could exact a full revenge for the injuries done him by Antonio and Alonzo. But he now knows that " even-handed justice commends the ingredients of the poisoned chalice to our own lips." Revenge only begets revenge; hatred perpetuates hatred. Prospero therefore shows his magnanimity by overlooking the offences committed against him, and rewards his enemies by awakening in them the consciences they have crushed : —

> Though with their high wrongs I am struck to the V i 25 ff.
>   quick,
> Yet with my nobler reason 'gainst my fury
> Do I take part: the rarer action is
> In virtue than in vengeance: they being penitent,
> The sole drift of my purpose doth extend
> Not a frown further. Go release them, Ariel:
> My charms I'll break, their senses I'll restore,
> And they shall be themselves.

His treatment of these wrongdoers makes him more honourable in our eyes than all his magic lore. He has won our love by his gentle tutoring of Miranda; but she was his daughter, and natural affection would lead him to care for her to the utmost of his power. We pardon his severity to Ferdinand, because we realize its purpose, and know that it is the mask of benignity; yet Ferdinand is to be his son-in-law and to make his child a queen, so that here too there is a possibility of self-interested motive. But when he forgives the unforgivable sin of his brother and Alonzo, we are sure that the divinity in man is authentically manifested. One can imagine that if

His forgiveness of his enemies.

the dream of a life after death comes true (and why may it not?), the awakening to reality may be such an experience as that of Alonzo and his company, when, after all their spellbound wanderings, they come at last into the visible presence of the merciful magician who has planned every step of their devious way, though he has remained unseen.

Miranda, the last of Shakespeare's heroines, is the crown and glory of them all. She is the fifth essence of the virtue of womanhood, the rich distilled perfume of outward loveliness and inward nobility, compacted of every creature's best. Mrs. Jameson has well said that

> We might have deemed it impossible to go beyond Viola, Perdita, and Ophelia as pictures of feminine beauty, to exceed the one in tender delicacy, the other in ideal grace, and the last in simplicity, if Shakespeare had not done this; and he alone could have done it. Had he never created a Miranda, we should never have been made to feel how completely the purely natural and the purely ideal can blend into each other.

But, in addition to those specifically womanly virtues which Mrs. Jameson ascribes to her, Miranda has qualities which are neither womanly nor manly, but super-sexual, and simply human: the chastity of honour, the "very virtue of compassion," gratitude and tender loyalty, humility and dignity in equal balance. Her first speech is an appeal to her father for mercy upon those in the wrecked ship. When Prospero tells her the story of his life, her one thought is to lament the burden that she must have been to him in their "sea-sorrow." In her spontaneous love and sympathy for Ferdinand, when he is bearing the yoke of Prospero's assumed displeasure, she does not abate a jot of her loyalty to her father.

Shakespeare has most exquisitely realized the significance of the fact that his heroine has seen no men but her father and the brutish Caliban, and that she remembers no woman's face, "save from my glass mine own." When she first sees the youthful and princely Ferdinand, her love goes out to him wholeheartedly and unaffectedly, with no coy posing to enhance her price. Prospero suggests to her that the young man is a tolerable sample of humankind: — The effects of her isolation.

> But he's something stain'd
> With grief that's beauty's canker, thou mightst call him
> A goodly person.

I ii 412 f.

But she, to whom humankind is an almost unknown world, is dissatisfied with so grudging a commendation: —

> I might call him
> A thing divine; for nothing natural
> I ever saw so noble.

Ibid. 415 f.

The courtship of Ferdinand and Miranda, the "fair encounter of two most rare affections," is characterized, over and above its alluring charm and naturalness, by a certain austerity of holiness, such as might have been imagined in the wooing of unfallen man and woman in paradise.

But, to my mind, the loveliest incident in the play is not this. It is the observation that Miranda makes when, in the last act, Prospero draws aside the curtain, revealing her and Ferdinand to the Neapolitan company, and showing her, for the first time in her life, a group of human beings. Hereupon she exclaims : —

V i 181 f.

O wonder!
How many goodly creatures are there here!
How beauteous mankind is! O brave new world,
That has such people in't!

Shake-
speare's
victorious
humanism.

That " How beauteous mankind is!" exposes the very secret of Shakespeare's triumph over the deadening influences of ordinary life. He had lived forty-seven years; he had known joy and sorrow, failure, the weariness of struggle and the disillusionment of success. He had lived amid the swarming egoisms of a great city, and laboured, with inconceivable strenuousness, in a profession that was scorned by the great and powerful. With the natural modesty of true genius, he had never dreamed of his own immeasurable superiority to the colleagues and rivals of his craft. He had known envy and self-scorn; he was familiar with the feelings analyzed in his own sonnet : —

Sonnet xxix.

When, in disgrace with fortune and men's eyes,
I all alone beweep my outcast state,
And trouble deaf heaven with my bootless cries,
And look upon myself and curse my fate,
Wishing me like to one more rich in hope,
Featur'd like him, like him with friends possess'd,
Desiring this man's art, and that man's scope,
With what I most enjoy contented least;
.   .   .   in these thoughts myself almost despising.   .   .   .

Yet, at the end of his years of creative work, he still could see the ever-present fact, of which we deny the existence because we have wilfully closed our eyes to it: the fact of the enthralling beauty of humanity and the world given to it to subdue. He retained the freshness and spontaneity of a little child; and therefore to him was it given to see the mystery of the kingdom of God.

The highest praise we can give to Ferdinand is to declare him not unworthy of the matchless maiden whose affection he has won. He is brave, chivalrous and loyal; and he has the quality, still rarer in the scion of a kingly house, that he is teachable. His acceptance of the task of carrying the logs is at once a splendid discipline for one whose soul was in danger from his having been born an idol, and a proof that his natural humility and common sense had enabled him to escape that danger. The lesson in obedience will teach him how to rule. *Ferdinand.*

Of the minor characters in *The Tempest,* Alonzo is the most pathetic figure, by reason of his supposed bereavement, and the contrast between his present predicament and his accustomed state. He does not know that his loss is unreal, and that the suffering laid upon him is for the purgation of his sin-stained soul. His trusty counsellor Gonzalo seeks to comfort him with diversions which are a trifle tedious and prosy; and of this Shakespeare makes a secondary use to reveal the infamous characters of Antonio and Sebastian, who mock the kindly old man at every word. The bitterness of their scorn is a sure sign of depravity: only to wickedness is anything human unqualifiedly contemptible. *Alonzo.* *Gonzalo.* *Sebastian and Antonio.*

The conspiracy of Antonio and Sebastian against Alonzo has its comic counterpart in that of Caliban and his two vinous associates against Prospero. Trinculo and Stephano have no necessary share in the working out of the main plot; yet who could wish them absent? The parallelism of their foolish wickedness with the wicked folly of the two princes *The comic conspiracy: Trinculo and Stephano.*

is one more instance of Shakespeare's constructive skill, his power of revolving wheels within wheels.

The Boat-swain.

Among the minor characters, too, that of the Boatswain is noteworthy, especially for his finely inspired rebuke to Gonzalo during the tumult of the storm: "What care these roarers for the name of king?"—a sentiment that may be commended to those stern democrats who are fond of assuring us that Shakespeare was a sycophantic snob, who worshipped monarchs and pandered to them.

The interlude.

The masque in Act IV, as we have seen, was chaffed by Jonson — not necessarily in an unfriendly spirit. It is perfectly consonant with the romantic and magical nature of the play, and the speeches of Iris and Ceres are in the richest vein of Shakespeare's descriptive nature-poetry. But, even if the scene were not beautiful in itself, anything could have been pardoned that led up to and occasioned that most majestic speech of apology and explanation which Prospero makes to Ferdinand:—

IV i 146 ff.

> You do look, my son, in a mov'd sort,
> As if you were dismay'd: be cheerful, sir.
> Our revels now are ended. These our actors,
> As I foretold you, were all spirits, and
> Are melted into air, into thin air;
> And, like the baseless fabric of this vision,
> The cloud-capp'd towers, the gorgeous palaces,
> The solemn temples, the great globe itself,
> Yea, all which it inherit, shall dissolve,
> And, like this insubstantial pageant faded,
> Leave not a rack behind. We are such stuff
> As dreams are made on, and our little life
> Is rounded with a sleep. . . .

What godlike opulence is this, which can scatter such largesse with a careless hand! And how we are dwarfed and beggared beside it!

The gigantic energy, which in an earlier chapter we noted as the distinguishing characteristic of the Elizabethan age, manifested surprisingly in Marlowe and uniquely in Shakespeare, is again forced upon our attention by the fact that Shakespeare's last play creates a new poetic genus. There has been no successor to *The Tempest* that can be mentioned in the same breath with it. The progress of poesy has produced other new genera, but none that appeals so universally as Shakespeare's native woodnotes.

The last play a new type.

Science has advanced with mammoth strides. The veils that hid from him and his contemporaries the surface of the earth and the dark backward and abysm of time have been torn aside. The globe has been explored from pole to pole, and the rocks beneath our feet have yielded up their ancient secrets. We peer down vistas of antiquity that he could not have dreamed of, and the world that our instruments measure is vaster beyond imagination than the one that was known to his time. Yet from the colossal realities of our experience we cannot extract such emotions of grandeur and mystery as his power of perfect sympathy and stately speech enabled him to distil from his little world. Nor shall our science ever enable us to search more deeply into the human heart than his inspired vision penetrated effortlessly. His revels are not ended; and his dream-children are more secure of immortality than the real men and women of the fleeting generations, each of which in its day learns to love them and him with a love that shall not die.

CHAPTER X

THE SONNETS: FUNDAMENTAL IDEAS IN SHAKESPEARE

Attempts to portray the personality and beliefs of Shakespeare.

SHAKESPEARE is the most elusive of all men. If any proof of this be required, apart from his works themselves, it is given in the multiplicity of the constructions placed by his admirers upon them. Some of the interpreters, mistaking the perfection of dramatic art for the sincerity of personal confession, have imagined it possible to find in his writings (particularly in the Sonnets) an extensive autobiographical revelation; others, from the plays, have ventured to tell the world what were Shakespeare's religious, philosophical and political opinions.

Emerson thought this easy;

Emerson is quite confident that " Shakespeare is the only biographer of Shakespeare," though he prudently hastens to add that " even he can tell nothing, except to the Shakespeare in us; that is, to our most apprehensive and sympathetic hour." In subsequent comments, Emerson lets us see that he had used the word "biographer" in a Pickwickian sense. What he meant was not that Shakespeare's life-story is told in his works, but only that these reveal the poet's convictions as to what is right and wrong, true and false, beautiful and ugly, in character and conduct: which need not be disputed, though we must resist the temptation to find Shakespeare's personal expression only in what *we* most like in the plays.

[270]

Matthew Arnold, placing himself at the opposite extreme, pronounces Shakespeare inscrutable:— Arnold de-clares it impossible.

> Others abide our question; thou art free:
>   We ask and ask, thou smilest and art still,
>   Out-topping knowledge. . . .

>   . . . Thou, who didst the stars and sunbeams know,
>   Self-school'd, self-scann'd, self-honour'd, self-secure,
> Didst walk on earth unguessed at.

According to Arnold, this spiritual *incognito* was the necessary condition of Shakespeare's becoming the interpreter and spokesman of all the joys and sorrows of humanity.

The Sonnets are the only portion of Shakespeare's writings in which we get even the appearance of direct personal disclosures. At first glance, we seem to have in them the story of an intense friendship, marred by betrayal but subsequently restored; and a record of love, made tragic by the perfidy of the beloved, who guiltily seduces the man friend of the preceding poems. We have glimpses of a philosophy, according to which all that happens in the world is but the endless and inevitable repetition of what has happened before. The air of deep melancholy in these poetic epistles conspires with their seeming intimacy of self-revelation to produce the impression of unaffected sincerity. The delusive semblance of self-revelation in the Sonnets.

Taking it for granted that the Sonnets actually are what they thus seem to be, many critics have erected romantic structures of interpretation upon them. Shakespeare is assumed to be veraciously recording his own joys and sorrows, his own sin, suffering and repentance. We are told that he is addressing the Earl of Pembroke, as his adoring intimate. Some have even perpetrated the extrava- Hasty con-clusions from this.

The Dark
Lady.

gance of construing the Sonnets as evidence of a
scandalous sexual connection between the writer and
his man friend — an accusation for which no jot or
tittle of evidence is anywhere to be found. The "Dark
Lady" addressed in a number of the poems has been
identified with a certain Mary Fitton, who is alleged to have been by turns the mistress both of
Shakespeare and of Pembroke. Others, on the
basis of reckless posthumous gossip, have identified
her with the wife of a country innkeeper, the mother
of Shakespeare's godson, Sir William D'Avenant.[1]

Evidence against the autobiographical interpretation.

In building up such speculations on the meaning of
the Sonnets, the writers forget that they are dealing with the greatest of *dramatists:* that is, with
the man who had the most consummate skill in
placing himself in imaginary positions, submerging
his own identity in that of other persons, and expressing feelings that had been engendered in his
heart quite otherwise than by immediate experience.

The sonnet-teering craze of the 1590's.

They also forget, or remain unaware, that during the
last decade of the sixteenth century sonnetteering
was a literary craze in England, and that many se-
quences of such poems were written, almost all of
them revolving around themes identical with those
treated in the Sonnets of Shakespeare. The evidence on this point has been amassed with crushing
completeness by Sir Sidney Lee, who, to my mind,
has amply proved his contention that there is no
reason to suppose the friend and lover of the Sonnets a real person identical with Shakespeare, or the
experiences they relate genuine. The "I" of the

Lee, chaps. x-xii and Appendices v-ix.

[1] The gossip is to the effect that D'Avenant, when a boy,
spoke of Shakespeare as his godfather, and was wittily told
not to "take the name of God in vain." But there is no
evidence for the implied charge against Shakespeare.

Sonnets may well be as purely a dramatic phantom as Romeo or Valentine, or any other of the characters in the plays.

Against the identification of the man friend of the Sonnets with the Earl of Pembroke there are two conclusive objections. The one is that Shakespeare never had anything to do with that nobleman; and the other is that the "Mr. W. H." to whom the Sonnets were dedicated *(not* by Shakespeare, but by the piratical editor "T. T.," Thomas Thorpe) cannot by any possibility have been the Earl of Pembroke, or any other earl. Such a man would naturally and necessarily have been accorded his full ceremonious designations — as, indeed, Pembroke was, by this very Thomas Thorpe, in a volume dedicated to him a few years later; and again by Heminge and Condell in the Folio. If he had not been, the dedicator would have suffered a Star Chamber prosecution for an insult to the orders of nobility.

" Mr. W. H." cannot have been Pembroke,

With the refutation of the Pembroke theory, the Mary Fitton legend, which depended upon it, falls also to the ground. There is no evidence that Shakespeare ever spoke to that lady in his life. Apart from this slight difficulty, the Fitton theory is open to the further objection that Mary was not a dark lady at all, but is proved by authentic portraits to have been fair. It is perfectly possible that the woman subject of the Sonnets may have been a purely fictitious personage.

nor the Dark Lady Mary Fitton,

who was fair.

There is only one man to whom Shakespeare's flattering protestations of friendship and appeals for continued favour apply in a fashion consistent with what is known from other sources: namely, Henry Wriothesly, the young Earl of Southampton, to whom the poet in his own name dedicated *Venus*

Shakespeare's friendship for his patron, Southampton.

and Adonis and *Lucrece.* In the letter prefixed to the *Lucrece,* Shakespeare, putting into prose a sentiment that to modern ears sounds almost as unrestrained as the poetical avowals of devotion in the Sonnets, begins by declaring, "The *love* I dedicate to your Lordship is without end." The seeming intensity of such expressions, however, is diminished when we remember that in the Elizabethan period the word "love" was currently used as a mere synonym for friendship or liking, and that all authors used similar extravagant language in addressing their patrons.

The most crucial illustration of this state of things is found in the way in which men were wont to apostrophize Queen Elizabeth, with all the seeming ardour of lovers for their mistresses. Many of the dedications of books and poems to Elizabeth, after she was sixty years old, would make it seem that she was still a paragon of personal beauty, and the "soul's idol" of her implorers. Even such first-rank men as Spenser and Sir Walter Raleigh were guilty of absurdities of this kind.

The opening sequence of Shakespeare's Sonnets consists of appeals to a beautiful young man to marry and perpetuate his name and qualities in offspring. Southampton at the time was young, unmarried, and conspicuously handsome, and was the only male representative of his line. That he knew Shakespeare and befriended him is a well-established fact. But even this plea for posterity was one of the stock themes of the sonnetteers, several of whom confess unequivocally that the passions and affections that informed their verses were all feigned.

Almost every point in the Sonnets,— their themes, their metaphors, their violences of flattery and de-

nunciation,— can be demonstrated to be the stock-in-
trade shared in common at the time among a host of
English writers, who were consciously imitating the
poets of France and Italy, from Petrarch down to
the third quarter of the sixteenth century. It is
amazing to find how many of Shakespeare's
thoughts, and even his words, in these poems are but
repetitions (however enhanced in beauty or splendour) of what others had thought and said. The
philosophy is an echo from Ovid, Shakespeare's lifelong favourite. The pretence that the sonnetteer is
old, and the man he addresses youthful, is common
form with most of the exploiters of the prevailing
fashion; we find it adopted by one writer at the mature age of twenty. So, too, is the promise of "immortality" through the poems to their subject. Such
expressions as—

> Not marble nor the gilded monuments   Son. lv.
> Of princes shall outlive this powerful rhyme,

and

> Thou in this shalt find thy monument   Son. cvii.
> When tyrants' crests and tombs of brass are spent,

— which Mr. Bernard Shaw construes as proof that
Shakespeare's modesty was of the same novel variety
as his own, prove nothing but that Shakespeare was
following the fashion with almost slavish consistency. He was, in fact, avowedly "keeping invention
in a noted weed" when he used such phrases; and
that his modesty was not of the peculiar Shavian
cast is shown where, departing from the fashion, he
flatly contradicts his claim of immortality, and de-
preciates his own work, in words which, being less
conventional, have less the air of unreality:—

> If thou survive my well contented day,   Son. xxxii.
> When that churl Death my bones with dust shall cover,

And shalt by fortune once more re-survey
　　These poor rude lines of thy deceasèd lover,
Compare them with *the bettering of the time;*
　　And, though they be *outstripp'd by every pen,*
Reserve them for my love, not for their rhyme,
　　Exceeded by the height of happier men.
Oh, then vouchsafe me but this loving thought:
　" Had my friend's Muse grown with this growing age,
A dearer birth than this his love had brought,
　　To march in ranks of better equipage:
　　　　But since he died and poets better prove,
　　　　Theirs for their style I'll read, his for his love."

Shake-
speare did
not arrange
the Sonnets
in the order
in which we
have them,
A further point to be remembered in connection with the Sonnets is that there is no reason for supposing them to have been arranged by Shakespeare in the order in which Thorpe printed them. We cannot discover from internal evidence how many different people they were addressed to, and there is no external evidence on the subject.[2] Instead of one friend and one "mistress," they may have been addressed to half a dozen men and as many women. Several of them, in all probability, were written singly. The glorious Sonnet cvii, which there is strong reason for believing the latest of them all, was almost certainly written by itself. It congratulates the Earl of Southampton on his release from prison, and refers unmistakably to the death of Queen Elizabeth and the accession of King James in 1603:—

Not mine own fears, nor the prophetic soul
　　Of the wide world dreaming on things to come,
Can yet the lease of my true love control,
　　Suppos'd as forfeit to a confin'd doom.
The mortal moon [3] hath her eclipse endur'd,

　[2] Unless, indeed, we take Meres's phrase, "sonnets among his private *friends*," to imply that they were addressed to a number of people; but this would be to overstrain the words.

　[3] *I. e.*, Queen Elizabeth, perpetually compared to "chaste Luna" by contemporary poets.

And the sad augurs mock their own presage; [4]
Incertainties now crown themselves assur'd,
    And peace proclaims olives of endless age.
Now with the drops of this most balmy time
    My love looks fresh,[5] and Death to me subscribes,
Since, spite of him, I'll live in this poor rhyme,
    When he insults o'er dull and speechless tribes.

Most of these 154 Sonnets were probably composed not later than 1594. They were circulated in MS. among Shakespeare's personal friends, in accord with what we know to have been the fashion of the time; for this we have the explicit testimony of Meres in 1598. The fact that they were published with a dedication not from the author's hand is proof positive that he had nothing to do with their appearance in printed form. *neither did he publish them.* The publication (in 1609), like that of the quarto editions of the plays, was a speculation on the part of the "stationer" (in this case Thomas Thorpe), who, by fair means or foul, had become possessed of a MS. copy. Under these circumstances, and in view of the vagueness and generality of most of their expressions, it is fantastic to attempt to construct from them a record of actual experience of friendship, betrayal, guilty love and repentance on the part of Shakespeare.

On the other hand, it would be equal folly to affirm positively that there is nothing at all reminiscent of personal experiences in the Sonnets. I am not seeking to maintain that Shakespeare was a saint. *Possible touches of autobiography.* There is a definite likelihood that the "W. S." of Willobie's *Avisa* was Shakespeare; and the thesis of that poem *Willobie and "W. S."*

---

[4] King James succeeded peacefully and with unanimous acceptance, whereas a revolution had been foreboded.

[5] Southampton had been imprisoned for life, owing to his participation in the Earl of Essex's rebellion in 1601, but was released after two years, by one of the first acts of James as King of England.

is that "W. S.," having himself vainly sought to conquer the stubborn virtue of "Avisa," afterwards egged his friend Willobie on to make the like attempt, in order that he might laugh at his failure. If this is a genuine episode of Shakespeare's life, however, it has none of the tragedy suggested by the sonnets addressed to the Dark Lady. We must remember that the poet, after some years of married life, was condemned to a decade of grass-widowerhood in London. He belonged to a profession which, even in that none too precise age, was considered exceptionally lax; and not without reason. The fate of Greene and Marlowe and the anecdotes of Peele are there to remind us of the kind of society he shared, and the temptations to which he must have been subjected.

But, whatever may have been his actual trips in life, we have no warrant for drawing up an indictment against him on the strength of histrionic utterances, made in confessed imitation of a literary fashion, and almost certainly understood, by those for whom they were written, to deal with imaginary incidents.

Neither a rounded system of philosophy nor a definite body of theological teaching is reasonably to be looked for in the work of a creative poet. Such men as Milton, Wordsworth, Browning and Tennyson are to some extent exceptions to this rule, but those who know them most intimately are least ready to offer us with confidence, from their poems, the organic formulation of their thinking. It is certain that Milton's personal beliefs did not correspond exactly with the theology of *Paradise Lost*. If it be true that even epic and lyric poets cannot give full

Marginal notes:

Shakespeare's life and professional associates.

Poetry (especially dramatic) not a suitable vehicle for systems of philosophy or theology.

and satisfactory expression in song to their thought on the fundamental issues of life and destiny, still more difficult is it for such doctrine to be incorporated in systematic fashion in the work of the dramatic poet. The very nature of his medium forbids it. The necessity for dialogue to be in character, and to explain and justify action; and the requirement that the ideas expressed must be those which the persons described may be supposed to have entertained, make it impossible for a play to serve as the vehicle for the author's convictions. However emphatically he may speak, we cannot easily determine when he is speaking for himself as well as for his characters. The less the author's private views are obtruded through the personages of a play, the better play is it likely to be; and *vice versâ*.

Didacticism has, indeed, been carried to such lengths as are possible, and to some that are not, in many modern plays, notably those of Ibsen and Mr. Bernard Shaw; yet even here the philosophy and religion of the authors are not clearly set forth. One cannot learn from the *Doll's House,* for example, how Ibsen thought the relations of the married should be modified, or from the *Enemy of the People* what he considered the real duty of a man in Dr. Stockmann's position. Mr. Shaw's failure to express his gospel through his plays is so complete that he has to write enormous prefaces, often much longer than the plays themselves, to tell us what he intends them to mean; and, even so, he frequently fails to make himself understood. *Failure of Ibsen and Shaw to preach through plays.*

The difficulty of determining the opinions of a dramatic author, when we have no other of his writings with which to compare the views expressed by his characters, is brought vividly home to us by *Variety of guesses at Shakespeare's religion.*

the variety of theories which have been promulgated with regard to Shakespeare's religion. One book has been written to prove that he was a Papist; another that he was a Protestant; a third, that he was a Puritan,—or at least of Puritan family; a fourth, that he was an atheist. Have we not here a sufficient caution against joining in the wild-goose-chase by which men have sought to decide when the dramatist is expressing his own convictions and when not? Any such theory can at best be held tentatively, and no dogmatic affirmation is tolerable. We must guide ourselves not by a phrase here and there, but by the general trend of the plays. We must seek to elicit the broad conception of man and the universe which is indicated by a consideration of all of them together. One is almost tempted to declare that the four volumes which claim Shakespeare as an adherent of four different religious schools succeed collectively in proving that he belonged to none of those schools. But this again would be an unwarrantable stretch of inference.

Sectarianism excluded by his universal sympathy. The improbability, however, of his having been a dogmatic upholder of any special set of theological or anti-theological beliefs is strongly suggested by the fact that he was indubitably one of the greatest of humanists. I use this term not to denote any particular philosophic or theological theory, but to indicate that capacity for delighted interest in and sympathetic self-identification with all things human which is vouched for by his dramatic achievement. He does not tell us that nothing human is alien to him, but he proves it by his creations. He has the inner secret of every creature he portrays; he lives in each of them successively. Men and women, old and young, kings and queens, soldiers, statesmen, ecclesiastics, royalists and republicans, Alsatian sharpers and bucolic buffoons, — all alike are brought to life before us, in their habits as they lived, with appropriate thought and characteristic speech, limned as they would have been proud to depict themselves. His kings are more majestic than their historic prototypes; his cockney tavern-haunters are as funny as any of the wonderful people of Dickens, and more lifelike. This is why we call him a humanist. The term in his case is not an intellectual pigeon-hole, but a psychological label.

As regards ultimate problems, theological or philosophical, Shakespeare's attitude would seem to have been permanently governed by a reverent awareness of the limitations of human knowledge, both actual and possible. I do not mean that he was irreligious or anti-religious; on the contrary, this non-dogmatic attitude in him, as in many other great men, was a profoundly religious one. There has been far too much talking about God as though He were (to use Matthew Arnold's expression) a man in the next street; and stories of miraculous interventions on behalf of particular persons or causes are commonly less an expression of faith than of egoism on the part of those who tell them. *His contempt for religious cocksureness.*

Now, Shakespeare cannot for a moment be declared a disbeliever in the possibility or the occurrence of miracles; but again and again in his plays he seizes opportunities to rebuke the towering presumption of persons who asserted that the order of nature had been interrupted for their behoof. One or two such passages I have found occasion to cite in preceding chapters. The remarks of Julius Caesar, concerning the prodigious portents which disturbed his wife and others, are further illustra- *His references to miracles and portents.*

tions of this recurrent thought. In the First Part of *King Henry IV,* the merciless chaffing by Hotspur of the braggart Glendower is yet another case in point.[6] We have seen, too, how invariably Shakespeare treats supernormal or supernatural manifestations as mere incidental or accidental parallels to a moral drama which is begun, continued and ended wholly within the souls of men and women.

Problem of his attitude regarding immortality. The deliverances of his characters on the question of human immortality are so various that, here again, we may not confidently dogmatize as to his own beliefs. The Ghost of Hamlet's father describes himself as enduring purgatorial punishment, in terms of the orthodox theological doctrine; yet Hamlet, later on, soliloquizes about the after-life in a decidedly agnostic fashion. At the close of the play, again, we find Hamlet with his dying breath **Hamlet's dying words.** declaring, " The rest is silence." This would not be worthy of remark, were it not that in the first quarto edition of the tragedy, instead of these words, we have, " Heaven receive my soul." The imperfections of that version, however, are so glaring that we may not confidently conclude this to have been the form in which Shakespeare originally penned the **Prospero's agnosticism.** line. On the other hand, it would be difficult to over-stress the significance of such a sentence as that oft-quoted one of Prospero, the character who seems most of all to resemble Shakespeare, in his apology to Ferdinand after the disappearance of the vision: —

> We are such stuff
> As dreams are made on, and our little life
> Is rounded with a sleep.

[6] On this subject, cp. the author's *Religion of Experience,* pp. 103-4. (New York: Macmillans, 1916.)

The man to whom such thoughts were familiar companions must at least have been one who did his thinking for himself, and did it with much greater independence of traditional teaching than was general in his day.

As to Shakespearean deliverances on the subjects of politics and national patriotism, the common opinion (that the poet was a snobbish and sycophantic king-worshipper) would seem to be somewhat undiscriminating. A full analysis of his historical plays, of the characters of his kings, and of his attitude towards them, would be needed before one could pronounce on the subject with anything like confidence; and such a study I am at present unable to undertake, though I am not without hope of finding opportunity for it in a future volume. Here it may be remarked that a man who had such unparalleled insight as Shakespeare into human nature, cannot conceivably have been imposed upon by titles and trappings after the fashion of the average superstitious monarchist. He often uses the conventional language of his time, to be sure; and, as a man of business, he was not above resorting upon occasion to the flattery which was necessary in his day as a means to business success, and was used by the greatest of his contemporaries. Yet the irony which the world's fopperies and struttings awaken in every man of keen insight and sense of humour is, as we have seen, by no means absent from him. The lesson of *Lear* was a fairly daring one for any man to read to the monarchs of that age.

Shakespeare's alleged sycophancy to kings.

Shakespeare has respect for greatness only when the greatness is real and intrinsic. He can revere a high office without revering the man who holds it. It is into the mouth of a murderous and incestuous usurper that, with poignant irony, he puts the familiar phrase about the divinity that doth hedge a king. He is an aristocrat, not in the conventional but in the etymological sense: a believer in the best, and in government by the best. His contempt for the "base mob," of which we are told so much, is a contempt for the baseness rather than for the mob. He can admire a great scoundrel — but for his greatness, and not for his villainy: as we see in the cases of Richard III, Iago and Macbeth.

His English patriotism.

His nationalism is in part a just pride in the great achievements of his countrymen, in part also the spontaneous patriotism which comes by nature, and is independent of the actual deserts of one's motherland — though to be forfeited, like loyalty to a parent, by grave misdoings on the part of kings or governors. It is, further, a romantic and imaginative delight in the picturesque adventures of such a monarch as Henry V. That Shakespeare could discriminate in this matter, too, is shown by the admirable study of the patriot Faulconbridge in *King John,* and by the lines in *King Richard II* with which John of Gaunt describes

II i 40 ff.

> This royal throne of kings, this scepter'd isle,
> This earth of majesty, this seat of Mars,
> This other Eden, demi-paradise,
> This fortress built by Nature for herself
> Against infection and the hand of war,
> This happy breed of men, this little world,
> This precious stone set in the silver sea, . . .
> This blessed plot, this earth, this realm, this
>   England. . . .

No man of British birth or blood can read unmoved that stirring paean. Yet, before it concludes, it becomes a lacerating indictment of the shame and disgrace which the irresponsible folly of the King was entailing upon the beloved land; and thereby it is redeemed from being mere idolatry.

The most startling comment that can be made upon the Elizabethan period in England is that it received Shakespeare without surprise. To us, after three hundred years of familiarity, he still comes as a perpetual revelation and rebuke, turning our complacent dreams of progress into misgivings lest we be backward-moving and degenerate. Already before the end of the seventeenth century, Dryden, looking back not only to Shakespeare, but to all the men eminent in letters and in active life who flourished before the Civil War and the days of Cromwell, exclaimed,— *Contrast between Shakespeare's age and ours.*

Dryden's "Epistle to Congreve," 1694.

Theirs was the giant race before the Flood!

And so indeed it still seems to us, whether we look solely to the work of Shakespeare, or whether we regard the entire galaxy of stars of the first magnitude whose orbits centred in the throne of the Tudors. These dwellers in a little world uttered thoughts beyond the reaches of our souls, in a speech too majestic for our harassed and utilitarian times. The scope, the dignity, the plasticity of their tongue wrought masterpieces too perfect for our imitation. More and Spenser, Raleigh and Hooker and Bacon, each in his own way stirs us with the suggestion of a mightier breed than that which lives around us.

The Book of Common Prayer is a specimen of the hurried work which Cranmer and his fellows could rush together to meet an exigency. The heavenly music of its diction, the large humanity of its outlook, and the tender and catholic piety of its *The language of the XVI century.*

spirit have been life and peace to millions. The English Bible, a greater work than any single mind could have brought forth, stands for the collective labour of a century. It is in large part the work of obscure men, none of whom in his own time was looked upon as a supreme literary artist. Yet to-day, when for the sake of accuracy we revise it, we cannot change a syllable without marring the felicity of its phrases.

The illusion of progress.

The notion that we have progressed, in any true spiritual sense, beyond these men, and the age in which they were at home, is an illusion, from which, for the sake of our souls, we must speedily awaken. We have indeed gained a knowledge of facts unknown to them; but in the vast abysses of space and time we have not found the splendours which inspired them. Their little world was a home to them,—perhaps because it had many exits; our vaster one, having none, has become a prison for us. We have multiplied machinery and enslaved ourselves to it. We have extended democracy and abridged freedom. We have lost the old sense of the unexplored possibilities of life; we cannot respond, as did the men of the time which we rightly call the New Birth, to the challenge of the future and the unknown. The soul of the wide world ceases to be prophetic, and dreams no more on things to come. We are materialists: which means that we think of ourselves as products and effects of that world which to them was the instrument and opportunity of the spirit of man.

We must regain belief in the reality and freedom of the spirit.

To renew our sense of the scope of the soul, of human freedom, and of the unexhausted possibilities of the spirit, we need to turn back from our universe of repetitions and inevitabilities, our worldwide empires and colossal republics, to the little world and the tiny nations of the past. We must unlearn the childish error which mistakes bigness for greatness, numbers for quality, and money for wealth. Spiritual grandeur has commonly dwelt with material littleness. The insignificant Palestine and Greece; the little England, with a population less than that of London to-day, and no colonial empire; the tiny Italian republics, unsecured even by the "scraps of paper" of their more potent neighbours,— from these have come forth the imperishable glories of the race of man.

We need not infer, indeed, that the huge nations of the modern world cannot do things even nobler than were done by the little ones of the past; my unswerving faith is that they can and will. But certain it is that these achievements will not be realized unless the power of vision and creation can be renewed in us. In the Elizabethan time, most men, from our lordly and emancipated point of view, were ignorant and superstitious. We are wise and sceptical. We have exchanged poetry for science — we have bartered the heavenly promise of the rainbow for a knowledge of its chemistry. By the patient labour of three centuries we have gained infinitely, and it behooves us to be grateful for the potent wizardry wherewith science has armed us. But, alas! we have lost one secret that was known to the superstitious people of the older world: the secret that Man is a spirit, and that the world of the senses, vast and impressive as it may be, is no more than the shadow of the soul, and its means of communication with other souls and with the universal spirit. Without that secret we cannot live. Until we have learned once more to recognize what a piece of work is a man, and how all things bow before him; — until we have ceased to be bullied and cowed by the world-machine which our own minds have framed, —we shall not see again the magnificence of the age that crowned itself with Shakespeare.

INDEX